ROUTLEDGE LIBRARY EDITIONS: SLAVERY

Volume 8

OUT OF THE HOUSE OF BONDAGE

OUT OF THE HOUSE OF BONDAGE

Runaways, Resistance and Marronage in Africa and the New World

Edited by
GAD HEUMAN

LONDON AND NEW YORK

First published in 1986 by Frank Cass & Co. Ltd

This edition first published in 2023
by Routledge
4 Park Square, Milton Park, Abingdon, Oxon OX14 4RN

and by Routledge
605 Third Avenue, New York, NY 10158

Routledge is an imprint of the Taylor & Francis Group, an informa business

© 1986 Frank Cass & Co. Ltd

All rights reserved. No part of this book may be reprinted or reproduced or utilised in any form or by any electronic, mechanical, or other means, now known or hereafter invented, including photocopying and recording, or in any information storage or retrieval system, without permission in writing from the publishers.

Trademark notice: Product or corporate names may be trademarks or registered trademarks, and are used only for identification and explanation without intent to infringe.

British Library Cataloguing in Publication Data
A catalogue record for this book is available from the British Library

ISBN: 978-1-032-30942-2 (Set)
ISBN: 978-1-032-33103-4 (Volume 8) (hbk)
ISBN: 978-1-032-33106-5 (Volume 8) (pbk)
ISBN: 978-1-003-31822-4 (Volume 8) (ebk)

DOI: 10.4324/9781003318224

Publisher's Note
The publisher has gone to great lengths to ensure the quality of this reprint but points out that some imperfections in the original copies may be apparent.

Disclaimer
The publisher has made every effort to trace copyright holders and would welcome correspondence from those they have been unable to trace.

OUT OF THE HOUSE OF BONDAGE

Runaways, Resistance and Marronage in Africa and the New World

Edited by
GAD HEUMAN

FRANK CASS

First published 1986 in Great Britain by
FRANK CASS AND COMPANY LIMITED
Gainsborough House, 11 Gainsborough Road,
London, E11 1RS, England

and in the United States of America by
FRANK CASS AND COMPANY LIMITED
c/o Biblio Distribution Centre
81 Adams Drive, P.O. Box 327, Totowa, N.J. 07511

Copyright © 1986 Frank Cass & Co. Ltd

British Library Cataloguing in Publication Data

Out of the house of bondage : runaways, resistance
and marronage in Africa and the New World.
1. Fugitive slaves—History
I. Heuman, Gad
305.5'67   HT867

ISBN 0-7146-3287-2

This collection of essays first appeared in a Special Issue, 'Out of
the House of Bondage', of *Slavery and Abolition*, Vol. 6, No. 3,
published by Frank Cass & Co. Ltd.

*All rights reserved. No part of this publication may be reproduced,
stored in a retrieval system, or transmitted in any form, or by any
means, electronic, mechanical, photocopying, recording, or otherwise,
without the prior permission of Frank Cass and Company Limited.*

TO THE MEMORY
OF MY PARENTS

Contents

List of maps		xi
Acknowledgments		xii
Notes on Contributors		xiii
Introduction	**Gad Heuman**	1

PART I: RESISTANCE IN AFRICA

Some Thoughts on Resistance to Enslavement in Africa	**Richard Rathbone**	11
Runaway Slaves and Social Bandits in Southern Angola, 1875–1913	**W. G. Clarence-Smith**	23

PART II: RUNAWAYS AND RESISTANCE IN THE NEW WORLD

'They are Indeed the Constant Plague of Their Tyrants': Slave Defence of a Moral Economy in Colonial North Carolina, 1748–1772	**Marvin L. Michael Kay and Lorin Lee Cary**	37
Colonial South Carolina Runaways: Their Significance for Slave Culture	**Philip Morgan**	57
From Land to Sea: Runaway Barbados Slaves and Servants, 1630–1700	**Hilary Beckles**	79
Runaway Slaves in Nineteenth-Century Barbados	**Gad Heuman**	95
On the Eve of the Haitian Revolution: Slave Runaways in Saint Domingue in the Year 1790	**David Geggus**	112

PART III: MARRONAGE

Cimarrones and *Palenques*: Runaways and Resistance in Colonial Colombia	**Anthony McFarlane**	131

(continued overleaf)

The Maroons of Jamaica, 1730–1830:
  Livelihood, Demography and Health   **Richard B. Sheridan**   152

A Comparison between the History of
  Maroon Communities in Surinam and
  Jamaica   **Silvia W. de Groot**   173

Bibliography   185

Index   197

List of Maps

Southern Angola	24
Barbados: parish boundaries	96
Saint Domingue: parish boundaries and towns	113
New Granada (1778–1780)	133
Jamaica, showing the main areas of Maroon settlement	153
Surinam, showing locations of the Maroons	175

Acknowledgments

This volume grew out of a session at the Association of Caribbean Historians' Conference held in Barbados in 1984. The panel was entitled 'Runaways in the Caribbean' and was co-organized by Hilary Beckles and myself. Delegates to the conference showed considerable interest in the topic, and it has since been possible to expand the scope and theme of that original session.

In the process, I have incurred a number of debts. Hilary Beckles not only joined me in convening the session; he also contributed his conference paper to this volume. James Walvin critically read all the manuscripts and offered his usual sage advice. Stanley L. Engerman and Michael P. Johnston suggested potential authors. Two of my colleagues at the University of Warwick, Edward Countryman and David Dabydeen, encouraged the search for an appropriate title. As usual, my wife stoically put up with more discussions of runaways and resistance than she might care to remember.

Notes on Contributors

Hilary Beckles teaches in the Department of History, University of the West Indies, Cave Hill, Barbados. Educated at the University of Hull, he has also taught at the Jamaica campus of the University of the West Indies. He is the author of *Black Rebellion in Barbados: The Struggle against Slavery, 1627–1838* (1984) and has written extensively on 17th-century Barbadian history. He is presently working on a study of comparative rebel slave leadership in the West Indies.

Lorin Lee Cary teaches Labour History at the University of Toledo, Ohio. Educated at Antioch College and the University of Wisconsin–Madison, he was a Fulbright–Hays Senior Scholar at the University of New South Wales during 1980. In addition to joint work on North Carolina slavery, his publications deal with various topics in labour and social history. Co-author of *No Strength without Union: An Illustrated History of Ohio Workers, 1833–1980* (1983), he is presently completing a book on slavery with Marvin L. Michael Kay and studying labour organizers after World War II.

Gervase Clarence-Smith teaches in the History Department, School of Oriental and African Studies, University of London. Educated at King's College Cambridge, the Institut d'Etudes Politiques in Paris, and the University of London, he has worked on slavery and the slave trade as practised by the Portuguese and Spaniards in the nineteenth century. He is the author of *Slaves, Peasants and Capitalists in Southern Angola, 1840–1926* (1979), and *The Third Portuguese Empire, 1825–1975* (1985). He is currently working on a general economic history of Equatorial Africa, and on a detailed study of cocoa cultivation in the islands of the Gulf of Guinea in the late 19th and early 20th centuries.

Silvia W. de Groot taught for many years at the University of Amsterdam. She studied history and anthropology at Utrecht and Amsterdam and has also taught in the United States, the Caribbean, Latin America, and Africa. She is the author of *Djuka Society and Social Change* (1969), *From Isolation Towards Integration: The Surinam Maroons and their Colonial Rulers* (1977), and numerous articles on Maroon societies. She is currently working on a study of Maroon women in Surinam.

David Geggus is Associate Professor of History at the University of Florida, Gainesville. He has held research posts at Oxford and Southampton Universities, and has been the recipient of research fellowships from the British Academy and the Guggenheim Foundation. In 1980, Cambridge University Press awarded him the Roger Brew Memorial Prize for Latin American History. He is the author of *Slavery, War and Revolution* (1982) and of some thirty articles and chapters.

Gad Heuman is a member of the Department of History and the Centre for Caribbean Studies at the University of Warwick. Educated at Columbia College and Yale University, he is especially interested in the transition from slavery to freedom in the Caribbean. He is the author of *Between Black and White: Race, Politics, and the Free Coloureds in Jamaica, 1792–1854* (1981) as well as several articles in this field. He is presently working on a study of the Morant Bay Rebellion in Jamaica.

Marvin L. Michael Kay is Professor of History at the University of Toledo, Ohio. He received his Ph.D. at the University of Minnesota and has taught at various universities including the University of Queensland, Australia. Formerly editor of *Studies in Burke and His Time*, he has published numerous essays on colonial North Carolina. Currently, he is completing a book on slavery in colonial North Carolina with Lorin Lee Cary and is working with Karl Vezner on a study of the North Carolina Regulators.

Anthony McFarlane teaches in the Department of History and the School of Comparative American Studies at the University of Warwick. Educated at the London School of Economics and Political Science, he has worked extensively on colonial Colombia. He has published articles on Colombian social and economic history; these have appeared in the *Hispanic American Historical Review* and in Colombian historical journals. He is presently working on crime and society in colonial Colombia.

Philip Morgan holds a visiting appointment this year at the University of California, Berkeley, but is otherwise Editor of Publications at the Institute of Early American History and Culture in Williamsburg. Educated at the universities of Cambridge and London, he is the author of *Slave Counterpoint: Black Culture in the Eighteenth-Century Lowcountry and Chesapeake* (forthcoming). He is presently working on a study of the world of Thomas Thistlewood, the Anglo-Jamaican.

Richard Rathbone teaches modern African history at the School of Oriental and African Studies, University of London and is currently Chairman of the University of London's Centre for African Studies. He has written extensively on modern West and Southern African history and is completing a study of colonial attitudes and colonial policy in Africa. His interest in the history of slavery developed out of teaching a trans-regional course on slavery in London University's Afro-American and Afro-Caribbean graduate studies programme.

Richard Sheridan is a member of the Department of Economics at the University of Kansas. He received his Ph.D. from the London School of Economics and Political Science, and is interested in the economic, social, and medical history of slavery and plantation economy of the British Caribbean colonies. He is the author of *Sugar and Slavery: An Economic History of the British West Indies, 1623–1775* (1974); *Doctors and Slaves: A Medical and Demographic History of Slavery in the British West Indies* (1985); as well as a number of articles in this field. He is presently working on a short history of the last years of slavery in Jamaica.

INTRODUCTION

The past twenty years has witnessed a remarkable outpouring of material on slavery and slave societies. While much of this literature has been devoted to the workings of the slave system, a considerable body of it has also dealt with various forms of resistance to slavery. In the past few years, much important work has been done specifically on slave revolts. Two recent books, Eugene D. Genovese, *From Rebellion to Revolution: Afro-American Slave Revolts in the Making of the New World* (1979) and Michael Craton, *Testing the Chains: Resistance to Slavery in the British West Indies* (1982) have filled important gaps in our knowledge of slave rebellions. Two further monographs on Caribbean rebellions and slave conspiracies by Hilary Beckles and D. Barry Gaspar have been published within the past year.[1]

Such rebellions were of crucial importance; yet slave revolts, by their very nature, could hardly have been everyday occurrences. In the United States, for example, most slaves would never have encountered a rebellion. Even in the Caribbean, where revolts were more frequent, rebellions generally affected a small minority of the slaves. If we are looking for forms of resistance which directly impinged on the lives of the slaves, it is day-to-day patterns of resistance that we need to study.

Some important research has been published on this aspect of resistance, especially for the United States.[2] But there are relatively few such studies for other parts of the Americas, or for Africa. This volume is intended to widen the study of runaways and resistance geographically and to use runaways as a means of further analysing slavery and the wider slave population. Some attention is also devoted to the Maroon communities established by runaway slaves in Jamaica, Surinam, and Colombia. The chapters on the Maroons seek to bring together our knowledge of these communities and to highlight similarities and differences among the various groups of Maroons in the Americas. The articles also remind us of the ultimate goal of at least some of the runaway slaves: complete freedom.

Much of the information on runaway slaves comes from newspaper advertisements for fugitive or caught slaves. These are an important source, partly because they are unbiased. The advertisements were not written for pro- or anti-slavery advocates, let alone for future historians. They also sometimes contain quite revealing material which is unavailable elsewhere. For example, they shed light on the internal economy of the slave societies as well as on the ability of slaves to remain undetected for long periods of time, even in relatively small colonies. Writing on St Domingue, David Geggus recorded the story of an African runaway who had been missing for two years. The slave survived by buying rum at the gates of sugar estates in one part of the colony and then selling the produce elsewhere, receiving stolen goods in exchange. In the case of nineteenth-century Barbados, there is evidence of a slave who had been a runaway for at least 25 years and had been living in the slave quarters of a plantation all that time. Such accounts not only help describe the runaways themselves but also highlight significant aspects of their societies.

As with other sources, however, it is important to ask questions about the material. For example, what prompted an owner to advertise for a missing slave? It is probable that owners living closer to cities with easier access to the press advertised more frequently than their more rural or distant counterparts. Advertisements may also be related to the time of year and the demands of the plantation, to the value of a particular slave and to the cost of the advertisement, to a change of ownership, or to the length of time a runaway had been absent. As a result, it is clear – as Philip Morgan has concluded in his chapter on South Carolina – that advertised runaways 'represent only the most visible tip of an otherwise indeterminate iceberg'.

There is another feature that is worth noting about the advertisements. They were placed for fugitive slaves as well as slaves who had been caught and were often in gaol. Those slaves who had been apprehended represented a particular type of runaway: there were generally more Africans in this cohort and a larger proportion of slaves who were not proficient in the language of the colony. On the other hand, fugitive slaves were usually highly acculturated and often highly valued slaves. It may be that captive slaves are therefore more representative of the broader slave population, and that greater attention needs to be paid to that group of runaways.

Several of the authors here are agreed about the need to go beyond advertisements in the press. Independent checks on the degree and significance of running away should be possible through the use of planter correspondence, plantation accounts, and inventories. Yet however useful these additional sources prove to be, newspaper advertisements, especially for areas outside the United States, remain to be fully utilised.

Whatever the source, the evidence on runaways is revealing at a number of different levels. At the very least, runaways were resisting their own enslavement by denying labour to their owners. Many runaways were seeking personal freedom while some worked against the system of slavery itself. But patterns of resistance were not just a feature of the New World; Richard Rathbone has described this process for Africa as well. On the enforced marches to the coasts, in the baracoons awaiting shipment, on board ships crossing the Atlantic, Africans resisted their enslavement. It is interesting that many slaves in the forts of west Africa may have known about resistance on board slave ships; Rathbone speculates that such information could have been part of the popular knowledge of the baracoons.

INTRODUCTION   3

Some of the slaves also managed to escape from the forts and to establish communities which pre-figured Maroon societies of the Americas.

Resistance took different forms as well. Gervaise Clarence-Smith notes that a majority of the runaway slaves in Angola joined bandit groups in the mountainous interior of the colony. These bandits were initially helped and protected by the peasantry; moreover, the bandits often returned to raid their former plantations. Clarence-Smith reports on one attack against the wealthiest planter in the area who was known for brutally treating his slaves. The escaped slaves directly attacked the planter and an employee, but left his property and cattle untouched. This was clearly an act of revenge, but flight from the Angolan plantations generally had more serious consequences: it helped to devastate the settler economy first by the withdrawal of labour and then by the raids on the estates.

Maroon communities in the Americas were also a serious threat to the early plantation economies. These autonomous societies, initially consisting almost entirely of African-born runaway slaves, were established before the end of the sixteenth century in New Granada and by the seventeenth century in Jamaica and Surinam. Communities of this type posed a number of challenges to white society. They were inevitably an inspiration for other slaves to abandon slavery. Moreover, the Maroons were almost never totally independent; they relied on the plantation society for various material goods as well as new recruits, especially women. Maroons therefore raided the estates, impeding the development and growth of the plantations.

As a result, white society was forced to come to terms with the Maroons. In the case of Jamaica, the Maroons agreed to a treaty which obliged them to return runaway slaves to their owners. As Richard Sheridan points out, the Jamaican Maroons generally carried out their treaty obligations. The Surinam Maroons, on the other hand, cooperated far less with the colonial authorities: for instance, they continued to absorb runaway slaves into their communities long after they had made peace with the whites. In comparing Jamaica and Surinam, Silvia de Groot notes that those in Surinam negotiated with the planters as equals. Unlike the Jamaican Maroons, they did not regard themselves as a conquered people. Ultimately, the Surinam Maroons enjoyed a far greater degree of internal autonomy than their Jamaican counterparts.

The *palenques* of eighteenth-century Colombia shared some of the characteristics of the Maroon societies of Jamaica and Surinam. However the Maroons in the Colombian *palenques* never became an instrument for policing the slave society. Moreover, as Anthony McFarlane suggests, they were not seeking to recreate entirely African traditions. Instead, the Maroons in eighteenth-century Colombia were adapting to the mores of their creole culture: they were less intent on restoring an African past than on integrating themselves into the Colombian economy. They had a vision of becoming free peasants and even of working as gold prospectors. Some of them also attacked the institution of slavery itself rather than divorcing themselves from it. Whether in Genovese's terms this reflected a bourgeois-democratic outlook, it nonetheless represented a very different world view from that of their Maroon ancestors.[3]

Yet most slave runaways did not aspire to establish or join Maroon communities. Indeed, a large proportion of the slaves studied in this volume ran away to visit kin or friends or attempted to merge into free black and brown urban communities. It is important to note that slaves attempting to 'pass as free' did not pose the same threat as slaves who sought to live as Maroons. It is possible that owners saw running away of this kind – which has been characterised as *petit marronage* as opposed to the *grand marronage* of the Maroons – as almost inevitable and at times perhaps even useful as a safety-valve within the system.

The authors of these essays generally agree about the composition of the runaways: they were predominantly young and male. Sixty-three per cent of runaways in Barbados were male, while in North Carolina males represented almost 90 per cent of the runaway population. Young men under 30 years of age generally lacked the family ties of older slaves; in fact, some may have run away to seek mates elsewhere. Even males who were tied to families ran away with greater frequency than females in the same category. As Kay and Cary suggest for North Carolina, male slaves were more often separated from their spouses and families than females. Moreover, a larger percentage of men than women had skilled occupations and were therefore likely to have had experience in travelling outside of their communities. One such group of slaves in North and South Carolina, watermen, were overly represented in the sample of runaways, but this was hardly surprising given their access to a relatively easy means of escape.

In general, skilled slaves were represented in greater numbers among the runaways than their proportion in the slave population. In both St Domingue and nineteenth-century Barbados, carpenters were the most numerous of the skilled runaways. These slaves were clearly in great demand and could probably find employment without much difficulty. Yet some skilled occupations rarely appeared in the lists of runaways: drivers, for example, were generally absent. This reflects their position as part of the administrative hierarchy of the plantations; moreover, they represented stability in the slave community and may have had too much to lose by trying to flee.

There were some noticeable differences in the various societies examined here. In St Domingue, for instance, creole and coloured slaves were unrepresented among the runaways, while the reverse was the case for Barbados.[4] Similarly, Barbadian skilled slaves were a much greater proportion of runaways than their counterparts in the Carolinas. Field slaves in

INTRODUCTION 5

Barbados made up a tiny fraction of the runaways, although they were far more statistically significant elsewhere. It may be that the size of Barbados affected the varying proportions of runaways; alternatively, the sample could reflect a more urban slave population than in the other societies being examined here. More comparative work will clearly be necessary to explain such differences.

However, there is little doubt that it was the skilled slaves who were most likely to flee successfully. Similarly, coloured and creole runaways had a greater chance of eluding capture. Not surprisingly, it was African-born slaves who were most frequently captured. In the case of North Carolina, 48 per cent of the runaways were either captured or killed, but 77 per cent of Africans who fled were in this category. Africans also tended to run away more in groups, while creole slaves ran away more frequently individually. Many newly-landed African slaves who escaped were trying to get back to Africa. For example, the following advertisement in the Jamaican press reported on the flight of four newly-arrived Africans; they told their ship-mates 'that they would proceed to the sea by night and remain in the bush through the day, and the first canoe they found, they would set sail for their country'.[5]

While Africa was the destination of some slaves, others were fleeing elsewhere. Slaves escaped to other plantations, to towns, and to different colonies. They fled by a variety of means, but among the most ingenious were those who escaped by boat from seventeenth-century Barbados to nearby islands. Citing the work of Neville Hall on the Danish West Indies, Hilary Beckles has adopted the term 'maritime marronage' to describe these runaways.

Once away, slaves were harboured by a variety of people. The kin of runaways were prominent among the harbourers, but so were whites, free coloureds, and free blacks. Those who protected runaway slaves did so for a variety of reasons: family considerations were, of course, important, but the prospects of employing runaways could also be crucial. From Angola to Barbados, slaves ran away to other owners; in some cases, especially at times of labour scarcity, owners may have enticed slaves with offers of better conditions of work. Since there is evidence of runaways working for slaves as well, the whole nature of the employment of runaways needs further research.

Runaway slaves tended to escape at particular points in the year. In Barbados, July and August were peak periods for running away. Since this was just after the crop had been harvested, it may reflect a number of possibilities, some of which were reported for other areas as well. It could have been in the owners' interest for slaves to flee at a time when there was less work for slaves to do. Masters would thereby have been spared the cost of feeding their slaves. Barry Higman has pointed out that the period after

6 OUT OF THE HOUSE OF BONDAGE

the crop had been harvested was known as the 'hungry-time' or 'hard-time' by Barbadian slaves; this was the season when food supplies – both from the plantations and from the provision grounds – were most stretched. Seasonal nutritional stress may therefore have been a factor in adding to the number of runaways during this time of year.[6] In St Domingue, some owners let their slaves scavenge for food during the severe drought in 1790, and some of these slaves would have been arrested as runaways.

Political considerations also affected the extent of running away. In Angola, there was a significant increase in the number of runaways as expectations of the abolition of slavery rose. Similarly in Barbados, there were more runaways in the year prior to the 1816 slave rebellion, which broke out in part because slaves believed they were about to be free.

It is possible therefore to discuss the slave runaways in some detail. The material in these papers shows us who the runaways were, suggests when and where they went, and who harboured them. But some of the authors here are also concerned about another point: what the runaways reveal about the wider slave population. Runaway slaves should not only be seen as an isolated subset of the slave population or merely as an aspect of resistance to slavery. Instead, the study of runaways can provide an additional perspective on slave culture and on the institution of slavery itself.

One of the most important areas which runaways highlight is the role of slave women and the slave family. Women were heavily underrepresented among the runaway slaves; furthermore, women tended to escape to visit kin rather than to remain away permanently. In addition, female runaways took their children with them far more frequently than men. Since it was kin who so often harboured slaves, what is apparent is the existence of a highly developed sense of family, including the extended family. The evidence can be looked at another way. Women may have refrained from running away in larger numbers because of the strength of kin ties which kept them attached to a particular plantation or a particular area.

The data on skilled runaways are also revealing. As such a high proportion of skilled slaves were male, the evidence reinforces our understanding of the lack of occupational mobility for female slaves. Research on skilled runaway slaves in eighteenth-century South Carolina points to an additional conclusion: that the relatively steady increase in the number of such slaves may help to explain the absence of slave rebellions throughout the last 60 years of the century. Philip Morgan suggests that an increase in responsibility and in status associated with gaining skills may have made it possible for these slaves to create a more meaningful world of their own, one that was not worth shattering in overt suicidal resistance. Studying skilled runaways may therefore be useful in analysing patterns of mobility among slaves as

INTRODUCTION 7

well as helping to account for the various forms of resistance or even the lack of it.

There is another aspect of resistance that is raised by Kay and Cary in their work on North Carolina. They deal with crimes committed by slaves, analysing their nature and frequency as well as the extreme punishments meted out by white society. This work on resistance and repression in North Carolina needs to be extended to other areas as well. Similarly, the policing arrangements of the slave societies are worth further attention. From seventeenth-century Barbados to Angola, slaves were sent after runaways. Yet when stopped, runaways sometimes used the excuse that they themselves were hunting for escaped slaves.

When they ran away, slaves did so for a variety of reasons. One was to put pressure on their masters, either to sell them or to improve their conditions. In Barbados, runaway slaves were sometimes promised freedom to choose new owners, if they returned of their own accord. Colombian runaways actually petitioned the viceroy about the loss of specific customary rights they regarded as inviolate. Anthony McFarlane argues that these slaves were behaving more like peasants than slaves; they were seeking to protect traditional labour practices. Such slaves were, in McFarlane's terms, less concerned about seeking freedom outside of slavery than about preserving some form of freedom within slavery itself. Sidney Mintz and Richard Price have also commented on various aspects of slave autonomy and proposed that we look at the degree to which slaves could affect and sometimes even control particular aspects of their masters' world.[7]

There are therefore many issues which call for further research. This collection will have succeeded if it inspires more detailed work in the area of runaways, resistance, and marronage. In the process, it should highlight the complexity of slavery by also examining the wider implications of those who chose to flee.

NOTES

1. Hilary Beckles, *Black Rebellion in Barbados: The Struggle Against Slavery, 1627–1838* (St Michael, Barbados, 1984); D. Barry Gaspar, *Bondsmen and Rebels: A Study of Master–Slave Relations in Antigua* (Baltimore, 1985).
2. Gerald W. Mullin, *Flight and Rebellion: Slave Resistance in Eighteenth-Century Virginia* (New York, 1972); Peter H. Wood, *Black Majority: Negroes in Colonial South Carolina from 1670 Through the Stono Rebellion* (New York, 1974); Michael P. Johnson, 'Runaway Slaves and the Slave Communities in South Carolina, 1799–1830', *William and Mary Quarterly*, 3rd series, 38 (1981), 418–41; and Betty Wood, *Slavery in Colonial Georgia, 1730–1775* (Athens, Georgia, 1984). See also the collection of runaway advertisements for the South by Lathan A. Windley, comp., *Runaway Slave Advertisements: A Documentary History from the 1730s to 1790* (4 vols., Westport, Conn., 1983).

8   OUT OF THE HOUSE OF BONDAGE

3. Eugene D. Genovese, *From Rebellion to Revolution: Afro-American Slave Revolts in the Making of the New World* (Baton Rouge, 1979), chap. 3.
4. *Creole* is used here to refer to slaves born in the Americas. *Coloured* means slaves of mixed colour, often described as mulattoes.
5. P.A. Bishop, 'Runaway Slaves in Jamaica, 1740–1807: A Study Based on Newspaper Advertisements Published During that Period for Runaways' (unpublished M.A. thesis, University of the West Indies, 1970), p. 11.
6. B.W. Higman, *Slave Populations of the British Caribbean, 1807–1834* (Baltimore, 1984), p. 215.
7. Sidney W. Mintz and Richard Price, 'An Anthropological Approach to the Afro-Caribbean Past: A Caribbean Perspective', *ISHI Occasional Papers in Social Change* (Philadelphia, 1976), p. 16.

PART ONE

RESISTANCE IN AFRICA

Some Thoughts on Resistance to Enslavement in West Africa

Richard Rathbone

Despite the obvious importance of integrating scholarship on pre-nineteenth-century African societies with research on black societies in the New World, the Atlantic appears to have remained a formidable barrier to such exchange. Few Africanists can read the Caribbean and American material without wincing when it adverts to the 'African background'. For the most part such allusions are generalised, often based on rather ancient scholarship and shy of both the complexity and the dynamism of the history of Africa. This remark points no finger of blame but rather seeks to emphasise that historical studies of Africa are now so numerous, detailed and sophisticated that a researcher whose commitment is to understanding the diaspora scarcely has time to master both bodies of data. Students of African history are no more successful in their understanding of the American material. Certainly North American and Caribbean scholarship has had a profound impact upon methodology,[1] but the rich material on black life on the other side of the Atlantic has never been seriously combed for what it might tell us about the continent from which its subjects had been so recently and rudely forced. An ultimate and obviously desirable synthesis seems remote and it is a matter of regret that a more thorough understanding of the African elements in the world the slaves made is still denied us.

This paper does very little to redress this situation. Its proposition is fundamentally very simple indeed. In the analysis of slave resistance in the Americas there is frequent reference to the significance of the activists' African past. For some authors, the propensity to revolt is in part conditioned by whether slaves were African born or 'creole'. Others have tangentially suggested that leaders and followers may well have been people traditionally attuned to 'jungle warfare', a position betraying a profound ignorance of West African geography but no less attractive for that. Similarly, 'African' patterns of social and political organisation from chieftaincy, through secret societies, to religious structures have been invoked to explain how rebellion could be mounted in the most disadvantageous circumstances.[2] All such thinking might be true, partly true or even wrong; what is missing is perhaps a more thorough understanding of a culture of resistance that is discernible through the records and which is rooted very firmly on African soil. By culture of resistance is meant no generalised notion of opposition of the spirit but actual evidence of physical attempts to prevent the forcible removal of people from their home environment. By the time of the high-tide of the Atlantic slave those acts of forcible removal appear to have been more commonly initiated by abduction, kidnapping and social and economic methods than by outright war and its repercussions. Thus it is not a question of 'national' mass resistance, which doubtless was part of the story, but of individual acts and especially the actions of those enslaved but awaiting shipment to the Americas. The evidence for resistance at the point of enslavement is thin; a partial explanation of this is undoubtedly that flight was the preferred method of avoiding the raiders' intentions. The abandonment of villages and fields for the bush whilst slaving parties were in the vicinity was undoubtedly a frequently repeated episode in many peoples' lives but its lack of drama has tended to play it down so far as the record is concerned.

Nonetheless there is clear evidence of the use of main force to prevent capture from the early period when, of course, it was more common for European crews to come into direct contact with their putative victims. The record of Hawkins' third voyage recalls that at Cape Verde 'our Generall landed certaine of our men, to the number of 160 ... to take some Negroes. And they going up into the Countrey for the space of six miles, were encountered with a great number of Negroes: who with their invenomed arrowes did hurt a great number of our men ...'.[3] By the end of the period such resistance appears to have been as strong. The Commissioner for Sierra Leone reporting to Canning on 15th May 1824 said that

> In the course of the last year some boats from Bissao ... sacked some of the villages there and carried off ... to be sold ... as many of their inhabitants as they could take. Besides the barbarity of this practise, its consequence is that the natives within the reach of such kidnapping expeditions are rendered savage and intractable, so much so that they are always disposed to deal harshly with such Europeans as may fall into their hands.

He went on to relate the story of some islanders' seizure of a Portuguese boat's crew who were ultimately released with great difficulty after the payment of a ransom by the Governor of Bissau.[4]

Once captured there is no doubt that attempts at escape were frequent. On the long march to the coastal assembly points, captives were frequently manacled as well as harnessed to one another by neck irons. Pinioning was resorted to in some cases as slaves might 'strike or stab' their captors.[5] Wadstrom's report goes further in relaying his informant's insight that manacling also prevented captives from suicide attempts. Escape at any point along the extended trails from point of capture to eventual embarkation was clearly perceived as a major risk by the purveyors, and the harsh circumstances of such journeys attest to the vigour and frequency of such attempts.

Despite the forbidding architecture of the coastal forts of West Africa it is clear that captives once ensconced on the coast were no more secure than they had been on the march. The long periods spent awaiting transhipment, periods on occasion in excess of a calendar year, provided the factors with the equally costly alternatives of the risk of escape or more systematic supervision and confinement. If the labour of the awaiting captives was to be used then risks had to be taken. But those risks could result in flight. The strong documentation for the 1680s for the Royal African Company allows us to get some idea of its scale. Conduitt, the chief factor for the Company in Accra, reported in June 1681 that flight from the barracoons was common; he complained that he received insufficient assistance from local African political authorities, and in an attempt to force their hands threatened to close down the trade. This threat apparently elicited a guarantee of recompense by the local rulers.[6] Although escape and failure to recapture was clearly being used here as a bargaining counter in local politics, there is less equivocal evidence for escape later in the same year from Accra. The new chief factor, Hassell, complained of the lack of leg-irons in October and other requests from him and his successors for restraining devices are notable aspects of the exchanges between the RAC and its local agents.[7] Visitors to the castles and trade forts today from Gorée southwards are struck not merely by the menacing gloom of the dungeons which let out on to the Atlantic surf, but also by the proliferation of ring-bolts in their walls. It is clear that at no point in the long misery of the march out of Africa were captives safe in the eyes of their captors.

Commodore Collier's second annual report on the settlements on the coast of Africa of 11 September 1820 recalls a recent visit to the disused barracoons of Bance Island:

> During the period of the slave trade . . . the walls of the slave-yards still prove the whole to have been so contrived as to prevent the chance of escape to the most resolute and infatuated of the miserable victims they inclosed, yet with all these precautions, insurrections, as on board the slave ships, were not uncommon and on one occasion the white managers were threatened; in the very moment they had dedicated to revelry and licentiousness; for which the unhappy slaves were all held responsible and condemned to an atonement, by undergoing indiscriminate butchery or suffering dreadful scarification. . . . Armed only with the irons and chains of those who were so confined the slaves audaciously attacked the lock-up keeper, at the moment he made his entré to return them to their dungeons after a few hours of basking in the sun; but thus bringing upon themselves the close fire

14   OUT OF THE HOUSE OF BONDAGE

of musketry ... which they probably neither saw nor contemplated
... many obtained their only wish, a relief from their misery by the
hand of death, for it can be scarcely be supposed that much value was
attached to the life of these beings when a few rusty muskets or three
or four bars of iron was the cost per head.[8]

Although we cannot trace the insurrectionary careers of such remarkable
rebels, an earlier reference suggests that there was more continuity to
resistance than is often supposed. Atkins, the Royal Navy surgeon, in his
Voyage to Guinea ... of 1735, recalls looking over the slave holdings of a
dealer rather aptly called Cracker.

> I could not help taking notice of one Fellow among the rest of a tall,
> strong make and bold stern aspect. ... He seemed to disdain his fellow
> slaves for their readiness to be examined ... scorned looking at us,
> refused to rise or stretch his limbs as his master commanded; which
> got him an unmerciful whipping ...; this same fellow, called Captain
> Tomba, was a leader of some country villages that opposed them and
> their trade at the River Nunes; killing our friends there, and firing
> their cottages ... by the help of my men [says Cracker] surprised and
> bound him in the night ... and made my property.

Captain Tomba clearly remained intractable and his subsequent career
leads one to suspect that he was not so isolated amongst his fellow captives as
Atkins suggested, for he was to lead a mutiny on the Bristol ship *Robert*
under Captain Harding's command, a mutiny which Atkins tells us nearly
succeeded. What happened to Tomba is unclear although imaginable.[9]

Unsurprisingly some of the most dramatic testimony arises out of the
circumstances of the Middle Passage. Resistance seems to have taken a wide
variety of forms. The Commissioner for Sierra Leone reporting to Canning
in April 1825 speaks of something rather like modern industrial action:
'A slave vessel entered this river (the Nunes) last November, the residents
however refused to load her and she was eventually supplied by the
Portuguese from Bissao'.[10] Thomas Phillips' account of the voyage of the
Hannibal at the end of the seventeenth century presents us with evidence of
suicide which is slightly less equivocal than the log entry of the *James* on
17th April 1675, which records that 'a stout man slave leaped overboard and
drowned himself'.[11] Phillips writes:

> the negroes are so wilful and loth to leave their own country that they
> have often leap'd out of the canoes, boat and ship into the sea and kept
> under water till they were drowned to avoid being taken up and saved
> by our boats. ... We had about 12 negroes did wilfully drown them-
> selves, and others starved themselves to death for 'tis their belief that
> when they die they return home to their own countries and friends

RESISTANCE TO ENSLAVEMENT IN AFRICA

again. I have been inform'd that some commanders have cut off the legs and arms of the most wilful, to terrify the rest.[12]

Phillips' information helps us to understand the circumstances in which insurrection took place, and perhaps to marvel at the clear evidence of the frequency of revolt. Phillips, by no means an inhumane monster,[13] tells us that

> When our slaves are aboard we shackle the men two and two, while we lie in port and in sight of their own country, for 'tis then they attempt to make their escape and mutiny; to prevent which we always keep centinels [sic] upon the hatchway and have a chest of small arms ready loaden and prim'd constantly lying at hand upon the quarter deck together with some granada shells [grenades]; and two of our quarter deck guns pointing on the deck thence; and two more out of the steerage, the door of which is always kept shut and well barr'd; they are fed twice a day, at 10 in the morning, and 4 in the evening, which is the time they are aptest to mutiny, being all on deck; therefore all that time, what of our men are not employed in distributing their victuals … stand to their arms; and some with lighted matches at the great guns that yawn upon them, loaden with partridge [another word for langrage or case-shot].[14]

Phillips additionally tells us about how intelligence might prevent mutiny: 'we have some 30 or 40 gold coast negroes make guardians and overseers of Whidaw [Whydah] negroes and sleep among them … in order … to give us notice, if they can discover any caballing or plotting among them, which trust they will discharge with great diligence'.[15] This evidence of the extremely careful policing of slave ships in the relatively early stages of the trade must be seen alongside the frequency of reports of slave revolt aboard ship.

Snelgrave's *New Account of some parts of Guinea and the slave trade* … of 1734 itemises those revolts known to him and they are worth quoting *in extenso*. 'Mutinies', he writes,

> are generally occasioned by the sailors' ill-usage of these poor people. … In 1704 … on board the *Eagle* galley … commanded by my father [with only 10 crew, and 400 slaves from Old Calabar on board] … these circumstances put the Negroes on consulting how to mutiny, which they did at four in the afternoon just as they went to supper [adding weight to Phillips' nomination of the 'danger time'] … the Mate fired his pistol and shot the Negroe that had struck my father … at the sight of this the mutiny ended … I went in 1721 in the *Henry* … we were obliged to secure them very well in irons … yet they nevertheless mutinied … 'what had induced them to mutiny?' [the crew

enquired]. They answered that I was a great rogue to buy them in order to carry them away from their own country and that they were resolved to regain their liberty if possible. ... A few days after this we discovered that they were plotting again and preparing to mutiny ... I knew several voyages had proved unsuccessful by mutinies; as they occasioned either the total loss of the ship and the White men's lives; or at least by rendering it absolutely necessary to kill or wound a great number of Slaves. ... I knew many of these Cormantine negroes despised punishment and even death itself ... a month after this ... I met ... the *Elisabeth* [upon which a mutiny had taken place] ... above one hundred of the Negroes then on board ... did not understand a word of the Gold Coast language and so had not been in the plot. But this mutiny was continued by a few Cormantee negroes who had been purchased about two or three days before ... [the Captain of the *Ferrers*] had on board so many negroes of one town and language it required the utmost care and management to keep them from mutinying.

Snelgrave learnt later that Captain Messervy's 'utmost care and management' had failed to prevent a mutiny ten days out from Africa in which Messervy was killed and the mutiny was in the event only put down after the slaughter of 80 of the *Ferrers*' slaves.[16] John Newton, active in the mid-eighteenth century stressed the significance and frequency of such challenges to his and others' commercial success. He believed that insurrection was always 'meditated; for the men slaves are not easily reconciled to their confinement and treatment ... they are seldom suppressed without considerable loss; and sometimes they succeed. ... Seldom a year passes but we hear of one or more such catastrophes'.[17] The reference to frequency of uprisings seems not to be the 'hard-sell' of a merchant group eager to exaggerate the rigours of their business and thus justify the high prices they charged. William Bosman, a man rightly credited with an alert mind and a good eye, wrote in 1705:

I have twice met with this misfortune; and the first time proved very lucky to me, I not in the least suspecting it; but the up-roar was timely quashed by the master of the ship and myself by causing the abettor to be shot through the head. ... But the second time ... the male slaves ... possessed themselves of a hammer ... with which ... they broke all their fetters in pieces ... they came above deck and fell upon our men ... and would certainly have mastered the ship, if a French and English ship had not happened to lye by us ... (and) ... came to our assistance ... before all was appeased about twenty of them were killed. The Portuguese have been more unlucky in this particular than we for in four years time they lost four ships in this manner.[18]

Newton's own ship the *Duke of Argyle* was subjected to what he argued was a wide conspiracy which was detected but hours before the rising.[19] In 1752 Captain Belson's snow[20] was lost to slaves who later decamped on the Sierra Leone coast. Owen in his *Journal of a slave dealer on the coast of Africa and America* tells of the successful takeover of a French vessel by its captive cargo who managed to kill all the crew. In command, the slaves, or rather ex-slaves, were apparently seeking a safe anchorage when Owen's ship encountered them and attempted to capture both them and their prize vessel. So formidable was their defence that Owen was forced to retire from the exchange, and although he tells us little more, it seems fair to conclude that the slaves made good their escape. Owen blamed his officers for this reverse; in another of his accounts he blames his own ill-health for his loss of an entire cargo who rose and decamped to a man off Sherbro Island in 1750.[21]

These are only a few examples of a very large tally of successful and unsuccessful slave risings on ship-board. While there is little direct evidence of a continuum of resistance from capture through the long process of trans-shipment to arrival in the Americas, we can at least ask some questions and provide fewer answers about such evidence. Firstly they, and other sorts of incidents, were frequent enough to merit quite prominent mention in the available contemporary sources. There are good reasons to treat these with care. Some of the literature is manifestly 'abolitionist' and hence eager to draw attention to examples of barbarism. How generalisable some of the material is can only be a question. Clearly it would be wrong to presume a rebellion in every barracoon, a mutiny on every ship. But through the route of the anti-slavery material *and* importantly through that of the slaving interest itself, we do get a picture of geographically and temporally widespread incidence of insurrection. This was equally clearly part of the widespread trader's information about the coast of West Africa. It is notable just how international the examples of insurrection are. Dutch traders, say, knew all about what happened to American or French ships. Africans involved in the trade in a variety of roles were presumably no less aware than their white trading partners whose knowledge of the interior was so slight. Wadstrom, for example, uses African informants extensively in his reasoning. Thus it is fair to assume that these epics, and the smaller and possibly more frequent incidents, were part of the 'trading climate' and part of popular knowledge. Given that most slaves destined for the Americas spent long periods within the general confines of the trading establishments, it is by no means outrageous to suggest that many of them were well acquainted with the possibly embellished accounts of past events.

Some of the evidence points to the existence of just such an awareness and the prevalence of a 'lore' amongst slaves. Phillips writes of Africans whilst still on their native shores 'having a more dreadful apprehension of

18   OUT OF THE HOUSE OF BONDAGE

Barbadoes than we can have of hell'.[22] Bosman furnishes us with his ideas of the kinds of fear that gave rise to resistance.

> We are sometimes sufficiently plagued with a parcel of slaves which come from a far in-land country who very innocently persuade one another that we buy them only to fatten and afterwards eat them ... they resolve ... to run away from the ship, kill the Europeans and set the vessel ashore.[23]

Bosman's implication was, presumably, that such an outrageous idea could only emerge from a 'far in-land' and hence provincial sensibility, though as with most imputations of anthropophagy a closer examination of the terms being used in the several languages might have yielded him a rather more rational but no less horrific set of apprehensions. But not all captives were from 'far in-land'. In a very suggestive passage the Commissioner for Sierra Leone writing again to Canning in April 1825 tells of the fate of a French slaver, the *Deux Soeurs*. 'The crew', he says,

> were overpowered by the slaves who killed eight of their [French] number leaving only three persons to navigate the vessel and that under a promise they should land them on some part of the coast near to the Plantain Islands ... *The catastrophe on board may be attributed to several of the slaves who had been employed as labourers and boatmen* [in Sierra Leone] ... *these men were aware of the consequences of being taken to the coast which no doubt induced them to have recourse to force to effect their liberation.*[24]

All institutions have traditions; and prisons and even concentration camps are and were replete with their own customs and folklore every bit as much as regiments, colleges and public schools. Although we know far too little about the social history of the growing coastal towns in which many slaves spent their last months in Africa, they were indubitably hot-beds of rumour both false and true. Against this notion of something akin to 'working class consciousness' must be put the plurality of languages spoken within those outposts. The cultural heterogeneity of these forts must be acknowledged and, because of the enormous inaccuracy of 'ethnic' description, it is unlikely that we will ever know what that 'cultural mix' was at any point in time.[25] Given the nature of capture and the ways in which trading posts acted as collection points, it is highly unlikely that slave 'consignments' were often homogeneous, however much the traders wished to satisfy the stereotyped preferences of the putative purchasers. But communications clearly did exist, as many of the bigger escape attempts and ship-board mutinies are on a relatively large scale. Moreover it is equally clear that informal leadership emerged within the barracoons. Some will be tempted to see such people as African chiefs, but it would only be the most

RESISTANCE TO ENSLAVEMENT IN AFRICA

unlucky chief who found himself enslaved. It would be my suggestion that leadership in the forts and on ship-board depended less upon traditional status (a status that would have meant little to strangers to that particular polity) than upon the sorts of factors that throw up group leadership in adverse circumstances. While the world we are dealing with is light-years from the *Colditz Story* it is not ridiculous to suggest that leaders were, *inter alia*, the most knowing and those who consistently defied restriction. Francis Moore's description of an attempted break-out of the particularly gloomy confines of Cape Coast Castle in November 1730 (by sawing through the bars at the windows) tells us that the leader had led several such bids for freedom; his prominence and courage were rewarded by one hundred lashes.[26]

Part of that 'knowing' must have included the formidable problem of what to do with liberty once attained. The coastal belt – and indeed the areas under the control of the great forest states – were hardly comfortable safe-houses for the self-liberated. Treaty relationships, as we have seen, operated in areas polluted by the trade and the capture of a runaway – often a fairly obvious figure in an area dominated by kinship ideology and reality – was often a commercial act. A runaway could be sold or returned for a reward. It is safe to assume that escape routes and safe territories were part of the essential knowledge of the captive group contemplating escape. The fascinating pre-figuring of maroon societies in the Americas is visible here, in and just off the African mainland. There are many accounts of liberated slave societies in the eighteenth century. The Upper Guinea coast has innumerable clusters of islands from Sherbro island northwards. Some of these certainly became favoured sites for the protection of hard-won independence from servitude. John Matthews in his *Voyage to the River Sierra Leone* of 1788 speaks of the Iles de Los just off modern Conakry as just such a haven.[27] But such free societies also took root on the mainland. The escape following successful mutiny aboard a Danish vessel in 1788 lying in the Rokel estuary led to establishment of a free settlement which was called the Deserters' Town a few miles out of Freetown in the hills.[28] The fact that the narratives of a great many of the initially successful mass escapes end with mass re-captures, sometimes months or even years later, suggests that groups stayed together and forged some kind of new society rather than scattering and attempting to return to their motherlands.

The frequency of escapes, rebellions both successful and unsuccessful, and the intelligence about places of safety for the fugitive, suggest a mounting challenge not only against the Atlantic trade but also against indigenous institutions of slavery. The nineteenth century was indubitably the period in which slavery became a particularly significant economic and social institution within Africa, but it was also a period of extensive self-liberation which threatened domestic and export economies as well as political

20 OUT OF THE HOUSE OF BONDAGE

control. It was, after all, the rapid recognition of this that led both British and French to abandon their opposition to slavery in general and to maintain hostility to the trade in humanity only, whilst smiling upon what they now dignified as 'domestic slavery', a position which was held until the mid-1920s in some areas of West Africa. Slavery was a state which few passively accepted or became resigned to. Fear of captivity haunted all who had any knowledge of its processes and by the eighteenth century it was only people fortunate enough to live beyond its compass who could have been innocent of it. There are innumerable accounts of men and women, like the 'free native mariner on board our ship Providence ... who once in irons lost his spirits irrecoverably' and died 'by the "sulks" '.[30] The counterblast to this sense of despair was of course the hope of salvation. Throughout the course of the slave trade, West Africa had become a place in which one could trust few people and, still less, luck to provide such salvation. That much is 'fact'. What is more elusive is the sense of a growing resistance in thought and action that gave rise to instances where 'slaves rose to a man, knocked off each others fetters and ... attacked the barricade'[31] as well as the 'sulks'. As Wadstrom reported, a captain 'who surpasses most others in effrontery and hardness of disposition' informed him how best to restrain a cargo: 'I put them all in leg-irons; and if these be not enough, why then I handcuff them; if hand cuffs be too little, I put a collar round their neck, with a chain locked to a ring-bolt on the deck; if one chain won't do, I put two, and if two won't do I put three; you may trust me for that ... these are not cruelties; they are matters of course; there's no carrying on the trade without them'.[32] It would seem as a matter of commonsense, for it is not something that we are likely to be able to prove, that such resistance was part of the cultural baggage the unwilling emigrants took with them to the Americas. It is not a collection of experiences and feelings that will fall easily within the notion of 'Africanisms' but it seems likely that they were vital elements in the making of the black diaspora.

NOTES

1. This has a long history; for example all Africanists would happily acknowledge their debt to the pioneering work of scholars on Amerindian language, society and history in the period before the Second World War. More recently there has been a more obvious relationship between the growth of both African and Afro-American historical studies, especially in the United States of America, which is perhaps most obviously seen in the work of and composition of the history group at Johns Hopkins University at Baltimore, Maryland. More generally the work of scholars like Eugene Genovese, Herb Gutman and Nate Huggins has had an inspirational impact upon the growth of a lively school of 'revisionist' historians working on the history of Southern Africa, a debt directly acknowledged by some of its most notable figures like Charles van Onselen and Martin Legassick. Recognition of the need to work together and across the canvas is implicit in the career of the late Walter Rodney and is explicitly evoked in published conference proceedings such as David W. Cohen and Jack Green's *Neither Slave nor Free*, Baltimore 1972 and Shula

RESISTANCE TO ENSLAVEMENT IN AFRICA

Marks and Richard Rathbone's introduction to the special number of the *Journal of African History* (Vol. 24 no. 2 1983) devoted to the history of the family in Africa.

2. These ideas, crudely caricatured for reasons of brevity, can be found in a large number of works such as Orlando Patterson's *Sociology of Slavery*, London 1967, Roger Bastide's *African Civilisations in the New World*, New York 1972, Eugene Genovese's *From Rebellion to Revolution*, Baton Rouge 1979 and Herbert Aptheker's *American Negro Slave Revolts*, New York 1978, and have found their way into much of the more general reading.

3. From Hakluyt's *Principall Navigations*, Glasgow 1903–5, pp. 398–445. Hawkins had in fact encountered no less resistance on the 2nd voyage (1564) where *Principall Navigations* (pp. 9–63) records, *inter alia*, that they 'were landing boat after boat, and divers of our men scattering themselves, contrary to the Capitaine's wishes ... in the mean time the Negros came upon them and hurt many thus scattered'.

4. Commissioner to Canning, 15 May 1824 in Correspondence, class A, *Parliamentary Papers* (IUP reprint), vol. XXVII. This and other comments from this useful source suggest on this, and on other occasions, that the anti-slavery squadrons were far from being the only local opponents of the outlawed trade.

5. From Wadstrom's *An Essay on colonisation*, London 1794, Part 2, p. 14 (the David and Charles reprint of 1968).

6. This and the following example come from the collection of letters from the *Outfactors of the Royal African Company to the Chief Agents of Cape Coast Castle* which are to be found in the Bodleian Library, Oxford.

7. *Vide supra*.

8. From 'Further papers relating to the suppression of the slave trade' in the *Parliamentary Papers* 1821, Vol. XXIII. Collier's writing is unusually sensitive and observant and although this worthy baronet's political heart is worn clearly on his uniform sleeve he seems not to be an elaborator.

9. From John Atkins, Surgeon, R.N. *A voyage to Guinea* ... London 1735, cited and quoted in *Documents illustrative of the slave trade* edited by E. Donnan, Vol. II, pp. 265–6, Washington 1930. Other than Atkins' second-hand provenance for Captain Tomba his origins remain obscure. It is however a remarkable portrait.

10. From the Class A Correspondence, *Parliamentary Papers*, Vol. XXIX, 1826. See my comment in note 4, supra.

11. In Donnan, *op. cit.*, vol. 1, p. 199.

12. *The voyage of the Hannibal, 1693–4* ... by Thomas Phillips to be found in Churchill's *Collections of voyages and travels* ... London 1732, vol. IV, pp. 218–19.

13. This comment is based on remarks of Phillips which chime in oddly with his actual role in the trade. Writing of Africans he says, for example, 'nor can I imagine why they should be despised for their colour being what they cannot help and the effect of the climate it has pleased God to appoint them. I can't think there is any intrinsick value in one colour more than another, nor that white is better than black'. Phillips *ibidem*. Such comment is less obviously apologetic than for example that of Atkins (*op. cit.*, pp. 168–73): 'it is advisable at all times to have a diligent watch on their actions, yet (abating their fetters) to treat them with all gentleness and civility'.

14. Phillips, *op. cit.*, p. 229. Such elaborate precautions were not of course the result of a history of fatalistic Africans who had no option but to play the role of victims in this repulsive commerce.

15. *Ibidem*. Whether the Gold Coasters were free or slave is not indicated. P. 407.

16. W. Snelgrave, *A New Account of Some Parts of Guinea and the Slave Trade*, London 1734, pp. 162–5.

17. *Ibidem*. The reference to language homogeneity or heterogeneity in the case of Messervy's ship the *Ferrers* is an important one which I touch on below. The whole question of communication between captives is, to my knowledge, largely untouched. Snelgrave suggests that a large group of mutually intelligible slaves demanded especial care which, to stretch this slight evidence further, suggests that slavers would have taken steps to avoid such a situation. It is interesting to note the drift of the interrogation of John Jackson, a factor for the African Company for 16 years in Africa in the Minutes of Evidence on the settlements of Sierra Leone and Fernando Po on 5 July 1830 in the *Parliamentary Papers* (Cmnd. 661) p. 91. He is asked: 'Are you aware that the liberated Africans generally

22 OUT OF THE HOUSE OF BONDAGE

speaking speak different languages, and are unable to form a society among themselves from the want of a common tongue?' Jackson replies: 'I have understood so; but we have some natives at Cape Coast who, I believe belong to the same nations from which the slaves come and have learnt the language of the place; they continue to speak also the languages of the countries from which they have come'. The contemporary evidence of very widespread multi-lingualism in coastal West Africa and the large scale of many of the risings briefly looked at here seem to suggest dynamic processes at work both in the coastal factory area and on ship-board through which usable *linguae francae* emerged. The evidence of the non-participation of some slaves in the revolt in the *Elizabeth* does, of course, suggest a contrary picture and it is, above all, clear that the composition of every slave consignment had its own character and that generalisation is probably dangerous.

18. William Bosman, *A new and accurate description of the coast of Guinea* ..., London 1705, pp. 363–5.
19. B. Martin and M. Spurrel (eds.), *The Journal of a slave trader (John Newton) 1750–54*, London 1962, pp. 54–5.
20. In Donnan, *op. cit.*, Vol. III, p. 315. A 'snow' is described by the *O.E.D.* as: 'a small sailing vessel resembling a brig, carrying a main and a foremast and a supplementary trysail mast close behind the mainmast; formerly a warship'.
21. E. Martin (ed.), N. Owen's *Journal of a slave dealer on the coast of Africa and America from the year 1746 to the year 1757*, London 1930, p. 24.
22. Phillips, *op. cit.*, pp. 218–19. The specificity of this comment seems to cast real doubt upon notions of the unawareness or naivety of slaves as to the real nature of what they were enduring.
23. William Bosman, *op. cit.*, pp. 363–5. I suggest the linguistic problems with this quotation in the text. Those acquainted with, for example, the ambiguity of the word 'chop' in contemporary West African creole and pidgins will be able to imagine some of the difficulties involved in interpreting Bosman's 'throw away' lines.
24. Commissioner Sierra Leone to Secretary Canning, 10 April 1825. Class A Correspondence, *Parliamentary Papers*, Vol. XXIX 1826. My italics. This late but fascinating comment contributes to a wider appreciation of the heterogeneity of slave consignments as well as to the generation of coastal communities in which, I would argue, slaves played an important and not always brief part. Although the French crew do not succeed, on this occasion, in the impressing of labourers there must have been many cases where such men were carried off. Although it is dangerous to build on single examples, this case raises important questions about the nature of consciousness with which this paper is concerned. The men the Commissioner writes about were manifestly not rural producers nor were they necessarily people clinging in adverse circumstances to older traditional cosmologies.
25. The inaccuracy either accidental or intended of trader descriptions of slaves are clear to anyone with a working knowledge of the social and political geography of pre-colonial West Africa. There are no fewer problems with ethnic attributions of slave-owners on the other side of the Atlantic, or for that matter, with the ethnic self-identifications of slaves themselves, for names, customs and even languages can be acquired. Ethnic categories in pre-colonial West Africa were only rarely the water-tight and unvarying identities that a later scholarship infected with 19th century and later nationalisms tended to stress. Most African social systems were absorptive rather than exclusive and, given the area's vivid history of inter-regional trade, human movement and interaction there is an enormous risk in the over-stretching of traders' taxonomies, some of which are clearly casual and ignorant in any case.
26. Francis Moore, *Travels into the inland parts of Africa* in T. Astley, *A new and general collection of voyages*, London 1745. Vol. II, p. 49.
27. London 1788, p. 16.
28. See C. B. Wadstrom, *op. cit.*, Part II, p. 79. The information comes from Wadstrom's edited version of the *Report of the Directors of the Sierra Leone Company* of 1791.
29. Wadstrom, *op. cit.*, Part II, p. 82.
30. *Ibidem*, p. 83.
31. *Ibidem*, p. 87.
32. *Ibidem*, p. 85.

Runaway Slaves and Social Bandits in Southern Angola, 1875–1913

W. G. Clarence-Smith

As the Atlantic slave trade slowly came to an end, slavery enjoyed a new lease of life in Africa. Most of the expansion in the use of slave labour occurred in African societies.[1] However, Portuguese colonists also seized upon the opportunities of employing slaves in Africa. Like the Sultans of Zanzibar, the authorities in Lisbon came under strong British pressure to abolish slavery, and legislation to this effect was promulgated in 1875. But in the two chief colonies of Angola and São Tomé, *de facto* slavery continued until the republicans seized power in Lisbon in 1910. The diplomatic controversy which this provoked has been studied in some detail, but little is known as to the lives of slaves themselves, especially in Angola.[2] Elsewhere I have attempted to shed light on slave conditions in the southern part of Angola, and here I wish to concentrate more specifically on the question of escaped slaves, after a brief survey of the general situation.[3]

The slave population of Southern Angola was concentrated in the coastal strip, in spite of the arid conditions prevailing in this northward prolongation of the Namib desert. The cold maritime current which gives rise to desert conditions also provides rich fishing, and the desert is broken by a handful of oases, fed by temporary streams running off the highlands of the great African escarpment inland. Both fisheries and oases came to be intensively exploited by slave-owning Portuguese settlers from the middle of the nineteenth century. Roughly dried and salted fish was sold over a wide area of Equatorial Africa, while foodstuffs serviced the fisheries and rum oiled the wheels of trade with the interior. The highlands of Southern Angola were settled by Boer trekkers and poor Madeiran peasants from the 1880s, but their economy did not require large labour inputs, based as it was on transport riding, hunting, mercenary service, extensive pastoralism and subsistence crop agriculture. There were thus few slaves owned by Europeans outside the coastal strip, although the highlands were of great importance as a refuge for escaped slaves. In all, the slave population of Southern Angola rose from between three and four thousand in the 1870s to around ten thousand by the time of abolition in 1913.

Slave conditions in the fisheries were almost certainly the worst in the whole Portuguese empire. The quality of food and drinking water was very poor in the isolated fishing ports on the edge of the desert, with water as the greatest problem. Housing was also wretched, owing to the lack of building

OUT OF THE HOUSE OF BONDAGE

Reproduced by permission of Cambridge University Press from G. Clarence-Smith, *Slaves Peasants and Capitalists in Southern Angola, 1840–1926*

materials in the desert, and temperatures could drop very low in certain seasons. Sex ratios were uneven, with a high preponderance of men. Women were only employed for the lighter work of drying and salting. Moreover, nearly all the slaves came from the interior of Angola and were totally unaccustomed to the sea and maritime jobs. Skilled Cabinda seamen from Northern Angola entered the area as free immigrants and had jobs as foremen or captains of fishing vessels. All the slaves, whether in the fisheries or other employment, suffered from the arbitrary violence inflicted on them by their owners and foremen.

The most common form of slave resistance was flight, but before looking at this phenomenon in more detail, it is worth surveying other forms of resistance. A serious crisis followed the legal abolition of slavery in 1875, which decreed that all slaves were to be freed within a period of three years. In 1876, the labour inspector attempted to make the slaves sign an initial obligatory five-year contract with their masters, after which, they were told, they would be entirely free. However, the slaves demanded that they should immediately be given their certificates of manumission. Slave resentment was increased by the fact that the Southern settlers had managed to get the legal minimum pay reduced from £0.27 per month, exclusive of food, lodging and so forth, to only £0.13 for men and £0.09 for women. The slaves discovered that original rates had been maintained in Central Angola, which added to their discontent. In view of this situation, punctuated by occasional acts of disobedience and even violence towards the employers, the authorities moved slowly in the drawing up of the new contracts.

However, in 1879, the three-year period of grace was over, and the new contracts had to be imposed. The governor of Southern Angola decided on a show of strength. On the basis of a denunciation of dubious value, he accepted that a great conspiracy was afoot in one of the larger plantations, with the aim of bringing out all slaves in a rebellion of the kind that Haïti had known. Six alleged ring-leaders were seized and sentenced to a flogging of 600 to 1,000 lashes, followed by deportation to São Tomé. At least two of the slaves died from the flogging before they could be deported. This action was quite illegal, and the governor was prosecuted and dismissed. Unfortunately, I was refused access to the thick file on the trial in the Lisbon archives, so that it is impossible to know what substance there was to the accusation of a slave conspiracy.

The new governor was one of the foremost Portuguese liberals of his time, and he attempted to ensure a real transition from slavery to contract labour. During his few months in office in 1880, he toured the fisheries and plantations, enforcing the payment of wages in cash, prosecuting settlers for illegal torture of workers, and encouraging labourers to lay their complaints before him. But he came up against the constant hostility of the settlers, and was revolted by the connivance of officials and the leniency of magistrates towards settlers convicted of homicide and torture. As a result he resigned and was replaced by a man who had lived for many years in the area and was close to the settlers' views.

Violence immediately flared up again. In December 1880 there was a riot involving some 200 slaves, which left nine people seriously wounded. Five young white girls were also said to have been raped and killed by a band of slaves. It is difficult to sort out how much violence was initiated by the slaves and how much was due to the provocations of the threatened settlers. Matters came to a head in 1884, when the bulk of the new contracts expired. Instead of allowing the slaves to choose whether to sign a contract and with whom, the authorities imposed the automatic prolongation of the initial contracts for a further five years, in flagrant violation of the law. When the slaves protested at this denial of their freedom, 400 were shipped off to serve as soldiers in Mozambique, being replaced at the government's expense by an equal number of newly purchased (or redeemed in official parlance) slaves from Central Angola.

After these ten agitated years, a tense calm returned to Southern Angola, as the slaves realised that the promise of freedom had been an empty one. Contracts were automatically prolonged every five years, and slaves were bought and sold freely through the practice of sub-contracting or endorsing contracts. The tiny salaries were grudgingly paid, but usually late and in alcohol or bonds redeemable only at settler stores. The slaves fell back on theft, sabotage and idling, and escaped whenever they could.[4]

It is usually said that escape was easier for slaves in Africa than in the New World, but Southern Angola was something of an exception to this general rule. The desert posed great obstacles to flight, and the slaves isolated in the fishing ports were in an especially awkward situation. It is possible that the geographical environment of the South contributed to the peculiar harshness of slavery in this part of Angola, which most observers commented upon.[5] Masters took further precautions by locking slaves up at night in compounds surrounded by high walls, which were topped with broken glass.[6] Moreover, the settlers generally did not buy local Africans, who knew the region, but preferred to purchase their labourers in the great slave mart of Novo Redondo, further up the coast. These slaves were drawn from a variety of Central Angolan peoples, with the Ovimbundu predominating from the 1880s, and they were brought to the South by sea.[7]

In spite of these precautions, the sources are full of references to slaves escaping. In the fisheries, the labourers were sometimes able to steal a fishing boat and escape by sea. In 1885, 14 slaves escaped in this way from the fishing port of Porto Alexandre.[8] Those who tried their luck across the desert were often befriended by the nomadic Herero inhabitants of the area, who bore a deep grudge against the settlers for the loss of the best pasture lands to European plantation agriculture.[9] For the slaves of the foothills, escape was relatively easy, as it simply involved finding a way up the escarpment.[10] However, the plantations in this area scarcely survived the twin blows of massive servile escapes in the late 1870s and the collapse of cotton prices on the world market. The slaves of the South came increasingly to be concentrated in the booming fisheries of the coast, and in the neighbouring oases, which turned more and more to the production of foodstuffs for the fisheries.[11]

The destinations of those who were successful in their bid for freedom come out less clearly from the sources, but it is possible to distinguish some tendencies. A few fugitives managed to return to their homes in Central Angola, in spite of the considerable distance involved.[12] It was even alleged that the chiefs who had originally sold them into servitude shared the proceeds of the sales with returning fugitives.[13] However, it is clear that for many slaves any return to their homes was out of the question. Those sold into slavery for a crime, usually witchcraft or murder, and those handed over as security for an unpaid debt could not go back to their societies of origin. Moreover, the distances and the insecurity of the backlands made it highly likely that fugitives would simply be re-enslaved by Ovimbundu or Ovambo slave raiders. And some slaves, born into servitude or taken to Southern Angola as young children, had become creolised and had no home to return to.[14]

For some labourers, escape was merely a way to change from a bad master to a slightly better one. When labour was scarce, masters did all they could to entice slaves away from other owners. In some cases, masters cynically utilised labour legislation to have a rival prosecuted and to obtain his workers in a process of redistribution. In these situations, masters welcomed runaways and took them on, instead of handing them over to the authorities for restitution.[15]

Although it is impossible to do any kind of quantitative analysis, it appears that the majority of slaves who successfully escaped joined bandit groups in the mountains of the interior. This phenomenon was not peculiar to the South, as the broken terrain of the great African escarpment was a magnet for similar groups of malcontents throughout the colony, in a period when Portuguese control was partial and fragile.[16] Three main groups contributed to bandit strength in the South, dispossessed local Africans, soldiers who deserted from the colonial army, and runaway slaves. Another group consisted of Africans from Namibia, who had either come with the Boers or fled on their own from the upheavals in that territory, but they appear to have stayed apart and distinct from other bandits, and were at times used as mercenary auxiliaries by the Portuguese.[17]

The distinction between runaway slaves and deserting soldiers is in some senses an academic one, given the nature of recruiting in Angola. As late as the 1890s, a high proportion of Angolan soldiers were simply purchased in

28 OUT OF THE HOUSE OF BONDAGE

the slave marts. Technically they were redeemed from servitude on condition that they served a fixed-term contract in the army, but in practice they tended not to be released and to be treated exactly as the state slaves of earlier days. Other soldiers were men captured by the Portuguese on military expeditions against 'rebels', and incorporated into the armed forces to avoid tiresome judicial proceedings. Many of these latter came from Mozambique, as it was judged safer to swap such captives between Portugal's two main colonies. Although soldiers were in this sense difficult to distinguish from runaway slaves, their weapons and military experience were of great utility to the bandit leaders.[18]

Some runaways were incorporated into Nyaneka societies as peaceful citizens,[19] but it is difficult to see the bandit groups as a simple extension of this situation. It is true that bandit leaders often were drawn from the traditional chiefly clans of the Nyaneka peoples of the highlands, and that many Nyaneka and Herero, the latter from the coastal strip, joined the bandits after losing their cattle, lands and political independence to the invading settlers.[20] Unfortunately, it is impossible to say whether such local Africans were numerically more important in the bandit groups, but descriptive accounts imply that runaways and deserters formed the hard core of the groups, even if they were dependent to a considerable extent on help from local peasants.[21] Moreover, the most famous bandit leader was both a nephew of one of the foremost Nyaneka chiefs and a deserter from the army. Mbundu was captured in 1882 and drafted into the colonial army in Luanda. He escaped with his rifle in about 1887 and returned home to lead one of the most successful bandit groups.[22] The entire life-style of the bandits differed from that of local peasants, for there were few women in the bandit lairs, little cultivation or other forms of economic activity apart from raiding, an insecure and sometimes wandering existence, and a premium awarded to military efficiency over chiefly birth.[23]

It needs to be said at this point that the use of the term bandit is not intended to reproduce settler stereotypes of the time, but rather to insert the Southern Angolan case into the broad comparative perspective of Hobsbawm's work on social banditry. As long as bandits are supported by part or all of the peasant population, they cannot be classed as common robbers. Robin Hood figures, who rob the rich to give to the poor, may be only figures of literature, but there can be little doubt that bandits have frequently been 'avengers', striking down the enemies of the peasants, and therefore helped and protected by the peasants.[24]

The first period of bandit activity was concentrated in the foothills of the escarpment in the late 1870s. When the 1875 law was not followed by the liberation of slaves, large numbers of workers fled from the plantations and took refuge in the mountains above. They were aided and abetted by the local Herero population, whose relations with the settlers were extremely

RUNAWAY SLAVES AND SOCIAL BANDITS 29

bad. The cotton boom of the 1860s had led to the extension of plantations in this area, and thus to the loss of grazing for the herds of the pastoral and semi-nomadic Herero. Serious drought in the late 1870s brought the situation to a head.[25] The settlers alleged that the Herero deliberately incited the slaves to abandon the plantations, in order to ruin the settlers and force them to leave the area, but this is impossible to verify.[26] It is more likely that the fall in cotton prices from the mid-1870s, and the drought, put strains on the planters in this marginal area with poor communications, and that this resulted in greater demands or worse material conditions being imposed on the servile population.[27]

In addition to general raiding, the escaped slaves returned to wreak vengeance on their former masters. Thus, in 1877, four ex-slaves led a raiding party of Herero and other fugitive slaves to the plantation of their former master, where they burned the house down and seized 70 head of cattle.[28] Even more notable was the attack on the wealthiest planter in the area in 1879, in which he and an employee were both wounded, but his cattle and other property were not touched. This planter had a particularly bad reputation for brutality in his treatment of slaves, and the attack was almost certainly one of pure revenge.[29] A year later, the Governor-General of Angola commented on the fact that raids were not directed against the plantations within easiest reach, but were concentrated against the property of settlers with whom ex-slaves and local Africans had a score to settle.[30] The government drafted in extra troops to deal with the crisis, but the plantations of the foothills did not recover from the combination of economic and social upheavals for many decades.[31]

From the mid-1880s, the focus of bandit activity shifted to the northern highlands, where the bulk of land and cattle alienation by Boers and Madeirans was concentrated. Although the Nyaneka chiefs led the resistance to the invasion, runaways and deserters provided many if not most of their fighting forces. In 1885, the Portuguese mounted an expedition against the principal stronghold of Kaholo. They found six kraals in an intensively cultivated little valley, which they burnt to the ground. However, they were unable to take the main fortification of the bandits, built on traditional lines on a rocky spur above the valley. The gaps between the boulders had been filled with stakes some three metres high and 30 centimetres thick, and the Portuguese decided that it was impregnable for a force without field artillery. Seizing all the cattle they could find, the Portuguese forces retired under constant harassment from the bandits.[32]

There were further expeditions mounted against Kaholo in subsequent years, but with no greater success than the first. The bandit stronghold continued to be a magnet for runaway slaves and deserters, who supplemented the proceeds from raiding by collecting wax and honey. The governor of Southern Angola in 1891 fulminated against the unscrupulous

30   OUT OF THE HOUSE OF BONDAGE

Portuguese petty traders who bought the cattle raided by the bandits in exchange for guns and ammunition, and acted as spies and informers for their bandit clients. However, the governor also revealed that the bandits were moving away from their original activities as avengers, and crossing the subtle but crucial line which separates social banditry from common robbery. The bandits were now raiding local Africans as well as settlers, and, even worse, were seizing African women and children to sell into slavery. Peasant support for the bandits was waning, with some Africans moving out of the area, and others cooperating with the Portuguese against the bandits.[33] By this period, the worst phase of land alienation was over, the Nyaneka chiefs had patched up some kind of peace with the Boers and Portuguese, and the Nyaneka peasants were drifting back onto their ancestral lands as squatters and herders for the whites.[34]

In 1892, the bandits therefore decided that it was dangerous to stay in Kaholo any longer, even though the Portuguese still had not managed to take the fortified *cipaka* (fort) by storm. Portuguese military resistance was slowly becoming more effective, with the formation of a squadron of irregular white cavalry in 1887, and the widely publicised impending arrival of a force of metropolitan cavalry to keep the peace.[35] Some of the Kaholo bandits moved north-east, but the greater part fell back on the southern highlands, where Bata Bata became their chief stronghold. The thick acacia forests of this region had the advantage of making the penetration of cavalry forces very difficult, and it was further away from the centres of white settlement. As in Kaholo, no single leader emerged. Instead, there was a somewhat uneasy juxtaposition of several warlords, of whom Mbundu was the most important.[36]

For over a decade, there was a kind of stalemate. The metropolitan dragoons, who finally arrived in the South in 1894, were able to protect the settlers to some extent, as the bandits never seem to have taken to using horses. But the Portuguese were quite unable to destroy the bandit lairs, which continued to attract the runaways and deserters who could make it to the fortified *cipaka*.[37] One bandit leader was betrayed, captured and shot by his escort in 1897, partly, it would appear, because local Africans became tired of his depredations.[38] The famous, or infamous, Mbundu was caught by surprise by the dragoons in 1901, who managed to enter his fortified *cipaka* in Bata Bata. The Portuguese took the *cipaka* with their bayonets, killed 46 men, took Mbundu's head back with them to expose in public, and set fire to the *cipaka*, burning alive some of the few women who had been caught. But the Portuguese were unable to follow up on this coup, and they retired very rapidly. Two traders who arrived on the spot a little later reported that over a thousand armed bandits had gathered at Bata Bata and were planning their revenge.[39] Four years later, Bata Bata was still a centre of bandit activity.[40]

RUNAWAY SLAVES AND SOCIAL BANDITS 31

The final eradication of bandit activity was a by-product of large military operations against the Ovambo peoples and the Germans in the far interior of the colony. The bandit *cipaka*, which were reported to be defended by stone walls, were taken one by one with the help of field artillery, and with the help of the Namibian auxiliaries, pardoned for their earlier bandit activity and newly christened 'native police'. The frustrations and humiliations suffered by the Portuguese in their campaigns in the far interior were taken out on the Nyaneka, who were submitted to a veritable reign of terror. Between 1906 and 1910, the southern highlands were 'pacified' and made to pay hut tax and provide forced labour.[41] And after the republican revolution of 1910 in Portugal, the disguised slavery and appalling military conditions which had contributed so much to banditry were finally reformed.

Slave resistance in Southern Angola correlated closely with rising expectations. Resistance was concentrated in the decade between formal abolition in 1875 and the final decision of 1884 to continue slavery under another name. Where flight was comparatively easy, in the plantations of the foothills, the slaves more or less destroyed the settler economy, by withdrawing their labour through flight, and then returning to raid the plantations of their former masters. In the isolated fisheries and oases close to the coast, slave resistance was largely broken after the mid-1880s, and reports of slave escapes became less frequent. At the same time, the bandits in the highlands slowly turned from attacks against their former masters to attacks against their African neighbours. When the ex-slaves began to enslave others and sell them to Portuguese petty traders, the cycle was complete.

After the republican revolution of 1910 in Portugal, all the suppressed resentment of the slaves burst once more into the open. In 1912, according to the British consul, the servile population of the coastal strip was in a state of 'unrest and ill will', as the republican authorities seemed to be stalling on their promises to eradicate slavery once and for all. The first liberal governor appointed by the new authorities was forced out under settler pressure, and in 1913 the slaves took matters into their own hands, paralysing one of the major fishing companies by strikes and desertions. The forceful governor-general of Angola was obliged to come to Southern Angola in person to enforce the anti-slavery legislation, braving settler threats to rise in open rebellion. The effects of abolition were hotly contested. The government claimed that no more than 10 per cent of slaves changed masters, and that less than 2 per cent left the area to return home. The settlers countered by asserting that some 85 per cent of workers had abandoned their masters. Whatever the truth of these conflicting claims, all were agreed that the infamous status of slavery had at last been eradicated in Southern Angola. The remnants of the former slave population moved up in

32 OUT OF THE HOUSE OF BONDAGE

the social spectrum, becoming skilled labourers or petty entrepreneurs, while their place at the bottom of the labour hierarchy was filled by short-term forced labourers under contract from the interior.

NOTES

1. P. Lovejoy, *Transformations in slavery, a history of slavery in Africa*, Cambridge 1983.
2. For the diplomatic controversy, see especially J. Duffy, *A question of slavery*, Cambridge, Mass. 1967.
3. W. G. Clarence-Smith, *Slaves, peasants and capitalists in Southern Angola, 1840–1926*, Cambridge 1979; 'Mossamedes and its hinterland, 1875–1915', Ph.D. Thesis, University of London, 1975; 'Slavery in coastal Southern Angola, 1875–1913', *Journal of Southern African Studies*, 2, 2, 1976, pp. 214–23.
4. Further details on slave conditions can be obtained from the items in note 3.
5. See for instance Great Britain, Foreign Office, Historical Section, *Angola, including Cabinda*, London 1919, p. 42.
6. P. Möller, *Journey through Angola, Ovampoland and Damaraland, 1895–1896*, Cape Town 1974, p. 24.
7. Arquivo Histórico Ultramarino, Lisbon (henceforth AHU), Repartição 2, Pasta 7, Curador Geral 16.8.1884.
8. Arquivo Histórico de Angola, Luanda (henceforth AHA), Avulsos 41-70-3, Governador de Mossamedes, 31.8.1885.
9. *Jornal de Mossamedes*, 8.5.1884.
10. AHU, Repartição 1, Diversos 1868–1888, Governador de Mossamedes, Relatório, 19.6.1877.
11. See Clarence-Smith, *Slaves*, chapter 3.
12. AHU, Repartição 1, Pasta 4, Governador Geral, Relatório, 9.4.1884.
13. AHU, Repartição 2, Pasta 7, Curador Geral, 16.8.1884.
14. For an appreciation of conditions in the Ovimbundu area, see the Swiss mission journal, *Le Philafricain*. For creolisation, see AHA, Avulsos, 41-91-1, Curador de Mossamedes, 30.11.1912.
15. D. Postma, *De Trekboeren te St. Januario Humpata*, Amsterdam 1897, p. 234, for this phenomenon in general; AHU Repartição 2, Pasta 9, Governador Geral, 17.4.1885, for a particular case followed by branding with the old slave brand.
16. For details, see R. Pélissier, *Les guerres grises, résistance et révoltes en Angola, 1845–1941*, Orgeval 1977.
17. *Jornal de Mossamedes*, 5.6.1885. For Namibians, see Clarence-Smith, *Slaves*, pp. 87–8.
18. For the military purchase of slaves, see Arquivo Histórico Militar, Lisbon, Pasta 5, 23, Governador Geral 6.5.1884 and 7.4.1884. For captives as soldiers, see AHU, Pasta 48, Secretário Geral 23.7.1878. For Mozambicans sent to Angola, see R. Pélissier, *Naissance du Mozambique, résistance et révoltes anticoloniales, 1854–1918*, Orgeval 1984, 2 Vols., *passim*.
19. *Jornal de Mossamedes*, 20.6.1883, and other issues in that year.
20. See W. G. Clarence-Smith, 'Capitalist penetration among the Nyaneka of Southern Angola, 1760s to 1920s', *African Studies*, 37, 2, 1978, pp. 163–76.
21. See for instance *Jornal de Mossamedes*, 5.6.1885.
22. Padre Wieder, 'O Jau', *Boletim da Sociedade de Geografia de Lisboa*, 11. 10, 1892, p. 719. Other sources indicate that he did not escape, but was released for lack of any evidence as to his alleged crimes, for instance *Jornal de Mossamedes*, 1.1.1887.
23. Clarence-Smith, *Slaves*, pp. 85–7.
24. E. Hobsbawm, *Bandits*, London 1969.
25. R. de Sousa, 'Mossamedes', *Boletim da Sociedade de Geografia de Lisboa*, 7, 6, 1887, pp. 403–4; AHU, Repartição 1, Diversos 1868–1888, Governador de Mossamedes, Rela-

RUNAWAY SLAVES AND SOCIAL BANDITS

tório, 19.6.1887.
26. *Jornal de Mossamedes*, 8.5.1884.
27. AHU, Repartição 1, Pasta 2, Governador Geral 27.3.1880, for harsh treatment of slaves by masters. For economic decline, see the description in H. Capello and R. Ivens, *De Angola à contra-costa*, Lisbon 1886, Vol. 1, p.128.
28. AHU, Repartição 2, Pasta 3, Curador Geral, 1.2.1877.
29. AHU, Repartição 1, Diversos 1868–1888, Governador de Mossamedes, Relatório, 16.7.1879.
30. AHU, Repartição 1, Pasta 2, Governador Geral 27.3.1880.
31. Clarence-Smith, *Slaves*, chapter 3.
32. *Jornal de Mossamedes*, 20.7.1885.
33. Details of successive expeditions in *Jornal de Mossamedes*. For 1891, AHA, Avulsos, 41-70-6, Governador de Mossamedes, 6.4.1891.
34. Clarence-Smith, 'Capitalist penetration'.
35. AHU, Repartição 2, Pasta 23, Governador Geral, 12.11.1897.
36. For north-east movement, *Jornal de Mossamedes*, 15.6.1892. For Bata Bata, Archives Générales de la Congrégation du Saint-Esprit, Paris, 477-A-V, Muraton 4.7.1893.
37. AHU, Repartição 2, Pasta 22, Artur de Paiva 18.11.1895, for complaints as to Portuguese passivity.
38. AHU, Repartição 1, Pasta 17, Governador Geral 20.4.1897 and annexes.
39. AHU, Repartição 4, Pasta 2, Governador de Mossamedes, 19.11.1901, and annexes.
40. AHU, Repartição 1, Pasta 22, Governador Geral 11.10.1905.
41. AHU, Repartição 4, Pasta 5, Alves Roçadas, Relatório, 29.12.1906; J. de Almeida, *Sul d'Angola, relatório de um governo de distrito, 1908–1910*, pp.219–32.
42. For post-1910 developments, Clarence-Smith, *Slaves*, pp.41–2.

PART TWO

RUNAWAYS AND RESISTANCE
IN THE NEW WORLD

'They are Indeed the Constant Plague of Their Tyrants': Slave Defence of a Moral Economy in Colonial North Carolina, 1748–1772

Marvin L. Michael Kay
and Lorin Lee Cary

In the summer of 1761 Sambo faced a personal crisis not uncommon among slaves in colonial North Carolina. Edward Williams of Pasquotank County planned to sell Sambo's daughter to a neighbouring planter whose wife, Mary Nash, was regarded as being 'bad to the Negro'. Sambo refused to accept this painful reality, but his options were few. He could plead with Williams, and may have done so. Or, since he had no recourse to the courts, he could respond with acts, albeit risky, that whites defined as 'criminal': fleeing with his daughter, covertly destroying or stealing the property of the owners, or openly resorting to violence to wreak havoc on those who would disrupt his family. Ultimately, Sambo collaborated with one of Josiah Nash's slaves, David, to poison Mary Nash. He promised David, a white witness testifed at Sambo's trial, that the 'touck' he would prepare would not kill Mary Nash but rather make her ill and thus 'better to him thaⁿ she was'. Sambo, David said, anticipated that this illness also somehow would ensure that Nash 'should not have the Negro girl he wanted to buy', Sambo's daughter. Whether or not Sambo's desperate manoeuvre achieved this objective is unclear. For Sambo personally, however, the outcome proved calamitous. On 2 August 1761, the Pasquotank County Court found Sambo guilty of preparing poison and conspiring and acting as an accessory to have it administered to Mary Nash. It sentenced him to be castrated.[1]

Sambo's plight illustrates the kind of dilemma which led American slaves and other eighteenth-century poor to shape popular cultures that departed from upper class laws, norms, and definitions of morality in part by their acceptance of certain crimes as legitimate acts. This criminality developed out of the existent if still emerging mores of the slaves which were, in turn, always significantly affected by their desperate social and economic needs and lack of access to more mature and effective forms of political or economic action and protest. Slaves in the colonies, therefore, like servants or poor freemen at home or abroad, wove criminal behaviour into their cultures and value systems to deal with immediate problems, sustain their sense of morality and justice, and redistribute some of the power and wealth which surrounded them. Varied contacts among slaves, other blacks, and poor white servants and freemen spread and reinforced the shared popular culture of the lower classes, but did not necessarily lead to joint criminal ventures or mutuality of interest.[2] Collaboration did occur, especially in theft, illicit trade, or social banditry, yet it typified neither white nor black criminality. And the willingness of poor whites to accept slave criminality, even when they condoned similar behaviour among themselves, was inhibited by the antagonism wealthy whites harboured about such acceptance and by the chasm of colour and status between freemen and slaves.

Since their range of options was fewer, slaves ran away more frequently and engaged in other criminal actions more often than did servants, though they had less reason to be sanguine about the chances of success.[3] This did not mean that slaves used or condoned criminality indiscriminately. They distinguished between taking the goods or lives of their masters or other whites and those of their fellow slaves. Slaves who committed crimes did not constitute a dangerous class to other slaves, although small thefts within the slave quarters undoubtedly occurred regularly.[4] They normally directed their major criminal acts against whites, the real targets of their revenge and the persons who had the power or goods which could most effectively relieve their wants. Thus, slaves often 'stole themselves' and 82 per cent of the slaves convicted of murder or related crimes chose white victims, their owners 41 per cent of the time.[5] Since slave criminality did not ordinarily disrupt the solidarity of their community, slaves could incorporate it into their value system with limited ambiguity and ambivalence and use it as a tool of resistance and an ethical means to correct existing social evils.

Slaves, then, chose from a variety of criminal acts to protect their 'moral economies' or vent their fury and frustrations. Sambo's choice to administer a harmful, mind-bending herbal potion undoubtedly reflected African religious practices which integrated conjuring with a sophisticated use of herbs for positive or destructive purposes.[6] But whatever the crime committed in individual cases, all provoked harsh responses from masters, and slaves understandably tended to differentiate among these crimes not so much in moral as utilitarian terms.

The matter may be understood even more holistically. Slaves lived organic lives in both a psychological and sociological sense, as do all human beings in touch with reality. To whatever degree they compartmentalized elements of their existence, they integrated their experiences and comprehended the complex interrelationships that exist among institutions, roles, values, and behaviour. Slaves, thus, interwove in complex, profound, if often hidden ways patterns of resistance and adjustment that historians commonly view as disparate responses to bondage: murder, arson, sabotage,

SLAVE DEFENCE OF A MORAL ECONOMY   39

flight, truancy, as well as a sustaining religiosity and expansive, powerful marital, familial, and communal ties. In so doing, slaves understood that in response to apparently identical or similar situations some slaves resisted and others did not, that some ran off and others murdered or committed suicide, and that the actions of individuals could equally vary over time. They dealt with these complex matters in practical ways each day of their lives.

At times divergent responses to similar situations occurred in especially dramatic fashion. Such was the shape dissatisfaction took among the slaves owned by Henry Ormond of Beaufort County. A member of one of the county's most powerful and prestigious families, Ormond treated his slaves harshly and in turn was deeply hated.[7] The *Virginia Gazette* of 6 September 1770 relates that four of his slaves, together with a female slave owned by Wyriot Ormond of a neighbouring plantation,

> conspired against their master, and on the Sunday night he was said to have rode from home in quest of one of his slaves who was missing, the conspirators, after their master was abed, went up to his room and with an handkerchief attempted to strangle him, which they thought they had effected, but in a little time after they left him, he recovered, and began to stir, on hearing which they went up again, and told him he must die, and that before they left the room; he begged very earnestly for his life, but one of them, his house wench, told him it was in vain, that as he had no mercy on them, he could expect none himself, and immediately threw him between two feather beds, and all got on him till he was stifled to death.[8]

Thus the mistreatments and punishments to which all slaves were subjected led them to respond in a variety of different ways, from running away even to murder. And their responses contributed to the sense of injustice held by other slaves on the Ormond plantation, as well as to that of those slaves who lived elsewhere and heard of the resistance.

We will now discuss in detail what is perhaps the most significant of slave crimes, running away. When slaves 'stole themselves' they dramatically challenged the carefully crafted controls their masters moulded to regulate the lives, labour, and destinies of their human property. Slaves understood this, however psychologically battered or physically threatened, maltreated, or constrained they might be and however different their individual reasons for flight. Running away, then, must be viewed as an act of resistance with significant political implications. Masters recognised this in their obsessive reference to the problem in their laws and slaves underscored it by their frequent escapes.[9]

If the political manifestations of running away had universal significance among New World slaves, then variations in geography, demography, and

40   OUT OF THE HOUSE OF BONDAGE

the social and psychological make-up of individual slave populations obviously affected specific runaway patterns. A number of scholars have analysed such factors in other mainland British colonies, but none have done so for North Carolina.[10] This portion of the essay attempts to fill part of this gap by examining the province's runaways for the years 1748–75.[11] It compares North Carolina runaways with those from neighbouring Virginia and South Carolina both to clarify the North Carolina story and to buttress our statistics, obtained from a too limited sample, with those derived from the more substantial samples available for bordering colonies.

Slaves who ran off to or formed Maroon settlements best illustrate the importance of setting as well as the political dimensions of running away. At times these slaves settled among Indians or sought the security offered by other European powers such as the Spanish in Florida. South Carolina slaves were closer to both the Spanish and the Indians in Florida than were the slaves of North Carolina or Virginia – and with enormous consequences. For not only did many South Carolina slaves successfully flee southward, but frequent related confrontations between slave runaways and whites also occurred. Both factors, in turn, tended to make South Carolina slaves particularly receptive to open revolt. The Stono Rebellion of 1739 must be considered in this context.[12] The more limited and dangerously unpredictable chances of escape to the westward and the Cherokees, on the other hand, normally constrained North Carolina's slaves.[13]

Other opportunities for marronage in South Carolina led to further differences between slave experiences there and in colonies to the north. The economic immaturity and the relative absence of political and legal organization in the South Carolina back country in the 1750s and the 1760s created a milieu in which whites and some blacks, a portion of them runaway slaves, lived as hunters and marginal farmers and joined together to practise social banditry. The Regulators, more substantial farmers importantly tied to the norms and values of commercial agriculture and the potentialities of slavery, sought by direct action and by establishing a serviceable legal and political organization to subdue the counter culture that threatened them.[14] Although rent asunder by other problems during this period, the North Carolina back country normally was made secure against such social banditry, as was Virginia's, by a well organized system of county courts, militias, and constabularies.[15]

Yet neither Virginia nor North Carolina was impervious to problems caused by Maroons. The Great Dismal Swamp, stretching southward from Norfolk, Virginia to Edenton, Chowan County, in the Albemarle Sound region of North Carolina, was an ideal hideout. Runaways deep in its watery isolation were 'perfectly safe, and with the greatest facility elude the most diligent search of their pursuers', J. F. D. Smyth noted in 1784, and blacks had lived there 'for twelve, twenty, or thirty years and upwards, subsisting

SLAVE DEFENCE OF A MORAL ECONOMY 41

... upon corn, hogs, and fowls ...'.[16] If by chance they were apprehended, Elkanah Watson observed, 'they could not be approached with safety' because of their belligerence.[17] Regions other than those within the Great Dismal Swamp were also threatened by groups of runaways.[18] Still, marronage apparently presented fewer opportunities to the province's slaves than it did to those in South Carolina and this helped minimize the conditions necessary to spark a revolt. To note this should not lead us to ignore the relationship between running away and still other forms of slave resistance in North Carolina, or elsewhere for that matter, and the political dimensions of escape.

We will now analyse what is quantifiable in the behaviour of runaways – the psychological and social situations that influenced how frequently slaves ran off and in turn throw light upon why, how, when, and to where they tried to escape. Since marronage is not mentioned in the records used to develop these statistical relationships, the only hint of it in the ensuing analysis is among slaves who ran off in groups. Others, however, may have attempted to settle in Maroon communities, including some of the unapprehended slave runaways in our sample and an even greater number not revealed by the few extant records.

An uneven distribution across the years of the handful of surviving North Carolina newspapers, the richest source of information on runaways, plus the actual advertising practices used by masters to recapture runaways, make it impossible to extrapolate from the 134 cited runaways to estimate how many slaves in the colony actually ran off during the years 1748–72.[19] Although variations in the quality of the extant data also hinder a social and psychological description of the runaways, it is likely that the resultant samples adequately reflect the runaways' age, sex, occupational characteristics, and geographical origins.

The ages of North Carolina runaways correspond with the pattern in other colonies: they were disproportionately young adults, 20 to 35. Forty-four (62 per cent) of North Carolina's runaways were in this age category although this population group comprised only about 30 per cent of the colony's slave population. Slaves 36 and older ran away slightly more frequently than their percentage of the population would indicate: 24 per cent of the runaways and 20 per cent of the colony's slave population. Slaves under 20 comprised about 50 per cent of the slave population but only 14 per cent of North Carolina's runaways.[20]

Eighty-nine per cent of slave runaways in North Carolina were males. This is identical with Windley's and Mullin's estimates for Virginia, but Windley, Morgan, and Littlefield compute percentages for males in South Carolina that range from about 7 to 11 percentage points less than was the case in the two provinces to the north.[21] Despite these differences, since male preponderance among runaways is far greater than sex ratios would

42   OUT OF THE HOUSE OF BONDAGE

suggest in all the surveyed colonies, other factors more substantially explain this disparity.[22]

The importance of marriage and the family to slaves and the consequent large number of slaves who ran away to rejoin spouses and kin, probably explains much of the predominance of males among runaways. Since husbands and fathers normally were the ones separated from their families, it was they who most often ran off to be reunited with wives and kin. The converse was also true. Marital and familial obligations limited the number of female slaves who ran away. Males also ran away in greater numbers because their experiences tended to enhance their knowledge of the countryside, social sophistication, and marketable skills to a far greater degree than was the case for females.

While North Carolina's small runaway sample makes suspect an analysis of the frequency distribution of various occupations among the colony's runaways, similarities between our findings and those based on much larger samples for other colonies lend credibility to our statistics. Field hands in North Carolina ran away in numbers slightly less than their proportion of the colony's slave population would suggest, comprising about 87 per cent of the runaways and perhaps 90 per cent of the slave population (see Tables 1–2). This closely parallels what occurred in South Carolina where field slaves ran away in numbers about 1.5 per cent less than one would predict from their proportion of the slave population.[23]

Domestics ran off in North Carolina in relatively few numbers, comprising 0.8 per cent of its runaways and 3.7 per cent of the slave population. This ratio of close to 1:5, however, is suspect because of the small sample involved (see Tables 1–2). South Carolina's statistics, obtained from a much more substantial sample, reveal that domestics ran away roughly in proportion to their percentage of the colony's slave population. Perhaps, then, too much should not be made of the discrepancy revealed by North Carolina's statistics.[24]

It is essential that a sex-specific analysis be used for artisans because almost all were males and it was preponderantly male slaves who ran off. In North Carolina male artisans ran off in slightly greater numbers, just under 11 per cent of the male runaways, than their proportion of the male slave population, 10 per cent (see Tables 1–2). A substantially smaller percentage ran off in South Carolina: there they totalled about 8 per cent of the male runaways, but 12.3 per cent of its male slave population.[25]

These findings do not substantiate Mullin's arguments that acculturated slaves, especially those with skills, fled in disproportionately large numbers because of greater chances of escaping successfully. Moreover, it is questionable if Mullin's figures for Virginia's artisans and domestics, equalling respectively 14.8 and 7.8 per cent of the slaves who ran away during the period 1736–1801, actually support his contentions for he does not estimate

SLAVE DEFENCE OF A MORAL ECONOMY

TABLE 1

SLAVE RUNAWAYS IN NORTH CAROLINA, 1748–75, BY OCCUPATION AND SEX

Gender	Occupation*	Number	Percentage
Both	Field Hands	117	87.3
	Artisans	13	9.7
	Watermen	3	2.2
	Domestics	1	0.8
	Total	134	100.0
Males	Field Hands	102	85.7
	Artisans	13	10.9
	Watermen	3	2.5
	Domestics	1	0.8
	Total	119	99.9
Females	Field Hands	15	100.0
	Artisans	0	0
	Watermen	0	0
	Domestics	0	0
	Total	15	100.0

*The sex of six field hands could not be determined. They were prorated between male and female field hand slaves in accordance with their respective percentages of the total numbers of field hands. See Note 19 in the text for sources used to construct this table.

their numbers in the colony's slave population. Indeed, given Virginia's comparative economic maturity and the fact that Mullin calculates occupational patterns for runaway male slaves only, it is quite possible that his reckoning for at least the runaway artisans is congruent with their running away in numbers commensurate with their proportion of the slave population. Such a conclusion is less likely for domestics who ran off; it is unlikely that they comprised as much as 8 per cent of the male slave population.[26]

An investigation of watermen who fled slavery adds to the element of doubt. North Carolina's statistics are again suspect because of the small sample. Since watermen were males, a sex-specific analysis is once more

TABLE 2

OCCUPATIONAL BREAKDOWN OF NORTH CAROLINA'S MALE AND FEMALE SLAVES ON THREE PLANTATIONS: 1770, 1809, 1809

Gender	Occupation	Number	Percentage
Both	Field Hands	145	90.1
	Artisans	9	5.6
	Watermen (Ferryman)	1	0.6
	Domestics	6	3.7
	Total	161	100.0
Males	Field Hands	70	87.5
	Artisans	8	10.0
	Watermen (Ferryman)	1	1.3
	Domestics	1	1.3
	Total	80	100.1
Females	Field Hands	75	92.6
	Artisans (Weaver)	1	1.2
	Watermen	0	0
	Domestics	5	6.2
	Total	81	100.0

Sources: Table 2 is based on occupational listings for three plantations on two slaveholdings: Pollock-Mitchell, 1770, and Mount Rose-Connicanary, 1809. This is a slender and biased sample on which to base a province-wide analysis. It overestimates non-field slaves and represents large plantations in later years. Yet it provides the most complete available data. See Pollock Papers, P.C. 31.1, NCSA.

required. Only 1.3 per cent of the colony's slaves are reckoned as watermen in contrast with 2.5 per cent of its runaways (see Tables 1–2). Findings for South Carolina are similar, the group comprising 1.7 per cent of the male slave population but 4.3 per cent of its runaways.[27] Despite the lack of comparative figures concerning the percentage of slaves who were watermen in Virginia, Windley's and Mullin's percentages for these runaways, respectively 5.2 and 7.5, are sufficiently high (certainly in the latter case) to suggest that watermen there also ran off in disproportionately large numbers.[28]

SLAVE DEFENCE OF A MORAL ECONOMY   45

Special characteristics prompted watermen to run away in comparatively large numbers and to do so with relative success. As with artisans and domestics, they had the advantage of being relatively acculturated and like artisans were able to sell their skills on the free labour market more readily than most other slaves. On the other hand, because of their preferred jobs and status all three groups had more to lose if they ran off than did field slaves. Also, although the skilled slaves' very knowledge of whites added to their capacity to run off successfully, it could paradoxically raise their level of apprehension because of a precise understanding of the power of whites and their willingness to use it without stint of violence if pressed. The special talents of watermen, however, their boating skills and geographical sophistication, somewhat countervailed against these inhibitions and enabled them to run off with uncommon frequency. Lastly, one may plausibly argue that relatively more Africans were watermen than were either artisans or domestics. Since Africans tended to run off with disproportionate frequency, this too would increase the number of watermen who escaped.

Field slaves in the Carolinas, despite their slim chances of success, fled in numbers only slightly less than their proportion of the slave population. Perhaps they chose to flee in such large numbers because they were less in touch with the full scope of white power, had fewer material advantages to lose than skilled slaves, and had fewer alternatives to relieve their harsher circumstances[29] (see Tables 1–2). But perhaps of even greater significance, a large number of field hands were Africans.

African-born slaves in the Chesapeake fell from about one-third of the adult slave population in the 1750s to one-tenth in the 1770s. In North Carolina during these years the proportion dropped from two-thirds to one-third. In South Carolina figures are available for the 1760s, 45 per cent, and 1775, 49.1 per cent.[30] During the years 1730–74 Windley estimates that about 31.5 per cent of Virginia's runaways were Africans, suggesting a comparatively high propensity to run away. Mullin presents a considerably lower estimate, 11 per cent, which can only partially be explained by the somewhat longer time span he reviews, 1736–1801. North Carolina's percentage of African runaways between 1748 and 1775, 54.1 per cent, accorded with the province's larger African slave population and the relative frequency with which Africans escaped[31] (see Table 3). Although estimates for South Carolina vary somewhat with the investigator and the time span studied – 40.4 per cent to 68.5 per cent for 1732–87 – the high percentages also reflect the comparatively large number of Africans in the colony's slave population and their greater propensity to run off than creole slaves.[32]

Africans, then, despite their greater difficulties in getting about, communicating, and passing as free still tended to run off in relatively large

TABLE 3

SLAVE RUNAWAYS IN NORTH CAROLINA, 1748–75, BY ORIGINS
AND FACILITY WITH ENGLISH

	Number	Percent
Origin[a]		
American Born	26	42.6
African Born	33	54.1
West Indies	2	3.3
Total	61	100.0
Facility w/English[b]		
Good	54	53.5
Some	33	32.7
None	14	13.9
Total	101	100.1

Notes

a. We could not determine the national origins for 73 slaves in our sample of 134.
b. We could not determine the facility with English for 33 slaves in our sample of 134.

numbers. They did so because of the especially wrenching separations and traumas they had experienced. Torn from their families, parents and spouses, shipped to a strange land, treated as objects, sold to masters who could not understand them, often isolated within the slave community, their behaviour was predictable. If opportunities existed, they fled. When they did, they fell back on their African sense of communality and family and tended to run away in groups. One-third of the North Carolina runaways, all of them field hands, escaped in groups and 88 per cent of the group runaways whose origins are known were Africans.[33]

In puzzling over the question of why some slaves chose to flee enslavement, it is not surprising that some white North Carolinians, despite overwhelming evidence to the contrary, doubted that their slaves could plot their own escapes.[34] However soothing such fantasies may have been to whites, slaves almost invariably determined when they would run off, under which circumstances, and what goals they would pursue. If often goaded by anger and despair, they still attempted to evaluate rationally their options and then plot the particularities of their escapes. This is not to suggest that slaves were not open to examples set by others. They were, and

SLAVE DEFENCE OF A MORAL ECONOMY 47

fleeing servants and apprentices may have animated some slaves, just as the converse may be true.[35]

Whatever the case, the decision to flee was not an easy one. It involved much risk and often departure from a familiar community peopled by friends and family. The brutality of enslavement, however, could offset such considerations. Behind the decision to flee, indeed, there sometimes lay a festering frustration born of an acute sense of self-worth and knowledge of the inherent limits of slavery. But the evidence of the psychological impact of slavery, such as the incidence of speech defects, is sparse and inconclusive for colonial North Carolina. Moreover, whatever inner conflicts existed, they had a varying impact upon the ability of many slaves to speak, how they looked when around whites, or, ultimately, their decision to flee. Thus Ned, 'a good sawyer and hewer, and part of a carpenter' with a 'very good sense', retained a 'bold look' even after repeated brandings before he fled from James Barnes of Halifax County in April 1768.[36] Outward appearance and behaviour, in any case, could be deceptive. As numerous masters learned all too well, their slaves could hide their innermost thoughts behind deferential, dissembling, even stuttering, masks. The 'Negro Wench' Joan, for instance, had a 'smiling Countenance', 'outlandish' Jack 'a pleasant countenance', and a slave who called himself Tom Buck 'an uncommon flippant Tongue, full of Complement'.[37] All were runaways.

The timing of departure is further evidence of how slaves rationally assessed their opportunities as runaways and often carefully planned their escape. The most popular periods for running away were the harvesting season of September to November, when 23 slaves (40 per cent of those for whom destinations are given) fled, followed by February–April, when the slack season ended and spring planting began. Seventeen slaves, or 29 per cent, ran off at this time. Another 15 ran off between May and August, and only three fled during December and January. No significant variation in the timing of escape set non-field runaways apart from field hands. Most North Carolina runaways, then, timed their flight to avoid both work and bad weather.[38]

The clothing slaves wore and took with them often hinted at prior planning, but also reflected the varying conditions of slaves. Artisans normally ran off with surplus clothes, field hands usually fled wearing only the seasonal issue of clothing, and most recent immigrants had the least clothing of all, at times only a blanket or jacket. Whatever they wore, North Carolina runaways usually took little else with them. Quantities of goods would have attracted too much attention. Concern not to appear too unusual, and lack of access to other forms of transportation, also dictated that the vast majority of runaways fled on foot. Only two rode off on stolen horses and, apparently, two Africans were the only ones who escaped by

48   OUT OF THE HOUSE OF BONDAGE

canoe. Runaways of all occupations and origins, however, frequently used waterways as paths and as means of sustenance.

Slave determination is apparent when we consider their destinations. Thirty-six of the 100 runaways who were captured or for whom a destination was given tried to or did escape from the province. The 64 runaways known to have remained in North Carolina stayed for various reasons and displayed no less resolution than those who crossed into neighbouring colonies. Twelve were thought to be headed for or actually captured in locations outside, and sometimes at quite a distance from, their home counties. Another 22 were captured in North Carolina, their home counties unknown. Finally, ten of the 64 were thought to be 'lurking about' their home plantations or seeking to get to other places within the same county. Whether on their own or harboured by relatives and friends, slaves who stayed close by not only risked recapture, but the heightened possibility of being declared outlaws. In all, 11 of the 18 runaways caught in their home counties were killed or committed suicide.[39]

A total of 61 field hands and three artisans were captured or killed, 48 per cent of the 134 North Carolina runaways. Twenty-four of the 33 African-born runaways, or 73 per cent, were among those who failed in their bid for freedom. And among the 40 captured or killed field hands whose ability to speak English could be determined, only five spoke it well. That Africans and those who spoke little or no English stood a poor chance of escaping is not surprising. Those slaves who could manipulate the language and their environment and most readily market their skills stood the best chance of eluding captors.

Deciding whether to flee was a complex, often painful process, for slaves confronted severely limited options as they pondered their needs. This sense of limits could generate among some an immobilizing despair. But for others the goals of freedom, economic reward, escape from harsh masters, reunion or escape with friends or family could be stilled by neither the probable risks nor the demands and preachments of masters. Thus field hands, despite their poor odds of escape, ran away in rough proportion to their numbers in the population. It is also understandable that Africans, though ill-equipped to remain at large for long in the white-shaped world into which they had been thrust, also fled in large numbers, mainly together.

Seeking to protect what was sacred and inviolable, including their memories and hopes, all of these slaves challenged their masters and slavery. The fact that they frequently ended up dead, jailed, whipped, or tortured only sadly testifies to the strength of their dreams and the indomitableness of their wills. These particular slaves attempted escape; others stole, assaulted, and killed. We turn to them now.

*   *   *

A comparative analysis of slave criminals other than runaways is not possible because figures for other colonies are lacking. Nor can the total number and numerical distribution of such crimes be extrapolated from the only available statistics, records relating to 100 slave felons who were executed and 15 who were castrated between 1748 and 1772. Still, an analysis of these statistics is revealing. The percentages of slaves executed or castrated within four time periods (1748–54, 1755–58, 1759–64, and 1765–72) almost exactly correspond with what one would predict from the slave population in each period (see Graph 1). Thus, neither changes in punishments nor political crises among whites during these years had perceptible effects upon the incidence of major slave crimes.[40] Minor slave crimes probably followed the same pattern. During the quarter century before the Revolution, then, slave criminality occurred in accordance with slave demography, the grimly exploitative nature of slavery, and the determination of slaves to defend their moral economy.

Of the 115 slaves known to have been executed and castrated, about 44 per cent were punished for murder or assault, six per cent for rape, three per cent for houseburning, and 26 per cent for theft. Another 21 per cent were runaways or outlaws killed on apprehension or who committed suicide to avoid capture. Although about twice as many slaves were executed for murder or rape as were executed or castrated for robbery, break-ins, or burglary, most slave crimes were directed against property. Adequate statistics cannot be compiled to demonstrate this, for criminal acts, other than those resulting in executions or castrations, were not systematically recorded. Such crimes were often dealt with on the plantations or remained unsolved or undetected. Nevertheless, the number and suggestive phrasing of provincial laws and town ordinances, together with comments by contemporary observers, leave little doubt that slave thefts occurred with great frequency.[41] Janet Schaw noted that blacks 'steal whatever they can come at, and even intercept the cows and milk them. They are indeed the constant plague of their Tyrants, whose severity or mildness is equally regarded by them in these matters.'[42] Slaves stole from one another as well as from whites to satisfy their immediate hunger and needs. But they stole from whites also to achieve the satisfaction that flowed from deceiving them and wreaking revenge upon their tormentors, to resist the proscriptions of masters, and to repossess that which masters stole from them through enslavement.

That harsh punishments did not deter slaves from resistance is demonstrated further by the fact that 71.5 per cent of North Carolina's executions and castrations during the years 1748–72 were perpetrated against slaves although they comprised only from 22 to 25 per cent of the colony's total population.[43] This record speaks not only of persecution, but also of refusal to submit to authority and an enduring capacity to resist the brutal realities

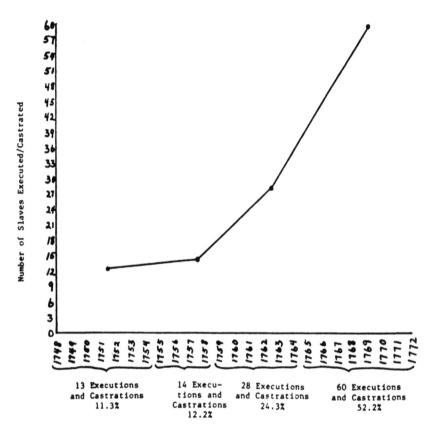

GRAPH 1
DATES WHEN SLAVES WERE EXECUTED OR CASTRATED
DELINEATED ACCORDING TO TIME PERIODS

of slavery. Those subjected to the harshest repression responded with the most destructive criminal resistance patterns.

A close look at the slaves punished for committing major crimes is also revealing. Slaveholdings for owners of 77 of the 115 executed or castrated slaves have been traced. Twenty-nine of these 77 slaves, or 37.7 per cent, came from plantations with 20 or more slaves. Since from 19 to 29 per cent of North Carolina's slaves lived on such plantations during the period in question, there is a positive correlation between the incidence of slaves committing major crimes and their living on large plantations. Perhaps this partially may be explained away by the greater tendency of large slave owners to discover and charge their slaves who committed major crimes before the slave courts. Whatever the case, regional patterns in the frequency of slave crimes also reflect this correlation. Regions with the highest concentration of large slaveholdings usually had the highest slave crime rates. The Lower and Upper Cape Fear regions had the greatest proportion of slaves living on large plantations and the highest major crime rate in the province; the west, with the smallest percentage living on large plantations, had the lowest crime rate.

Slave felons unsurprisingly were all adults and their gender distribution parallels that among runaways. Thus, males committed major crimes much more often than did females: 79 male slaves were executed and 15 castrated between 1748 and 1772, while only 10 female slaves were executed (9.6 per cent). Males and females who perpetrated major crimes, however, committed violent crimes with proportionate frequency. Among slaves whose crimes are listed in the records, four of eight executed female slaves were convicted of murder or murder-related crimes while 25 of 49 castrated or executed male slaves were convicted of such crimes.

Fully 97.4 per cent of the 115 slaves executed or castrated were field hands. Since field hands made up about 90 per cent of the adult slave population during these years, they probably committed major crimes in disproportionately large numbers. This tendency was most pronounced among field hands who came from plantations with 20 or more slaves. Artisans and domestics, on the other hand, probably committed such crimes less frequently than their share of the total slave population would suggest. About 10 per cent of the male slaves were artisans but they comprised 2.1 per cent of the executed or castrated male slave felons. Similarly, about 3.7 per cent of the slaves were domestics, but approximately 1 per cent of the slave felons were house slaves (see Table 2).

Both artisans and domestics eschewed felonious crimes because of their preferred position in slave society and the extremely hazardous nature of such criminality. They understood that their chances of successfully escaping after committing a major crime were remote and that capture meant death. Field hands, however, were less inhibited by close contact with and knowledge of whites, nor were they held back by a fear of losing a superior social and economic situation. Since they also could not appeal to their owners as effectively as artisans or domestics for a redress of grievances, they were driven more often to the point of desperation. Field hands consequently were more prone than other slaves to commit whatever crime best served their immediate needs.

Nearly one-quarter of the convicted slave felons (28 of 115) collaborated with one another. Twelve of the 29 slaves convicted of murder or murder-related crimes committed such crimes in groups of two or more, and two of the ten slaves executed or castrated for theft joined with two other slaves who escaped and thus evaded conviction. A review of such collaboration is highly suggestive. First, and almost by definition, slaves planned and implemented their crimes both with resourcefulness and, at times, ruthlessness. Second, female slaves collaborated in disproportionate numbers. Forty per cent of the major crimes committed by females involved two or more collaborators; this was the case for 23.4 per cent of the males. Third, collaborators from different plantations often directed their criminal activities not only against their owners, but also against the persons or property of other whites. In doing so they demonstrated their knowledge of the countryside and skill in handling boats and horses. Fourth, they recruited other slaves to aid them to avoid capture and to further their efforts.

Still, slaves committed most of their crimes individually. Such slaves also exhibited ingenuity and deep feelings of alienation and hostility to enslavement. Who knows the particulars behind the raging fury of Dick, owned by John Brevard, Esq.? In December 1764, Dick wounded his owner in an effort to kill him. He also sought to kill 'severall Negroes the property of Said Brevard'. And when 'Divers Subjects ... did attempt to take him', he armed himself and resisted them until subdued. Dick was hanged and his head was 'chopped off and set up at the Forks of the Road that Leads to George Davison's as an example etc.–'. To the slaves a grisly admonition, to the master, in compensation for his executed slave, £35 proclamation money.[44]

Such typically savage punishments did not end the needs or stem the fury, frustration, and desperation which kindled slave crime. It was indeed like a small but protracted war, albeit one in which whites, intent on regulating and exploiting their chattel property, controlled the guns and the mechanisms of power. Unequal as the contest was, whites hardly came through unscathed. Numbers were murdered, assaulted, robbed, burgled, or had their houses burned. They paid a price for their continued aggressions upon blacks.

'Criminal' acts coloured the outlook of all slaves. Some gained from the numerous examples an ability to follow in the footsteps of more adventuresome comrades. Many more were emboldened to defy authority in less overt ways. But almost all slaves derived from this criminality a heightened awareness of the destructive meanings of white treatment and definitions of slaves and of the necessity of constructing or using effective defence mechanisms and institutions to protect themselves. Accordingly, and whatever the heartrending, destructive paradoxes, slaves interwove in profound if often hidden ways murder, houseburning, running away, goldbricking, a sustaining religiosity, and expansive, powerful marital, familial, and

SLAVE DEFENCE OF A MORAL ECONOMY 53

communal ties. Doing this, they maintained and expanded their humanity and challenged the assertion by their masters that only they could define the parameters of slavery.

NOTES

1. Governor's Office, Committee of Claims Reports, 1760–1764; Pasquotank County Court Minutes, 1737–85, North Carolina State Archives (hereafter NCSA). Also see William L. Saunders, ed., *The Colonial Records of North Carolina*, 10 vols. (Raleigh, North Carolina, 1886–90), 6: 738–44.
2. This conceptual analysis has been influenced by studies of poorer folk and their resistance patterns in Europe. See especially: E. P. Thompson, 'Patrician Society, Plebian Culture', *Journal of Social History*, 7 (1974), 382–405; Thompson, 'The Moral Economy of the English Crowd in the Eighteenth Century', *Past and Present*, no. 50 (Feb. 1971), 76–136; Douglas Hay et al, *Albion's Fatal Tree: Crime and Society in Eighteenth-Century England* (New York, 1975); Jeffrey Kaplow, *The Names of Kings: The Parisian Laboring Poor in the Eighteenth Century* (New York, 1972).
3. Thirty-four servant and apprentice runaways are recorded in newspaper ads and a sample of county court minutes in the NCSA. As in the case of slaves, this total understates the number who actually ran off. For full discussion and documentation see our 'Slave Runaways in Colonial North Carolina, 1748–1775', *North Carolina Historical Review*, forthcoming.
4. The French criminal poor often were a dangerous class to other poor. See Kaplow, *The Parisian Laboring Poor*, passim. For the frequent incidence of petty thefts within the slave community, see John Brickell, *The Natural History of North Carolina* ... (Johnson, North Carolina, 1969; orig. pbd. 1737), pp. 272, 275; Janet Schaw, *Journal of a Lady of Quality* ... *1774–1776*, eds. Evangeline W. Andrews and Charles M. Andrews (New Haven, 1923), pp. 66, 177.
5. For sources see note 40. Peter Wood uses the phrase 'stole themselves' in *Black Majority: Negroes in Colonial South Carolina from 1670 Through the Stono Rebellion* (New York, 1974), p. 239.
6. Uppermost in the slaves' moral economy was a sense of the inviolability of marriage and the family, the significance of the bonds of community, and the necessity of maintaining traditional, if regionally varying, work schedules and treatment. The last might include privileges such as opportunities to visit other plantations or to plant gardens. See Albert J. Raboteau, *Slave Religion: The Invisible Institution in the Antebellum South* (Oxford, England, 1978), pp. 13–15.
7. For records dealing with Ormond's family see: A List of Members of the North Carolina Lower House of the Assembly, Compiled by the NCSA; Governor's Office, Lists of Taxables, Militia and Magistrates, 1754–1770, Undated; Treasurer's and Comptroller's Papers, County Settlements with the State, Tax Lists, Beaufort-Tyrrell, 1755, NCSA.
8. *Virginia Gazette* (Rind), 6 Sept. 1770.
9. North Carolina passed two basic slave and servant codes in 1715 and 1741. Five of the 21 articles in the 1715 law pertained directly to or mentioned runaways; 22 of the 58 articles of the 1741 act did so. Walter Clark, ed., *The State Records of North Carolina*, 16 vols., numbered 11–26 (Winston and Goldsboro: State of North Carolina, 1895–1906), 23: 62–6, 191–204. For subsidiary laws of 1753, 1758, and 1764 see pp. 388–90, 488–9, 656.
10. See, for example, Wood, *Black Majority*, pp. 239–68; Gerald W. Mullin, *Flight and Rebellion: Slave Resistance in Eighteenth-Century Virginia* (New York, 1972), pp. 34–123 and notes.
11. For North Carolina's slaves during the Revolution see Jeffrey J. Crow's excellent studies: *The Black Experience in Revolutionary North Carolina* (Raleigh, 1977); 'Slave Rebelliousness and Social Conflict in North Carolina, 1775 to 1802', *The William and Mary Quarterly*,

54 OUT OF THE HOUSE OF BONDAGE

3rd Ser., 37 (1980), 79–102.

12. See Wood, *Black Majority*, especially pp. 304–26. This is not to deny that other conditions, especially demographic factors, helped induce slave uprisings in South Carolina. See Wood, *Black Majority*, pp. 131–66; Marvin L. Michael Kay and Lorin Lee Cary, 'A Demographic Analysis of Colonial North Carolina with Special Emphasis Upon the Slave and Black Populations', in Crow and Flora J. Hatley, eds., *Black Americans in North Carolina and the South* (Chapel Hill, 1984), pp. 71–87; US Bureau of the Census, *Historical Statistics of the United States: Colonial Times to 1957* (Washington, D.C., 1960), series Z 1-19, p. 756.

13. See Theda Perdue, 'Red and Black in the Southern Appalachians', *Southern Exposure*, 12 (1984), 17–24.

14. See: Richard J. Hooker, ed., *The Carolina Backcountry on the Eve of the Revolution: The Journal and Other Writings of Charles Woodmason, Anglican Itinerant* (Chapel Hill, North Carolina, 1953); Richard Maxwell Brown, *The South Carolina Regulators: The Story of the First Vigilante Movement* (Cambridge, Mass., 1963); Rachel N. Klein, 'Ordering the Backcountry: The South Carolina Regulation', *William and Mary Quarterly*, 3d ser., 38 (October 1981), 661–80.

15. See: Kay, 'The North Carolina Regulation, 1766–1776: A Class Conflict', in Alfred F. Young, ed., *The American Revolution, Explorations in the History of American Radicalism* (DeKalb, Illinois, 1976), pp. 71–123; Charles S. Sydnor, *American Revolutionaries in the Making: Political Practices in Washington's Virginia* (New York, 1952), pp. 86–106.

16. J. F. D. Smyth, *Tour in the United States of America* (London, 2 vols., 1784), 1: 101–2.

17. Elkanah Watson, *Men and Times of the Revolution . . .* (New York, 1856), pp. 51–2.

18. In 1767, for instance, 20 armed slaves were sighted in New Hanover County. See New Hanover County Court Minutes, 1738–69, 1771–72, NCSA.

19. We analysed all extant issues of North Carolina's newspapers for the years 1748–75 for our analysis of runaways: *The North Carolina Magazine and Universal Intelligencer* (hereafter *NCM*), *Cape Fear Mercury* (hereafter *CFM*), *North Carolina Gazette*, New Bern, (hereafter *NCG*), and the *North Carolina Gazette*, Wilmington. In addition we examined the more numerous issues of the *South Carolina Gazette* (hereafter *SCG*), and the various editions of the *Virginia Gazette* (hereafter *VG*). Subsidiary sources used in the NCSA included county court minutes, Committee of Public Claims' records, private correspondence, and estate inventories. A detailed listing appears in Kay and Cary, 'Slave Runaways in Colonial North Carolina'.

20. See: Kay and Cary, 'A Demographic Analysis', pp. 71–121; Herbert G. Gutman, *The Black Family in Slavery and Freedom: 1750–1925* (New York, 1976), p. 265; Allan Kulikoff, 'The Beginnings of the Afro-American Family in Maryland', in *Law, Society, and Politics in Early Maryland*, eds. Aubrey C. Land, et al. (Baltimore, 1977), p. 187.

21. See Lathan Algera Windley, 'Profile of Runaway Slaves in Virginia and South Carolina from 1730 through 1787' (Diss. University of Iowa 1974), p. 65; Mullin, *Flight and Rebellion*, pp. 89, 103; Daniel C. Littlefield, *Rice and Slaves* (Baton Rouge, La., 1981), p. 144; Philip D. Morgan, 'Black Society in the Low Country, 1760–1810', in Ira Berlin and Ronald Hoffman, eds., *Slavery and Freedom in the Age of the American Revolution* (Charlottesville, Va., 1983), Table 12, p. 100.

22. Sex ratios in the Chesapeake, North Carolina, and the South Carolina lowcountry probably averaged about 117, 125, and 130 respectively during the years 1750–75. For sex ratios and proportions of African-born slaves in the three regions see: Kay and Cary, 'A Demographic Analysis', pp. 76–8, 93–103; Kulikoff, 'A "Prolifick" People: Black Population Growth in the Chesapeake Colonies, 1700–1790', *Southern Studies*, 16 (1977), 393–6, 403–6; Morgan, 'Black Society in the Lowcountry', pp. 90–2.

23. See Morgan, 'Black Society in the Lowcountry', pp. 99–102.

24. Morgan, 'Black Society in the Lowcountry', pp. 99–102.

25. Morgan, 'Black Society in the Lowcountry', pp. 99–102.

26. See Mullin, *Flight and Rebellion*, pp. 94–6, 103–5, 108–9.

27. See Morgan, 'Black Society in the Lowcountry', pp. 99–102.

28. See Windley, 'Profile of Runaways', pp. 68, 70, 71, 138; Mullin, *Flight and Rebellion*, pp. 94–6, 103–5, 108–9.

SLAVE DEFENCE OF A MORAL ECONOMY

29. See Morgan, 'Black Society in the Lowcountry', pp. 99–102.
30. See the works listed in note 22 for percentages of African-born slaves in each colony.
31. See note 19 for sources used to construct estimates of North Carolina's African runaways and note 28 for Virginia's runaways.
32. See Windley, 'Profile of Runaways', pp. 68, 70, 71; Littlefield, *Rice and Slaves*, pp. 129–31, 151–8; Morgan, 'Black Society in the Lowcountry', p. 92.
33. See note 19 for sources used to obtain these statistics.
34. *NCG*, 24 Feb. 1775; *SCG*, 17 Nov.–4 Dec. 1775.
35. For examples of slaves and servants who ran off together or perhaps affected each other see: Rowan County Court Minutes, Feb. and Aug. 1769, NCSA; *NCG*, 24 June 1768, ad dated 13 Oct. 1769, 10 Nov. 1769; *SCG*, 28 May–4 June 1750, 1 June 1769.
36. *VG* (Purdie & Dixon), 3 Nov. 1768, 24 June 1773; *CFM*, 8 Dec. 1769.
37. See, for example, *VG* (Purdie & Dixon), 26 Nov. 1772; *NCG*, 10 Nov. 1769, 2 Sept. 1774.
38. The above patterns differ somewhat from those in Virginia and South Carolina. See: Windley, 'Profile of Runaways', pp. 171–6; Cheryl Ann Cody, 'Slave Demography and Family Formation: A Community Study of the Ball Family Plantations, 1720–1896' (Diss. University of Minnesota 1982), p. 109. See note 19.
39. For slaves thought to be lurking about, see *SCG*, 15–22 Jan. 1750; Edgecombe County Court Minutes, 27 June 1758, NCSA; *NCM*, 4–11 Jan. 1765; *NCG*, 2 Sept. 1774, 24 Feb., 24 March, 5 May, 12 May, 14 July, 6 Oct. 1775.

For those thought headed for other parts of North Carolina, see *NCM*, 4–11 Jan. 1765; *VG* (Purdie & Dixon), 15 Aug. 1766; *NCG*, 22 Dec. 1775; Jacob Wilkinson to Col. Alexander McAllister, Nov. 1766, McAllister Papers, Southern History Collection, University of North Carolina.

For those caught within North Carolina but in counties other than those from which they fled, see Governor's Office, Lists of Taxables, Militia and Magistrates, 1754–70, undated, NCSA; Clark, ed., *State Records*, 22: 836–40; *NCG*, 7 July 1753, 2 Sept. 1774, 5 May 1775; *SCG*, 6–16 Dec. 1760; *VG* (Purdie & Dixon), 28 Sept. 1769; *CFM*, 8 Dec. 1769, 29 Dec. 1773.

For those captured within North Carolina and whose home counties could not be determined, see Rowan County Court Minutes, July 1755, Feb. 1772; Carteret County Court Minutes, 6 Dec. 1757; Bertie County Court Minutes, 24 July 1759; Stephen Blackman to Sheriff, Dobbs County, 19 Sept. 1767, Shaw Papers, folder, misc. papers, 1766–1883, NCSA; *VG* (Purdie & Dixon), 5 Nov. 1767, 14 Dec. 1769, 10 Jan. 1771; *NCG*, 10 Nov. 1769, 7 Jan. 1774, 24 Feb. 1775; *CFM*, 22 Sept. 1773.
40. From 1758 to 1764 provincial law required castration for male felons who were first offenders. See Clark, ed., *State Records*, 23: 488–9, 656; Kay and Cary, ' "The Planters Suffer Little or Nothing": North Carolina Compensations for Executed Slaves, 1748–1772', *Science and Society*, 11 (1976), 288–306.

For the sources used to obtain statistics concerning slave criminality cited in the text see the following in the NCSA: Treasurers' and Comptrollers' Papers – Payments to Masters for Executed Slaves; Secretary of States' Papers – Court Records, 1702–1898; Bertie County Slave Papers, 1744–1815; Chowan County Slave Papers, 1731–1819; Slavery Papers, 1747–75, Craven County; Craven County Court Minutes, 1747–75; Cumberland County Miscellaneous Papers, 1754–1867; Edgecombe County Court Minutes, 1757–84; New Hanover County Court Minutes, 1738–67, 1771–98; Orange County Court Minutes, 1752–66; Pasquotank County Slave Papers, 1734–1860; Pasquotank County Court Minutes, 1737–85; Pasquotank County Lists of Taxables, Miscellaneous Material, 1749–1814; Perquimans County Slave Records, 1759–1864; Rowan County Court Minutes, 1753–72; Legislative Papers, 1689–1756, 1764–66, 1767–Nov. 1768, Dec. 1768–Dec. 17, 1770; Governor's Office, Committee of Claims' Reports, 1760–1764. Also see: *VG* (Rind), 6 Sept. 1770; Clark, ed., *State Records*, 22: 815–66; Saunders, ed., *Colonial Records*, 5: 975–86; 6: 209–15, 738–44; 8: 141–3.
41. See note 9 for the basic laws dealing with slavery. Other laws also throw some light upon slave theft: Clark, ed., *State Records*, 23: 62–6, 82, 165–8, 172–3, 194–5, 201, 916, 955–6.

For Wilmington town ordinances and consequent slave trials see: Donald R. Lennon and Ida Brooks Kellam, eds., *The Wilmington Town Book, 1743–1778* (Raleigh, 1973), pp. 148,

56 OUT OF THE HOUSE OF BONDAGE

164–9, 187, 197, 204–5, 209–14, 219–21, 225–9. Our forthcoming book on slavery in colonial North Carolina will detail slave theft in the colony.

42. Schaw, *Journal of a Lady of Quality*, pp. 66, 177. See also Brickell, *Natural History of North Carolina*, pp. 272, 275.

43. For white trials and punishments see: Legislative Papers, 1689–1756, 1764–66, Nov. 1767–Nov. 1768, Dec. 1768–Dec. 17, 1770; Governor's Office, Committee of Claims' Reports, 1760–64; New Bern District Minutes of the Superior Court, 1768–72; Edenton Superior Court Minutes, Nov. 1760–67; Wilmington District Minutes, Superior Court, Oct. 1760–Nov. 1783; Salisbury District Minute Docket Superior Court, 1756–70; Hillsboro District Minute Docket, 1768–88, all in NCSA. See also: Clark, ed., *State Records*, 22: 404–5, 836–47, 863–6; Saunders, ed., *Colonial Records*, 5: 975–86; 6: 738–44; *VG* (Hunter), 10 Nov. 1752; *NCG* (Davis), 14–21 Sept. 1764; *VG* (Purdie & Dixon), 7 Jan., 28 July 1768, 28 March 1771. See Kay and Cary, 'A Demographic Analysis', pp. 82–3.

44. Saunders, ed., *Colonial Records*, 7: 856–7; Clark, ed., *State Records*, 22: 847–52. Secretary of State's Papers, Court Records, 1702–1898; Rowan Court of Pleas and Quarter Sessions Minutes, 1753–72; Governor's Office, Lists of Taxables, Militia and Magistrates, 1754, 1770; Legislative Papers, 1767–Nov. 1768, NSCA. See Kay and Cary, 'Compensations for Executed Slaves', pp. 288–306.

Colonial South Carolina Runaways: Their Significance for Slave Culture*

Philip D. Morgan

'What a History! Horses and Negroes! Negroes and Horses!' Such was the conclusion of Samuel Coleridge who was perhaps one of the first commentators upon slavery to assemble advertisements for runaway slaves (and horses), in his case, so as to indict the system.[1] More recently, there have been a number of studies of colonial slave runaway populations, but perhaps they too have been, in part at least, politically inspired, for the act of running away has often been conceived solely in terms of resistance. While many runaways were rebels, not all were. Indeed, such a simple interpretation wrenches the act of running away out of its social context. Few modern studies of slave runaways have attempted to relate the runaway population to a wider slave population, nor have they explored adequately the significance of slave mobility patterns for an understanding of slave culture.[2] These are the dual aims of the present essay.

I

How representative of the broader slave population were the runaway slaves recorded in colonial South Carolina newspaper advertisements? One crude indicator is available if we compare the size of the South Carolina runaway population with that of the most populous slave colony on the North American mainland, namely, Virginia. While South Carolina's slave population was less than a half of Virginia's for most of the eighteenth century, its runaway population, as measured in newspaper advertisements, was at least four times as large.[3] The runaway sample from South Carolina stands a greater chance of being a representative group than was the case in Virginia.

Much more certain is that these advertised runaways represent only the most visible tip of an otherwise indeterminate iceberg. Sixty-five South Carolina probate inventories in the colonial period include references to over a hundred slaves who were said either to be 'absent', 'out considerable Time', 'slid away', or simply 'runs in the woods'; none of these runaways

---

*This is a revised version of an article earlier published in French, 'En Caroline du Sud: Marronage et Culture Servile', *Annales, Economies, Sociétés, Civilisations*, 37 (1982).

were ever advertised in extant South Carolina newspapers.[4] Similarly, runaways mentioned in planter correspondence do not often find their way into the pages of the South Carolina press.[5] Running away was so common on one lowcountry estate that, rather than place single advertisements, notice was given 'that many of the slaves belonging to the plantation of JOHN WALTERS Esq are constantly running away', and space instead was devoted to the large rewards offered for their apprehension. Another owner warned planters and overseers not to let 'strange' Negroes come to their plantations 'as several of my negroes have been out of the plantation in neglect of their duty'.[6] Petit marronage was an accepted fact of life for South Carolina planters.

What then determined whether a master would advertise for his runaway slave? The likelihood of the slave's voluntary return was probably the most important, as one unusually revealing notice makes evident: Leonard 'has absented himself some time from me', the master stated, and 'this looks so much like running away that I will give a reward' for his capture.[7] But the degree of commitment of the slave runaway, or the length of his absence, were far from being the only determinants of a runaway notice. The idiosyncrasies of particular masters cannot be discounted;[8] proximity to Charlestown, and ease with which an advertisement could be placed, weighed in many a decision to advertise;[9] the cost of a runaway advertisement may have deterred some masters;[10] only when an owner had accumulated a number of runaways might he advertise;[11] one master only advertised for his valuable carpenter when he was 'about to depart the province';[12] other absentees were advertised when the master wanted to sell them or perhaps when a new master, who had bought them as runaways, made strenuous efforts to regain them;[13] many advertisements refer to a recent sighting, indicating that an owner might only advertise when he had some idea where his slave had gone.[14] For all these reasons, notices for runaway slaves are a gross underestimate of the extent of absenteeism among slaves.[15]

The notices for runaway slaves do permit one internal check on representativeness. To take advantage of it, we must distinguish between two different types of advertisement: one intending to recover a fugitive, the other informing readers of captured slaves. In colonial South Carolina newspapers, 3,558 slaves were listed as fugitives and another 2,041 as captives. An advertisement for a fugitive generally provided a full description. At the same time, however, fugitives tended to be acculturated, highly valued, and therefore probably atypical slaves. Conversely, advertisements for captives were rather perfunctory, but for a reason. They described slaves who tended to be recent arrivals, those less conversant with white ways, those unable to reveal much more than their own name. These slaves, we may suspect, more closely approximate the broader slave population.

Certainly, the birthplaces of the two sample groups were radically

COLONIAL SOUTH CAROLINA RUNAWAYS 59

different. Creoles, who tended to be the most highly valued of slaves and those most likely to evade capture, figure prominently in the fugitive population. Over half of the fugitives for whom a birthplace is known were born in the New World. Among the corresponding captive population, nine out of ten were African-born.

By combining both sample populations, a fairly constant relationship between Africans, forming two-thirds of the population, and creoles, forming the other one-third, is evident (see Table 1). This corresponds approximately to the proportion of Africans within the South Carolina slave population just before mid-century (see Table 2). However, toward the end of the colonial period, the proportion of Africans within the adult population and in the combined runaway populations diverged markedly. While the proportion of Africans in the wider population declined, their presence among advertised runaways remained constant. This can probably be explained by the increase in advertisements for captives, most of whom, as we have seen, were Africans. In the last two decades of the colonial era, two-thirds of all advertised runaways were captives. Better communications and the erection of gaols in outlying areas meant that gaolers throughout the colony began to forward lists of captives to the printers in Charlestown.[16] It is the changing nature of the evidence, therefore, rather than the changing disposition of African slaves for flight, that accounts for the divergence. Be that as it may, this exercise in comparison establishes the dominance of Africans in the runaway population, particularly among captives, and their sizeable, though diminishing, presence in the wider population.

Descriptions of African runaways in newspaper advertisements offer a unique insight into the appearance of this numerically predominant group. The typical slave in colonial South Carolina was far removed from the shuffling, grinning, affable slave of Sambo folklore. Indeed, the very act of grinning would often have revealed an exotic sight for many African slaves had filed teeth. One unusually detailed notice described one slave's upper tooth as 'filed about half way, and the one next to it broke above the gum by filing'[17] Another facet of the eighteenth-century slave's appearance that would heighten his strangeness would be the cicatrizations, which received descriptions, even diagrammatic sketches, in hundreds of advertisements.[18] African hair decoration – 'his hair plaited', 'her hair plaited after her country manner', 'his hair is twisted up like twine' – was another distinguishing characteristic of colonial slaves.[19]

Nor were all colonial slaves uniformly decked out in osnaburg overalls topped with canvas cap – the later stereotyped picture of the typical slave. In fact, many were virtually naked, so that descriptions such as 'has nothing on but an old rag about his middle', 'a clout round his loins', has on 'only an Arse-cloth', abound.[20] Certainly, slaves suffered from delays in the distribution of clothing and, of course, runaways out for some time would soon be in

OUT OF THE HOUSE OF BONDAGE

TABLE 1
THE BIRTHPLACES OF SOUTH CAROLINA RUNAWAYS, 1732–1782

Birthplace	Fugitives (Percent)	Captives (Percent)	Total (Percent)
Africa	45.5	89.1	65.0
North America	30.6	7.5	20.2
Mulattoes	6.3	0.5	3.7
Mustees	10.9	0.8	6.4
West Indies	3.8	1.4	2.7
Indians	1.9	0.5	1.3
Other	1.0	0.2	0.7
Total	100.0	100.0	100.0
Total Number	1,658	1,345	3,003
Number of Unknown	1,900	696	2,596

Years	Africans (Percent)	Creoles (Percent)	Total Number
1732–39	66.6	33.4	144
1740–49	42.7	57.3	157
1750–59	68.7	31.3	418
1760–69	69.5	30.5	929
1770–79	67.3	32.7	1,240
1780–82	39.3	60.7	56
1732–82	66.3	33.7	2,944

Notes and Sources: The lower half of the table omits 39 Indians and 20 'others'. See Charleston Library Society, *South Carolina Newspapers, 1732–1782* (microfilm).

want of clothing; but one wonders whether what appeared to be scarcity of clothing from a Euro-American perspective was not an expression of African cultural preferences. Display of African-style jewellery added to the variety and was another expression of cultural heritage. One 'Angolan' man had a 'silver Bobb in his right ear', another African had 'small wire rings in his ear', and a 'Guinea' woman had '5 brass rings in one ear and six in the other'. Necklaces of beads, often called 'negro beads', and bracelets consisting of metal rings were also common.[21]

African ethnic identities were not easily obliterated in the lowcountry. A 'Mandingo' slave belonging to the Charlestown workhouse was employed as an interpreter for his countrymen; when a slave from Angola was brought to

COLONIAL SOUTH CAROLINA RUNAWAYS   61

TABLE 2

THE PROPORTION OF AFRICANS IN THE ADULT SLAVE POPULATION OF
SOUTH CAROLINA

Year	Adult Slaves	Africans	
		Number	Percent
1730	14,379	c.9,000	62.6
1740	27,859	19,607	70.4
1750	25,478	14,335	56.3
1760	36,538	16,460	45.0
1770	53,595	23,788	44.4
1775	67,097	32,951	49.1

Notes and Sources: The adult slave and immigrant data will be presented in my forthcoming book, 'Slave Counterpoint: Black Culture in the Eighteenth-Century Chesapeake and Low-country'. To determine the number of surviving African immigrants, I employed the adult survivor schedule, with two small modifications, outlined in Allan Kulikoff, A '"Prolifick" People: Black Population Growth in the Chesapeake Colonies, 1700–1790', *Southern Studies*, 16 (1977), 421.

gaol, information was derived 'from the other negroes in the house'; and when some Bambara slaves were captured, the gaoler had to rely on 'a fellow who understands their country Tongue'.[22] Occasionally, South Carolina fugitives acted to maintain African ethnic ties. One runaway, who spoke 'very broken English though he has been many years in the province', was supposed to be 'at the plantation of Mrs. Edith Mathewes in John's Island, where he frequently used to visit a countryman of his'. An owner, advertising for an 'Angolan', pointed out that 'as there is abundance of Negroes in this Province of that Nation, he may chance to be harbour'd among some of them'.[23]

Africans, particularly 'New Negroes', as recent immigrants were known, also revealed a commitment to ethnic ties when they ran away together. In 1734 three 'Angola' slaves, two of whom were brothers, made off in a canoe, carrying their axes and hoes, presumably in an attempt to maintain themselves. Almost a half-century later, five 'Guinea' slaves, each identified by 'a piece of lead tied to their necks on which is engraved their names', ran off after three months in the province, carrying five duffel blankets and four or five felling axes. Perhaps most interesting, however, was the group of six runaways taken up at Indian-Land, 70 miles south of Charlestown in 1772. Two were 'new Guinea' slaves belonging to one master, one was a 'new Kishee' (Kisi) slave belonging to another master, and three others were also recently-arrived Kisi slaves belonging to a third owner. Africans of different ethnic backgrounds and different masters combined in runaway bands on the fringes of lowcountry settlement.[24]

62 OUT OF THE HOUSE OF BONDAGE

Not surprisingly, lowcountry owners became conversant with various African ethnic groups. One master, advertising for his fugitive, could assume that his fellow whites would be able to recognise somebody who looked 'much like an Ebo Negro'. Others made identifications on the basis of a slave's markings.[25] In fact, a comparison of the ethnic origins of imports and runaways suggests that contemporary opinions of the various ethnic groups may not have been all that far-fetched. Slaves from Senegambia, the Gold Coast and Angola – the regions most preferred by South Carolinians – were not notable runaways, given their proportions in the slave population as a whole. On the other hand, South Carolinians consistently expressed a dislike for slaves from the Bight of Biafra; and slaves from that region figured disproportionately in the runaway advertisements, as Table 3 indicates.[26]

TABLE 3

ORIGINS OF SLAVE RUNAWAYS AND AFRICAN IMMIGRANTS, SOUTH CAROLINA

Coastal Region of Origin	African Immigrants (Percent) 1733–1807	Slave Runaways (Percent) 1732–1782
Senegambia	19.5	21.2
Sierra Leone	6.8	2.2
Windward Coast	16.3	20.6
Gold Coast	13.3	13.4
Bight of Benin	1.6	0.9
Bight of Biafra	2.1	10.2
Angola	39.6	28.4
Miscellaneous	0.7	3.1
Total	100.0	100.0

Notes and Sources

The import figures are taken from Philip Curtin, *The Atlantic Slave Trade: A Census*, Madison, Wisc., 1969, 157. The ethnic origins of 1,164 fugitives and captives were given in newspaper advertisements. The maps and text in Richard Gray, ed., *The Cambridge History of Africa from c.1600 to c.1790*, Cambridge, 1975, vol. 4, espec., 172–3, 224–5, 277, 288, 326 and 330, were particularly useful in identifying the coastal regions of the various ethnic groups.

If birthplace is one sensitive indicator of the runaway sample's representativeness, occupation is another. Again, it is to be suspected that skilled slaves, like creoles, will figure prominently in advertisements designed to recover fugitives. In fact, one-fifth of the slaves in such advertisements were described as skilled. This proportion falls to less than fourteen per cent with the inclusion of those runaways advertised as captives, as Table 4 reveals. Our most reliable, though by no means in-fallible, guide to the representativeness of this combined figure is to be found in the probate inventories of lowcountry decedents. The level of skills among bondmen of inventoried estates was undoubtedly greater than that

COLONIAL SOUTH CAROLINA RUNAWAYS

found in the wider slave population. Probated estates tended to over-represent the more elderly and wealthy members of society who, in turn, owned more slaves, and certainly more skilled slaves, than the living. However, this bias does not seem to have been excessively pronounced.[27] Moreover, for our purposes, what is striking is the comparable fluctuations in the proportions of skilled slaves over time in both samples (see the time series in Tables 4 and 5).

There are interesting variations in the occupational structures of both samples. For example, drivers were conspicuously absent from the ranks of skilled runaways, an indication that they were a stable element in the slave community. On the other hand, the independent, self-reliant existence of watermen, with their obvious access to a means of escape, no doubt accounts for their prominence among skilled runaways, forming, in fact, one-quarter of the total, when they comprised less than ten per cent of the inventoried skilled.[28]

More important, however, is the overall trend in the numbers of skilled slaves. As Herbert Gutman has declared, 'it is of genuine importance to know roughly what percentage of slaves had ... skills. It is of even greater importance to know if these percentages changed over time. An occupational structure is a most powerful clue for understanding a social structure or community'.[29] From these two samples, it would seem that the proportion of skilled slaves fluctuated during the course of the eighteenth century, rising from about 9 or 10 per cent in the 1730s to about 13 to 16 per cent in the 1770s, exceeding that proportion in the 1780s, and reaching a low point in the 1750s of about 9 per cent. If the exact proportions are only approximate, at least both groups bear out the upward trend and both confirm the downturn of the 1750s.[30]

Apart from the 1750s, then, there would seem to have been a modest but real increase in opportunities for slaves. Late eighteenth- and early nineteenth-century evidence suggests the upward trend continued, perhaps even accelerated.[31] What is the significance of this phenomenon? One possible implication is suggested by Barry Higman's argument that declining occupational opportunities in early nineteenth-century Jamaica can be linked to the island-wide rebellion of 1831. Of course, expanding or declining occupational opportunities cannot mechanistically explain the incidence of overt slave resistance. However, if, as seems likely, the relative absence of overt slave resistance can be linked to the degree to which slaves could create a predictable and orderly world, then the acquisition of skills and preferred positions, much like the creation of dense kin and family ties, should be seen as part of that process. Skills and privileged positions certainly gave slaves a sense of responsibility, a measure of self-esteem and a degree of freedom. And, if these attributes could lead bondmen to take up arms against whites, they just as easily and much more significantly, given

TABLE 4
RUNAWAY SOUTH CAROLINA SKILLED SLAVES, 1732–1782

Period	Skilled Slaves	Total	Per Cent
1730s	44	519	8.5
1740s	80	621	12.9
1750s	83	872	9.5
1760s	202	1,427	14.2
1770s	309	1,928	16.0
1780s	54	232	23.3
1732–82	772	5,599	13.8

SKILLS

Tradesmen	411 or 53.2%	House Slaves	116 or 15.0%
Woodworkers	214	House Servant	23
Cooper	72(4)	Waitingman	33
Sawyer	40(3)	Seamstress	19
Carpenter	95(5)	Coachman	2
Cabinetmaker	7	Gardener	3
Wheelwright	9	Cook	7(1)
Shipwright	1	Waiter	1
Blacksmith	12(1)	Nurse	1
Shoemaker	34(1)	Hostler	3
Painter	5	Washerwoman	15
Tanner	12(1)	Barber	9(2)
Bricklayer	29(1)		
Butcher	10	Town	31 or 4.0%
Saddler	3		
Caulker	4	Market Slave	25(2)
Hired	36(2)	Shoptender	2(1)
Apprentice	10	Porter	3
Brickmaker	1	Labourer	1
Distiller	3		
Stocking Weaver	1	Agriculture	9 or 1.2%
Carter	1		
Baker	1	Ploughman	3
Waggoner	4(1)	Hunter	3
Sailmaker	2	Driver	3
Tailor	19		
		Miscellaneous	13 or 1.7%
Watermen	192 or 24.9%		
		Jeweller	2
Boatman	89(3)	Doctor	5
Sailor	88(10)	Saw Mill Worker	1
Fisherman	14	Regimental Drummer	4(1)
Ferryman	1	Indian Trader	1

TOTAL   772(39)

Note: Figures in parentheses represent those artisans who were captured.

COLONIAL SOUTH CAROLINA RUNAWAYS

65

TABLE 5

INVENTORIED SOUTH CAROLINA SKILLED SLAVES. 1730–1779

Years	Skilled Slaves	Adults	Per Cent
1730s	65	644	10.1
1740s	156	1,326	11.8
1750s	267	2,952	9.0
1760s	335	2,746	12.2
1770s	448	3,572	12.5
1730–79	1,271	11,240	11.3

SKILLS

Tradesmen	809 or 63.6%	House Slaves	249 or 19.6%
Woodworkers	634	Waitingman	21
Cooper	321	Barber	8
Sawyer	114	Coachman	3
Carpenter	196	Gardener	5
Woodman	1	House slave	92
Turner	2	Cook	61
Wheelwright	13	Midwife	1
Shipwright	10	Ironer	1
Blacksmith	22	Washerwoman	28
Shoemaker	43	Seamstress	20
Painter	6	Waitingwoman	1
Tanner	9	Nurse	4
Bricklayer	34	Maid	3
Butcher	8	Spinner	1
Tradesman	2		
Caulker	5	Town	10 or 0.8%
Currier	2		
Silversmith	1	Porter	3
Gunsmith	1	Chimney Sweep	1
Brazier	2	Labourer	5
Baker	2	Market Man	1
Taylor	7		
Stockkeeper/ Bookman	2	Agriculture	88 or 6.9%
Carter	6	Driver	70
		Ploughman	1
Watermen	110 or 8.6%	Herdsman	9
		Hunter	5
Boatman	103	Indigo maker	3
Fisherman	6		
Patroon	1	Miscellaneous	5 or 0.4%
		Doctor	5

TOTAL   1,271

Source: Inventories H to CC and Records of the Secretary of the Province. 1730–1736. SCDAH.

66   OUT OF THE HOUSE OF BONDAGE

the suicidal nature of that course, allowed slaves to create a meaningful
world of their own. Only in this way may greater occupational opportunities
for slaves in late colonial and early national South Carolina go some way
toward explaining the relative quiescence of that colony's slave population
in the period following the Stono revolt of 1739.[32]

II

Just as the representativeness of the runaway sample, particularly in terms
of overall size, internal composition, birthplace and occupational structure,
can tell us much about an emergent Afro-American slave culture, the same
is true of the patterns of mobility revealed in the advertisements themselves.
Of the 3,558 fugitives, just under a half were said to be making for a specific
destination and just under a third were said to have a specific motive in
mind. These are, of course, the motives and destinations attributed by
masters to their slaves. Can their judgements be trusted? Infallibility
certainly cannot be claimed, but there are significant reasons for accepting
the masters' word.

First and foremost, masters were advertising for valuable property. They
could be expected to give careful thought to the probable whereabouts of
their slaves. Furthermore, in some cases, there was precedent to guide
them, as with the runaways who were 'supposed to be gone towards
Winyaw, Harry having before (about a Year ago) run away and been taken
up in that Part of the Country'.[33] In other cases, precise information about a
runaway's whereabouts prompted an advertisement. Indeed, 8 per cent of
all fugitive advertisements reported a sighting, often a rather specific one, as
in the case of one slave 'harbour'd about Mr. Harvey's on Wappo and in
Town and on Town Neck, generally at Mr. Elliot's and Mr. Rose's' or
another who 'was seen at work in Town last Saturday at the House of one
Mr. Oliver'.[34] In addition, nearly one-fifth of all fugitives were described as
being 'well known in' a particular parish. In most cases, this was meant to
alert the citizens of that parish to the probability of the slave heading there.[35]

Occasionally, it is possible to check the accuracy of the master's pre-
diction as to his slave's supposed destination. The master of runaway Cyrus
noted that his slave was 'formerly the property of William Sealy, jun. at
Euhaws, Indian-Land', and had, therefore, probably 'gone to the Southward'. Four months later, it was confirmed that Cyrus had 'been seen at
Euhaws'. Another master thought his runaway would make for Charlestown. The slave was later captured at the Wando River, which is close to the
city.[36]

If the slaveowners' assessments, then, are relatively reliable, the various
destinations and motives they imputed to their slaves can be explored.
Plantations were the favored destinations of almost half the runaways,

COLONIAL SOUTH CAROLINA RUNAWAYS 67

towns were a magnet for another quarter, and other colonies accounted for fifteen per cent. Those said to be visiting relatives, friends, or acquaintances outnumbered those attempting permanent escape by about four to one. The divergences from this general pattern by particular groups of slaves will reveal much about the nature of South Carolina's slave community.

One such divergence is the difference a slave's occupation made in his response to bondage. Skilled slaves sought to pass as free more often than was the case among all runaways. While only 18 per cent of all runaways attempted to pass as free, almost a third of skilled slaves did so (see Table 6). However, twice as many artisans attempted to visit as pass as free. Similarly, skilled slaves ran to plantations more often than to towns, although they also headed out of the colony and to towns more frequently than the runaway population at large. Conversely, although field hands were overwhelmingly said to be making for plantations and to be visiting, they outnumbered skilled slaves in trying to escape out of the colony. Only about a quarter of those said to be leaving the colony were skilled slaves. The fact that only one-fifth of all those visiting or aiming for plantations were skilled slaves, and that well over a half of all those attempting permanent escape were field hands demonstrates that a slave's occupation in no way automatically determined the motive or destination of the runaway.[37]

A fugitive's ability to speak English was more crucial in determining his motive and destination than was the acquisition of a skill. Although visiting was still an activity favoured by runaways said to be proficient English speakers, almost a third of those attempting to pass as free spoke English well whereas only 2 per cent spoke English badly. Aiming to be free was more the preserve of the proficient English speaker than of the skilled slave. The same relationship is evident for the runaway's destination. Over twice as many skilled slaves were said to be making for plantations as opposed to leaving the colony, whereas those who spoke English well headed for both destinations in equal numbers (see Table 6).

A runaway's sex also influenced motive and destination. About two-thirds of fugitive men were said to be visiting; and just over a fifth were attempting to pass as free. Women, however, overwhelmingly preferred to visit. Over four-fifths of all female fugitives were said to be visiting; only one in ten were said to have freedom as an aim. Moreover, men outnumbered women by eight to one in those runaways said to be trying to leave the colony. A number of explanations for these dissimilar patterns suggest themselves. For one thing, proportionately, almost twice as many women as men were said to have a town as their goal, a reflection of the opportunities for female domestic and casual labour in Charlestown. For another, the absence of women from the ranks of those attempting to leave the colony can probably be explained by their strong kin ties and their reluctance to leave children (see Table 6).[38]

TABLE 6

MOTIVES AND DESTINATIONS OF SOUTH CAROLINA RUNAWAYS

| | A. Occupation | | | | B. Linguistic Ability | | | | | | C. Sex | | | | | |
	Skilled Slave		Field Hand		Speaks Well		Speaks Badly		Unknown		Male		Female		Total	
To visit	157	21.4	576	78.6	95	13.0	26	3.5	612	83.5	523	71.4	210	28.6	733	100
	61.6		71.9		57.6		55.5		72.5		65.3		82.3		69.4	
To pass as free	79	41.1	113	58.9	55	28.6	3	1.6	134	69.8	164	85.4	28	14.6	192	100
	31.0		14.1		33.3		6.4		15.9		20.5		11.0		18.2	
To avoid sale	.17	15.9	90	84.1	11	10.3	16	15.0	80	74.7	94	87.9	13	12.1	107	100
	6.7		11.2		6.7		34.0		9.5		11.7		5.1		10.1	
To avoid punishment	2	8.3	22	91.7	4	16.7	2	8.3	18	75.0	20	83.3	4	16.7	24	100
	0.8		2.8		2.4		4.3		2.1		2.5		1.6		2.3	
Total	255		801		165		47		844		801		255		1056	
	100		100		100		100		100		100		100		100	
Plantation	151	18.3	673	81.7	98	11.9	47	5.7	677	82.4	656	79.7	167	20.3	823	100
	38.6		49.4		34.3		57.3		48.9		48.9		40.7		47.0	
Town	121	26.5	335	73.5	62	13.6	18	4.0	377	82.4	298	65.4	158	34.6	456	100
	31.0		24.6		21.7		22.0		27.2		22.2		38.4		26.0	
Other Colony	74	28.2	188	71.8	91	34.7	6	2.3	165	63.0	233	89.3	28	10.7	262	100
	18.9		13.8		31.8		7.3		11.9		17.4		6.8		15.0	
Backcountry	7	13.7	43	86.3	8	15.7	8	15.7	35	68.6	50	96.1	2	3.9	51	100
	1.8		3.2		2.8		9.8		2.5		3.7		0.5		2.9	
Both plantation and town	38	23.6	123	76.3	27	16.8	3	1.9	131	81.3	105	65.2	56	34.8	161	100
	9.7		9.0		9.4		3.6		9.5		7.8		13.6		9.1	
Total	391		1362		286		82		1385		1342		411		1753	
	100		100		100		100		100		100		100		100	

Influences A: Occupation; B: Linguistic Ability; C: Sex. In roman character, the numbers; in bold type, the percentages.

One final factor, birthplace, also produced a divergence from the general pattern of mobility. Over a half of the Africans were said to be visiting and a further one-third were said to be avoiding sale, whereas only one in 20 were said to be attempting to pass as free (see Table 7). Creoles certainly attempted to pass as free more frequently than Africans. And yet, over three-quarters of the native-born runaways were said to be visiting. Only mulattoes diverged markedly from the general pattern, with twice as many of them seeking to pass as free as visit. When destination is considered, Africans headed for plantations in much the same proportion as the total runaway population but, understandably, fewer tended to have a town as a goal whereas, less obviously, more were thought to be trying to leave the colony. This surprising pattern reflected an urge to return to their home-land rather than an awareness of the greater degree of freedom possible in other colonies. Such was the aim of five 'Angolans' who ran away from their backcountry residence in 1761 and were 'supposed to have gone an east course as long as they could thinking to return to their own country that way'.[39] The destinations of American-born and mustee slaves closely followed that of the runaway population at large. Again, mulattoes diverged most markedly from the general pattern, with almost as many attempting to leave the colony as making for plantations.

A skilled, native-born, male runaway who was able to speak English well was more likely to pass as free or attempt to leave the colony than a runaway who was his exact opposite. And yet, only the attributes of interracial parentage and proficiency in the English language produced a significant divergence from the general patterns of mobility of all advertised fugitives. For male, skilled, creole slaves, visiting remained almost as popular as it was for all runaways.

III

The overwhelming majority of runaways travelled to plantations and tried to maintain contact with family and friends. It is visiting, rather than any simplistic equation of running away with resistance, that deserves closer scrutiny.[40] Many advertisements, for example, display a recognition of strong slave commitments to particular neighbourhoods and to friends and acquaintances. One slave woman, for instance, was thought to be on her way to Robert Cochran's plantation at Cainhoy, where she had 'a very good friend'.[41] Some advertisements simply referred to the runaway's former owners; others mentioned that the runaway had been recently bought or was about to be sold.[42] In both cases, it can be reasonably inferred that the runaway aimed to maintain or re-establish contact with old acquaintances. In the case of Betty, for example, no inference is necessary, for she was 'bought at the sale of the late Thomas Holman's Estate, the 14th of

TABLE 7

MOTIVES AND DESTINATIONS OF SOUTH CAROLINA RUNAWAYS:
INFLUENCE OF BIRTHPLACE

	Africans		North American		Mulatto		Mustee		West Indian		Indian		Unknown and others		Total	
To visit	73 **56.1**	**10.0**	157 **75.8**	**21.4**	16 **32.7**	**2.2**	52 **68.4**	**7.1**	5 **35.8**	**0.7**	5 **38.5**	**0.7**	425 **75.0**	**57.9**	733	**100**
To pass as free	8 **6.2**	**4.2**	41 **19.8**	**21.4**	32 **65.3**	**16.7**	22 **29.0**	**11.4**	7 **50.0**	**3.6**	7 **53.8**	**3.6**	75 **13.2**	**39.1**	192	**100**
To avoid sale	·41 **31.5**	**38.3**	9 **4.4**	**8.4**	1 **2.0**	**0.9**	1 **1.3**	**0.9**	1 **7.1**	**0.9**	1 **7.7**	**0.9**	53 **9.3**	**49.7**	107	**100**
To avoid punishment	8 **6.2**	**33.3**	0		0		1 **1.3**	**4.2**	1 **7.1**	**4.2**	0		14 **2.5**	**58.3**	24	**100**
Total	130 **100**		207 **100**		49 **100**		76 **100**		14 **100**		13 **100**		567 **100**		1056	
Plantation	127 **48.5**	**15.4**	153 **49.7**	**18.6**	22 **34.4**	**2.7**	53 **51.4**	**6.4**	1 **3.3**	**0.1**	10 **76.9**	**1.2**	457 **47.0**	**55.6**	823	**100**
Town	41 **15.6**	**9.0**	67 **21.7**	**14.7**	17 **26.6**	**3.7**	28 **27.2**	**6.1**	8 **26.7**	**1.8**	2 **15.4**	**0.4**	293 **30.1**	**64.3**	456	**100**
Other Colony	52 **19.9**	**19.8**	46 **14.9**	**17.6**	18 **18.1**	**6.9**	12 **11.7**	**4.6**	20 **66.7**	**7.6**	13 **7.7**	**0.4**	113 **11.6**	**43.1**	262	**100**
Backcountry	27 **10.3**	**52.9**	11 **3.6**	**21.6**	2 **3.1**	**3.9**	0		0		0		11 **1.1**	**21.6**	51	**100**
Both plantation and town	14 **5.7**	**9.3**	31 **10.1**	**19.3**	5 **7.8**	**3.1**	10 **9.7**	**6.2**	1 **3.3**	**0.6**	0		99 **10.2**	**61.5**	161	**100**
Total	262 **100**		308 **100**		64 **100**		103 **100**		30 **100**		13 **100**		973 **100**		1753	

In roman character, the numbers; in bold type, the percentages.

February last, and returned to his Plantation the next day where she is supposed to be harboured by Mrs. Holman's Negroes'.[43] Slaves even established ties independent of their own plantations. One slave, bought at an estate sale, was reckoned to be in the vicinity of 'an old settlement of [his former master's] at Wampee', presumably being supported by the neighbouring slaves.[44]

There are some extraordinary instances of attachment to a particular locale. Five slaves left Savannah in Georgia to make their way to North Carolina, where they had previously lived. West Indian-born slaves attempted to board vessels for the islands – and home. A 'Mandingo' slave, after spending most of his youth in South Carolina, was shipped off and sold in Jamaica; he was captured in Charlestown a year later.[45] This last example is indicative of the early identification of African-born slaves with particular New World neighbourhoods. Another is the 'Guinea' slave, who 'spoke indifferent English', but who had managed to form attachments in the Orangeburg district (in the South Carolina backcountry), where he had been captured on two occasions and was supposed to be heading for a third time. Planters were well aware of these formative attachments. One master advertised for a runaway who had been in the province five years and who had belonged to a planter in the parish of St. Thomas and St. Dennis 'by whom he was purchased [as] a new negro and with whom he lived until about 18 months ago when he was purchased at one of the Provost Marshall's sales, to which part of the Country it is most natural to suppose he is returned'.[46]

Closer attention to visiting also reveals the capacity of the slave community to harbour runaways. Fugitives could remain at large for long periods, even though their movements were known and publicised. The master of a sawyer, who spoke 'broken English' and who had been absent for two years, had a 'good deal of reason to think he is harboured sometimes about Fourhole Swamp, sometimes about Mr. Bacot at Goose Creek, and sometimes on the Town Neck, he having been frequently seen about them Places, and not long since on the latter'. Similarly, another runaway who had been absent for more than two years was 'suspected to be harboured by his father, and some other of Mr. Benjamin Mathews negroes either in Charles-Town or on John's Island at both which places he has been frequently seen'.[47] In fact, about 350 slaves, or one in ten of the fugitive population, were noted as having been absent for six months or more.

Certain identifiable groups tended to offer support to runaways. 'Fishing Negroes', market slaves, and 'kitchen Negroes' were three such groups often singled out in Charlestown. Thus, one slave woman, who had absented herself a second time, was expected to find employment in the Negro washing-houses or kitchens as she had done previously 'for 23 months together'.[48] Free blacks, both in town and countryside, were always a target of suspicion. Even groups of 'Jamaica negroes', 'Bermuda negroes' and, later in the century, 'French Negroes' were singled out for harbouring runaways.[49]

Supportive and cooperative arrangements among slaves are also suggested by the large number of slaves who ran away in groups. There were 710 such cases, involving 1,999 slaves, or 36 per cent of all advertised runaways. Just under a half of all these slaves ran away in groups of two. There were two significant trends. First, while Africans, particularly newly-arrived ones, were heavily represented in runaway groups, mixed groups of either creoles and Africans or acculturated and unassimilated slaves became increasingly common. By the 1770s, almost one in three of the 240 groups who ran away in that decade were of this type. Second, perhaps the most significant trend within group runaways was the growing evidence of kin ties. In the 1730s there were a mere five cases of a family group or men and women running away together – less than ten per cent of all group runaways in that decade. In the 1770s there were 70 such cases, forming about a third of all group runaways.[50]

Visiting itself is most significant in demonstrating the range and strength of slave kin ties. Of the 733 slaves who were said to be visiting, much the largest group – almost half – were said to be harboured by black relatives. Some runaways had a network of relatives thoughout the province. One native-born carpenter was 'well-known in Charlestown and adjacent parts [and had] a mother called Free Peg, [who lived] at Mr. Ladson's plantation on Ashley River and many other relations between that and Stono parish by some of whom it is probable that he may be harboured'. One slave woman was thought likely to board a vessel 'as she has a mother that lives at Winyah' and a father and brother at John's or James Islands. The destination of one married couple was difficult to pinpoint, for the wife had 'a mother and sister at the honourable William Bull Esq.'s plantation in Ashley River, a sister at the late Thomas Holman's, several relations at Doctor Lining's, a brother at Mr. William Elliott's and many others; amongst whom there is great reason to believe both are harboured'. Finally, a master, advertising for three runaways, noted that they had been bought from 'Mrs. Monck, in St. John's Parish, in whose neighbourhood they are well known, and have a long train of acquaintance and relations, by whom they are supposed to be harboured and entertained'.[51] It was not only near relations that sustained runaways. One absentee was supposed to be harboured by his aunt; another was said to be supported 'by Jonathan Scott's negroes, where he has an aunt and several cousins'; and a third was supposed to be with his brother-in-law.[52]

The attraction of visiting kin and friends is better understood when we remember that the vast majority of runaways were young men. Sixty per cent of the 1,525 runaways whose ages were listed were in their late teens or

COLONIAL SOUTH CAROLINA RUNAWAYS

early twenties. Presumably, these were precisely the slaves who found it hardest to find mates, who had often been separated from close kin, and who had not yet formed households of their own. Young men lacked the restraining ties of older slaves. Moreover, their incentive to renew or make acquaintance with fellow slaves was that much greater. Occasionally, young men acted desperately. In 1775 Toby, belonging to William Maxwell, broke into an out-house on William Roberts' plantation situated in James Island and carried off one of his slave women, Tenah. When Roberts put out a warrant for Toby's arrest, Toby apparently 'came armed ... with the Intention (from exceeding good Grounds) to take away the Life of' Roberts.[53] Even more occasionally, a young man might succeed in gathering a number of women around him. In March 1779 'young' Nero, a mulatto, ran away with Marianne, both of whom belonged to John McIllraith; in late May Nero was seen with another woman, named Cloe, belonging to Martin Pfeniger; and in September he was said to 'support and provide' for three runaway slave women, two belonging to Pfeniger and one to Thomas Caton.[54] Even young women, always in demand, ran away to find a compatible mate: 15-year-old Doll was said to have 'strayed or run away, supposed to have gone a courting', whereas Phillippa apparently went 'a-sweethearting at Jacksonburgh, where her mother Amey lives'.[55]

If the prevalence of visiting is indicative of the development of a more cohesive slave community and, more particularly, the emergence of slave kin networks, how can this be explained? In the first place, the composition of the slave population changed dramatically over the century. The adult sex ratio declined from about 170 in the 1730s to about 120 in the 1770s. Since men on average married or cohabited with women younger than themselves, nearly every man by the 1770s had an opportunity to marry. Second, the proportion of Africans in the slave population began to decline, although the decline was the least marked of all the North American colonies. A third related point is the considerable natural increase among creole lowcountry slaves, perhaps best evidenced by the increasingly balanced sex ratios, which occurred in the face of the large-scale African influx of the 1760s and 1770s (when more men were imported than women). There was a marked increase in the numbers of children in the lowcountry slave population from around the late 1740s onward. Kin ties began to supersede shipmate and ethnic ties.[56]

Turning from a demographic to more of a socio-economic explanation, there were additional developments within the fabric of lowcountry life that favoured the emergence of slave kin networks. First, large landholdings, the relatively non-exhaustive nature of the rice crop, and the development of tidewater rice production tied South Carolina slaves closely to the coast. Lowcountry slaves had a greater chance to remain in the same neighbourhood than was the case, say in Virginia, where tobacco production and small

74   OUT OF THE HOUSE OF BONDAGE

holdings necessitated westward expansion. The emergence of dense kin ties
was, therefore, in part a function of the geographic immobility of South
Carolina slaves who were, so to speak, 'servants forbidden to move'.[57]
Second, the large-scale nature of rice production meant that even in the
1730s almost half of the 5,000 slaves listed in South Carolina inventories
were resident on plantations of 30 or more slaves; by the 1770s this proportion had risen to about two-thirds. By 1790, almost a half of all slaves in
the Santee and Ashepoo regions belonged to planters who owned 100 or
more slaves.[58] If, as seems likely, this increased the opportunities for slaves
to form attachments within their own plantations, one final factor, the
growing density of the black population and their rising share of the total
population, facilitated the development of attachments between slaves of
neighbouring, even distant, plantations.[59] Slave kin networks developed
within and across plantation boundaries.

These basic demographic and socio-economic realities in turn encouraged
the development of more complex households and slave families. And it was
perhaps the consciousness of being part of an extended kin network –
including spouses, siblings, grandparents, aunts, uncles and cousins – that,
more than anything else, provided Afro-Americans with the foundation for
a sense of community. As a result of these relatively favourable conditions,
at least in comparison with those in other North American colonies, and
perhaps particularly through the agency of the slave family, a rich and
distinctive legacy of folklore, music, language, and religious expression was
continually being fashioned from African and American materials.[60]

A study of the colony's runaways can only serve as a small piece in this
overall jigsaw, but a significant one nevertheless, first, for confirming the
degree of local mobility among slaves and, more importantly, for suggesting
the ends to which that mobility was put; second, for documenting, in ways
that most other sources do not even approach, the extent and nature of the
African influence within the colony's slave community; and, finally, for
helping to establish the magnitude of the occupational opportunities to
colonial South Carolina slaves. Rather than simply equating running away
with resistance, it may be more useful to explore the social and cultural
significance of the phenomenon. Advertisements for slave runaways may
bear a superficial resemblance to advertisements for lost horses, but they
can be made to tell us much more than Coleridge ever envisaged.

                                    NOTES

1. Coleridge cited these advertisements (from Jamaica) in his 'Hint for a new Species of
   History', *Omniana or Horae Otiosiores* by Robert Southey and S.T. Coleridge, ed. Robert
   Gittings, Fontwell, Sussex, 1969, 1st pub. 1812, pp.167–71.

COLONIAL SOUTH CAROLINA RUNAWAYS

2. For previous studies of slave runaways, see Gerald W. Mullin, *Flight and Rebellion: Slave Resistance in Eighteenth-Century Virginia*, New York, 1972; Jean Fouchard, *The Haitian Maroons: Liberty or Death* trans. A.F. Watts, New York, 1981, 1st pub. Paris, 1972; Peter H. Wood, *Black Majority: Negroes in Colonial South Carolina from 1670 through the Stono Rebellion*, New York, 1974, pp.239–68; Lathan A. Windley, 'A Profile of Runaway Slaves in Virginia and South Carolina from 1730 through 1787', Ph.D. diss., University of Iowa, 1974; Daniel E. Meaders, 'South Carolina Fugitives as Viewed through Local Colonial Newspapers with Emphasis on Runaway Notices 1732–1801', *Journal of Negro History* (subsequently, *JNH*), 60 (1975), 288–319; Michael P. Johnson, 'Runaway Slaves and the Slave Communities in South Carolina, 1799 to 1830', *William and Mary Quarterly* (subsequently, *WMQ*) 3rd Ser., 38 (1981), 418–41; Daniel C. Littlefield, *Rice and Slaves: Ethnicity and the Slave Trade to Colonial South Carolina*, Baton Rouge, 1981, pp.115–73; Betty Wood, *Slavery in Colonial Georgia, 1730–1775*, Athens, 1984, pp.169–87. Runaway slave advertisements have been recently compiled for the Southern colonies: see Lathan A. Windley, comp., *Runaway Slave Advertisements: A Documentary History from the 1730s to 1790* 4 vols.,Westport, Conn., 1983.
3. In 1750 the slave populations of South Carolina and Virginia stood at 40,000 and 105,000 respectively. Windley counted about 1,300 slave runaways in Virginia newspapers between 1736 and 1787: 'A Profile of Runaway Slaves', 9; I count about 5,600 slave runaways in South Carolina newspapers between 1732 and 1782. While there are more extant issues of colonial newspapers for South Carolina than Virginia (twice as many, i.e., about 3,500 to 1,750), the discrepancy cannot be explained by this alone, especially since the Virginia slave population was so much larger than that of South Carolina. Although I do not propose to deal with the post-Revolutionary era in this essay, it is noteworthy that I count at least 2,000 runaways in South Carolina newspapers between 1783 and 1800, whereas Mullin counts only 400 Virginia runaways in the same period: *Flight and Rebellion*, 129 [this last figure is an estimate because Mullin divides his data by the year 1775].
4. Examples of inventories listing runaways include those of John Hays, May 8, 1731, Records of the Secretary of the Province I; Daniel McPherson, June 8, 1737, Inventory Book II; Josiah Baker, Sept. 1, 1743, Inventory Book KK, South Carolina Department of Archives and History (subsequently, SCDAH).
5. See George C. Rogers, et al., eds., *The Papers of Henry Laurens*, Columbia, S.C. 1968–, vol.4, pp.645 and 656. The extant South Carolina newspapers for 1764 and 1765 reveal no advertisements for runaway slaves belonging to Henry Laurens. At least 20 slaves absconded from Laurens' plantations in the 1760s and early 1770s, only one of whom merited a runaway advertisement. Similarly, four slaves from one of George Austin's plantations ran away for about six months and no advertisement survives for them. See Josiah Smith to George Austin, Jan. 31, April 11, and July 22, 1774, Josiah Smith Letterbook, Southern Historical Collection, University of North Carolina at Chapel Hill.
6. Isaac Chardon, *South Carolina Gazette* (subsequently *SCG*), June 28, 1735; Rachel Russ, *ibid.*, Dec. 31, 1763.
7. Job Colcock, *Royal Gazette*, July 18, 1781. Betty Wood has pointed out that over half the masters of runaway slaves in Georgia advertised their slaves within a month of their absence, suggesting that they did not expect them to return voluntarily. By the same token, just under half waited a considerable time before advertising, perhaps indicating that they did expect a speedy return or capture: *Slavery in Georgia*, p.171. My data corresponds: in the 1730s, for instance, about 60% of the advertisements were placed within a month of the runaway's departure.
8. Peter Wood has singled out Alexander Vanderdussen (who placed 11 advertisements for 12 slaves in the 1730s and early 1740s) and Francis LeBrasseur (who advertised four times for eight runaways in the 1730s) as masters keen to advertise and prone to cruelty toward their slaves: *Black Majority*, pp.245–6. Other masters who were quick to advertise include Humphry Sommers (who advertised for 22 runaways from the 1750s to the 1770s) and John Ainslie (who advertised for 19 runaways during the 1750s and 1760s).
9. One-fifth of the fugitives and captives whose residences could be determined (70% of all cases) left Charlestown, whereas only one in ten of the South Carolina slave population

76   OUT OF THE HOUSE OF BONDAGE

lived in the city.

10. At mid-century, it cost around £1 local currency to run a standard-sized notice in three consecutive editions of a South Carolina newspaper. In addition, the master could expect to pay a reward, mileage and workhouse charges.

11. James Parsons, *SCG*, Oct. 13, 1761; David Graeme, *ibid.*, Oct. 13, 1757.

12. William Henderson, *SCG*, March 19, 1763.

13. William Flud, *SCG*, March 13, 1775; Josiah Smith and Edward Darrell, *Gazette of State of South Carolina* (subsequently, *Gaz of State of SC*) Jan. 20, 1779.

14. Advertisements referring to recent sightings include William Killingsworth, *SCG*, Nov. 20, 1762; Robert Williams, *ibid.*, April 30, 1763; Stephen Miller and Isaac Legare, *ibid.*, Aug. 17, 1765.

15. By how much it is impossible to say. I certainly do not mean to suggest epidemic proportions. After all, advertised runaways in colonial South Carolina consistently form only about 0.3% of the adult slave population in any year throughout the period. Perhaps, at most, one in 100 adult slaves absconded during any given year. On the other hand, this may be more than one might expect. See, for comparative purposes, B.W. Higman, *Slave Populations of the British Caribbean 1807–1834*, Baltimore and London, 1984, pp.387–8.

16. Not only does the publication of lists of captives by the Workhouse become more regular, but by the 1770s captured slaves were being described by the Georgetown, Camden and Orangeburg gaolers.

17. Elias Robert, *South Carolina and American General Gazette* (subsequently, *SC & AGG*), Nov. 18, 1774. 119 runaways were described as having filed teeth (cf. Littlefield, *Rice and Slaves*, p.123).

18. The 'country marks' of 634 runaways were described (cf. Littlefield, *Rice and Slaves*, p.123). Examples of diagrammatic sketches include the Workhouse, *SCG*, Nov. 30, 1755; the Workhouse, *ibid.*, Nov. 4, 1756; and the Workhouse, *ibid.*, Sept. 14, 1765.

19. The Workhouse, *South Carolina Gazette and Country Journal* (subsequently, *SCG & CJ*), June 2, 1772; the Workhouse, *SCG*, Nov. 1, 1759; the Workhouse, *SCG & CJ*, Feb. 28, 1775.

20. The Workhouse, *SCG*, Oct. 10, 1754; Camden Gaol, *ibid.*, Nov. 8, 1773; Charlestown Gaol, *ibid.*, June 5, 1736.

21. William Martin, *SCG*, Jan. 19, 1738; the Workhouse, *ibid.*, Sept. 1, 1752; the Workhouse, *ibid.*, April 7, 1772. For evidence of necklaces and bracelets, see the Workhouse, *SCG*, Nov. 22, 1760; the Workhouse, *SCG & CJ*, Dec. 22, 1772; and Camden Gaol, *SC & AGG*, Nov. 27, 1777.

22. The Workhouse, *SCG*, Nov. 1, 1759; the Workhouse, *ibid.*, March 26, 1763; the Workhouse, *ibid.*, March 23, 1765.

23. Thomas Ladson, *SC & AGG*, Feb. 17, 1775; Isaac Porcher, *SCG*, Aug. 13, 1737.

24. James Paine, *SCG*, Feb. 9, 1734; Daniel Ravenel, *SCG & CJ*, Feb. 25, 1772; the Workhouse, *ibid.*, Dec. 1, 1772. Ethnically-mixed groups were particularly common by the late colonial period. In the 1730s almost 60% of the runaway groups involved Africans alone; by the 1770s, the proportion had been reduced to 45%.

25. John Champneys, *SCG*, Aug 30, 1773. For an example of an identification by markings, see the Workhouse, *SCG*, Aug. 25, 1757.

26. See Rogers et al., eds., *Laurens Papers*, vol. 1, 252, 258, 295, vol. 2, 93, 186, *passim*; Darold D. Wax, 'Preferences for Slaves in Colonial America', *JNH*, 58 (1973), 394–5; Littlefield, *Rice and Slaves*, pp.8–32, 125–8. Littlefield's table on p.127 is similar to mine, though there is a discrepancy in our respective numbers.

27. The inventory reporting rate for the St. James' Goose Creek taxpayers, listed in 1745, and St. John's Berkeley slaveowners, listed in 1762, was 58% and 54% respectively. The difference in inventory reporting rates between plantations with 30 or more slaves and those with 29 or less was statistically insignificant. For the St. James' listing, see my 'A Profile of a Mid-Eighteenth-Century South Carolina Parish: The Tax Return of Saint James' Goose Creek', *South Carolina Historical Magazine*, 81 (1980), 51–65; for that of St. John's Berkeley, see the Records of the Commissioners of the High Roads of St. John's Parish, 1760–1853, South Carolina Historical Society, Charleston.

28. Philip D. Morgan, 'Black Society in the Lowcountry, 1760–1810', in Ira Berlin and

COLONIAL SOUTH CAROLINA RUNAWAYS

Ronald Hoffman, eds., *Slavery and Freedom in the Age of the American Revolution*, Charlottesville, Va., 1983, pp.119–20.

29. Herbert G. Gutman, 'The World Two Cliometricians Made', *JNH*, 60 (1975) 99.
30. Morgan, 'Black Society', pp.99–102.
31. *Ibid*.
32. B.W. Higman, *Slave Population and Economy in Jamaica 1807–1834*, Cambridge, 1976, pp.212–32.
33. Benjamin Godin, *SCG*, March 30, 1738.
34. Thomas Drayton, *ibid*., May 11, 1738; *ibid*., Aug. 3, 1769.
35. Six hundred and thirty-one runaways were so described.
36. John Champneys, *SCG & CJ*, April 25, 1769 and *ibid*., Aug. 3, 1769; Robert Lewis, *SCG*, Sept. 14, 1769 and Workhouse, *SCG & CJ*, Oct. 3, 1769.
37. The basic assumption here is that, where an owner did not refer to a skill, the runaway was a field hand. Since masters generally aimed to identify their slaves as precisely as possible, it would be surprising if a slave's skill was omitted. My analysis of runaway motives and destinations is similar to that of Russell L. Blake who sampled runaway advertisements in 'Slave Runaways in Colonial South Carolina', unpublished paper, University of Michigan, 1972.
38. Philip D. Morgan, 'Black Life in Eighteenth-Century Charleston', *Perspectives in American History*, New Ser., 1 (1984), 200–203. See also Higman, *Slave Populations of the British Caribbean*, p.389. The evidence on the close kin ties of slave women is supported by the runaway material. Only one runaway man was accompanied by a young child, whereas 77 female fugitives were accompanied by one child, 24 by two, nine by three, and two by four children.
39. David Wallace, *SCG & CJ*, Nov. 21, 1767. See also Joseph Weatherly, *SCG & AGG*, Jan. 27, 1775.
40. Furthermore, the motive visiting was ascribed to proportionately more runaways as the century progressed: 57% in the 1730s, 56% in the 1740s, 67% in the 1750s, 70% in the 1760s, 72% in the 1770s. It then remained at that level for the rest of the century. See Morgan, 'Black Society', p.130. For a similar pattern among Chesapeake slaves, see Allan Kulikoff, 'The Origins of Afro-American Society in Tidewater Maryland and Virginia, 1700–1790', *WMQ*, 3d Ser., 35 (1978), 253–4.
41. Brian Cape, *SC & AGG*, Oct. 23, 1777.
42. 1,075 runaways were advertised as having had at least one former owner and another 146 two or more former owners. This represents over a third of all fugitives. For slaves running away on the day of, or shortly after, their sales, see, for example, John Narney, *SCG*, March 22, 1760; James Michie, *ibid*., April 16, 1754; Christopher Gadsden, *ibid*., Sept. 24, 1753.
43. Philip Tidyman, *SCG*, March 14, 1774.
44. Alexander Frazer, *ibid*., May 28, 1753.
45. McCarton and Campbell, *ibid*., June 28, 1760; for examples of West Indian slaves heading for the islands, see George McKintosh, *ibid*., Sept. 22, 1766 and Nathan Savage, *SC & AGG*, May 5, 1775; the Workhouse, *SCG & CJ*, April 29, 1766. See Isaac McPherson, *SC & AGG*, July 30, 1778, for an instance of an urban slave who 'did not chuse to live in the country'. Such cases can be multiplied particularly late in the century.
46. William Burrows, *SCG*, Aug. 3, 1769; John Mathews, *SC & AGG*, April 13, 1772.
47. Roger Saunders, *SCG*, April 27, 1738; John McQueen, *ibid*., Jan. 15, 1750; the Workhouse, *ibid*., Sept. 1, 1767.
48. Stephen Hartley, *SCG*, Oct. 13, 1757. The supportive role of 'fishing Negroes' can be glimpsed in Kennedy O'Brien, *SCG*, Nov. 15, 1737; Nathaniel Blundell, *ibid*., Feb. 26, 1763; John Ross, *SC & AGG*, Dec. 12, 1768. Examples of market slaves and 'kitchen Negroes' thought to be harbouring runaways include Mary Ellis, *SCG*, Feb. 3, 1757; John Forrester, *ibid*., May 7, 1763; William McKinny, *SC & AGG*, Aug. 27, 1778.
49. For an example of each, see Peter Timothy, *SCG & CJ*, May 20, 1766; John Champneys, *ibid*., March 3, 1772; White Outerbridge, *SCG*, Nov. 27, 1752; Jacob Valk, *SC & AGG*, March 19, 1778.
50. Moreover, whereas in the 1730s the largest groups, comprising five or six men, were

78 OUT OF THE HOUSE OF BONDAGE

composed of newly-arrived Africans, by the 1770s they were dominated by a combination of creoles and Africans, often with families as their nucleus. Thus, one group of nine runaways was composed of a native-born nuclear family of four, another creole lad, and four Africans. Another group of 14 were all native-born, except for one African woman. Once again, a nuclear family was the focus of this runaway group. See *SCG*, April 19, 1735; Richard Walter, *SCG & CJ*, July 3, 1770; John Ainslie, *SC & AGG*, Aug. 26, 1771.

51. Rawlins Lowndes, *SCG*, Aug. 25, 1757; John-Paul Grimke, *ibid.*, Aug. 14, 1762; Thomas Tucker, *ibid.*, Feb. 17, 1759; John Dawson, *Gaz of State of SC*, Oct. 3, 1779.
52. Andrew Letch, *SCG*, June 12, 1753; Francis Roche, *SCG & CJ*, Oct. 20, 1767; Richard Lamput, *SCG*, Oct. 24, 1775.
53. William Roberts, *SCG & CJ*, July 18, 1775. Interestingly, three years later, Toby carried Tenah off a second time. In 1778, both he and Tenah belonged to new owners and Tenah had become a mother: Samuel Bonneau, *SC & AGG*, July 30, 1778.
54. John McIllraith, *Gaz of State of SC*, March 17, 1779; Martin Pfeniger, *SC & AGG*, March 18 and May 29, 1779; and Thomas Caton, *ibid.*, Sept. 10, 1779.
55. Hampton Lillibridge, *ibid.*, Jan. 29, 1778; George Cuhun, *ibid.*, Nov. 5, 1778.
56. For full substantiation, see my 'Slave Counterpoint: Black Culture in the Eighteenth-Century Chesapeake and Lowcountry' (book manuscript, forthcoming).
57. Peter Laslett, *Family Life and Illicit Love in Earlier Generations*, Cambridge, 1977, p.252. This comparison between Chesapeake and lowcountry slaves is fully documented in my forthcoming book. Quite obviously, I am drawing a distinction between geographic immobility and local mobility.
58. Some of this documentation is presented in Morgan, 'Black Society', pp.93–6.
59. Slave attachments across plantations are suggested by the greater distances travelled by runaways as the century progressed. Advertisements for captives that state the location of the runaway's residence and the place of capture are available for 19 slaves in the 1730s, 30 in the 1740s, 37 in the 1750s, 134 in the 1760s, and 124 in the 1770s. The average distance travelled, as the crow flies, was, for successive decades, 31, 30, 39, 43, and 52 miles.
60. Again, for documentation, see my forthcoming book.

From Land to Sea: Runaway Barbados Slaves and Servants, 1630–1700

Hilary Beckles

In recent years there has been a rapid growth in the literature concerning runaway slaves and rebel Maroon communities that existed in a state of 'semi-freedom' in the peripheral mountainous and wooded zones of Caribbean plantations. Detailed analyses in both the traditions of the case study and the comparative methodology now exist so that much is known of this minority of rebel slaves who fled from their plantations in a precarious quest for freedom. The literature has concentrated primarily upon three features of this mode of rebellion. First, it attempted to evaluate the impact of lost labour upon the plantation economy and society. Second, it dealt with subsequent attempts by rebels to defend their new status against their masters' retrieving forces. Related to this aspect are studies concerning the difficulties posed for the governing officials, as well as individual planters, in combatting the persistence of the problem. Third, it focussed upon the internal organisation of Maroon rebel communities, as some scholars, particularly social anthropologists, have suggested that these communities offered alternative social models, with varying degrees of attractiveness, for the larger enslaved population.[1]

There is, however, another dimension to the study of slave runaways in the Caribbean which has been neglected, especially within the Anglophone region. This concerns the practice of 'maritime marronage' – the rebellious activities of those slaves who took to the sea in flight attempting to escape fully the geographical confines of their plantation bondage. Little is known of these 'overseas' rebels, though the available evidence suggests that at certain times, especially during major wars between rival colonial powers, they posed greater problems for their deserted masters than those rebels who took flight internally.[2]

The Barbados case is of particular interest, because there the act of maritime marronage touched upon various aspects of Eastern Caribbean colonial history which are also insufficiently researched. It reveals, for instance, much about the nature of international relations and the shifting balance of power within the region. Furthermore, because the labour force of the colony during the seventeenth century comprised, in addition to the black slaves, thousands of white indentured servants who were referred to by many contemporaries as 'white slaves' and 'white niggers' (because of the oppressive conditions under which they served), revolt and resistance, including marronage, at times cut across racial lines as both groups sought, separately but sometimes collectively, to escape their bondage.[3] This essay looks at the pattern of marronage established by slaves and servants in Barbados, emphasising the alliances they formed in their internal flight from the plantations as well as their external flight from the island.

In seventeenth century Barbados both slaves and servants planned armed rebellions against their masters as well as sought to flee the plantation on which they laboured. The servants revolted in 1634, and their general rising of 1647 which aimed to capture the island from the planter elite, was aborted by the militia in its final organisational stages. In this rebellious tradition established by servants there were aborted slave conspiracies in 1649, 1675 and 1692.[4] These structured eruptive events represent only one aspect of an overall culture of resistance, a most prominent feature of which was marronage – both petit (internal) and grand (external).

That servants and slaves should have participated in rebellious behaviour almost identical in form and intent is not surprising. Historians of early English American colonies have argued since the 1920s that the system of indentured servitude most closely approximated chattel slavery in the area of the masters' perceived notions of property 'rights' in servant labour and, in the case of runaways, in their responses to its retrieval. Herrick, for example, noted that 'as slavery had its worst features in the cruel treatment accorded those who sought to escape its effects, so the indenture system shows at its worst in the study of runaways'.[5] Smith accepted this view and stated that 'the institutions of indentured servitude appear at their worst in this matter of runaways, and there is little to distinguish a servant from a slave'.[6] In addition, Smith noted, if the servant 'ran away, he was brought back under the auspices of rigorous laws and he suffered heavy penalties. Although the point was not often discussed, the colonists felt that masters held property in the labor of their servants, and that the masters' rights were thus property rights.'[7]

The social and economic development of indentured servitude in Barbados during the seventeenth century supports these contentions. The brutal conditions under which most servants served their term were aggravated by their general inability to achieve even modest levels of social mobility and property accumulation after their contracts had expired.[8] These factors produced a psychological profile among servants which tended towards rebellious behaviour – marronage being a common expression of their discontent. From the formative years of colonisation servants are described as persistently attempting to escape their bondage by running away. Sir Henry Colt who visited the colony in 1634 noted that they spent their leisure idling about Carlisle Bay, the chief port of call, seeking every opportunity, both day and night, to secretly escape the island in a departing

FROM LAND TO SEA

vessel. Colt noted, furthermore, that the objectives of their 1634 defeated uprising were to kill their masters and put to sea.[9]

Evidence of internal servant and slave marronage is quite abundant for the pre-1670s period. During this time, they fled to the few caves and gullies, as well as the remaining, but rapidly diminishing wooded zones, in attempts to free themselves of the rigours of plantation labour. They sought both temporary respite from their bondage as well as long-term freedom. On 6 November 1655, for example, the Council was informed by Capt. Richard Goodall and Mr John Jones that 'there are several Irish servants and Negroes' who have run away from their masters' estates and are 'out in rebellion in ye thicket and thereabouts'. The thicket was a large part of the then internal frontier areas of the colony, comprising the south eastern region of the St Philip parish where the sugar plantation culture had not yet fully encroached. The council, on hearing this alarming evidence, ordered

> Lt. Col. John Higginbottom ... to raise any of the companies of Col. Henry Hawley's regiment, to follow ye said servants and runaway negroes, and if he shall meet with any of them, to cause them forthwith to be secured, and send them before the Governor, or some Justice of the Peace. But if the said servants and runaway negroes shall make any opposition, and resist his forces, and refuse to come in peaceably and submit themselves, then to use his utmost endeavours to suppress or destroy them, providing they do stand out in rebellion, and cannot be taken otherwise.[10]

Col. Higginbottom's purge was probably not immediately successful, as similar orders were issued by the Council during the following three years.

The minutes of Council for the period 1652 and 1660 give insights into the many discussions concerning runaway servants and slaves. Petitions were frequently made by masters to the Council requesting assistance in the pursuit of their runaways. For example, on 3 June 1656 the Council heard the petition of William Healthcott concerning his Scots servants who 'have for a long time absented themselves from their master's service upon a pretence of freedom from their service'. The Council ruled that the said servants should be taken up and returned to their service, but that the master was not to take advantage of the laws to enforce any penalties upon the servants.[11] Likewise, on 8 June 1657 Thomas Moore, a planter in the St Joseph parish, complained that several of his slaves had absconded from the estate and could not be found. The Council directed Col. Lewis Morris to order Capt. Weston of his regiment 'to levy six files, or more, to apprehend the runaways, but if the said Negroes shall make opposition, and cannot be otherwise taken and subdued, that such as so resist may be lawfully killed and destroyed'.[12] On 2 September 1657 the General Assembly decided that

82 OUT OF THE HOUSE OF BONDAGE

the number of runaway servants and slaves had grown to such a proportion that the Governor was asked 'to issue Commissions for a general hunting of runaways throughout the island'.[13]

Servants quite commonly ran away from the plantations as a result of irregularities over the terms and conditions of their contracts, particularly if they considered that these were being deliberately breached by their masters. In such cases, servant marronage was an attempt to resist the undermining of rights which the legal system did not effectively protect. Such was the case of Will Bowman who claimed that he ran away from his estate on account of being treated contrary to the terms of his indenture. The Council ordered in this case, on 15 January 1656, that he 'forthwith return home to his master's plantation, and from thence not to depart till further order, unless he have liberty to sue for his freedom'.[14] When in August 1656, the servants of Martin Bentley ran away from their estate over grievances concerning their indenture, the Council ordered that 'ye servants forthwith return to their master's plantation, and serve out their time'.[15]

In some cases, however, runaway servants and slaves launched attacks upon the persons and properties of their deserted masters. The most common act of hostility committed by runaway servants and slaves was the burning of the sugar canes. On this issue, the Assembly was most concerned, as arsonist attacks were seen as striking at the very core of the sugar plantation system. Planters frequently informed the Assembly that runaway slaves commonly burned the canes to revenge themselves on their masters, and that servants often did the same. Slaves convicted of such arsonist acts were generally executed. A 1655 ruling of Council, however, provided that if a servant, runaway or otherwise, should

> willingly burn or set on fire any sugar cane field, or other place where sugar cane do grown, in any place in this island, shall for every such offence to be proved, receive 40 lashes upon his naked back, and branded on the forehead with a hot iron with the letter 'R' and become servant to the party or parties that shall be so damnified by the burning ... for the term of seven years.[16]

A Common practice of runaway slaves and servants, while being pursued by the militia or specialist trackers, was to go from plantation to plantation in an attempt to draw others into their ranks. The objective was to strengthen their armed defence while complicating the business of their retrievers. In response to this development, Gov. Searle in 1656 instructed, by public proclamation,

> all masters, mistresses and overseers of houses and families and all constables ... to apprehend all strange negroes and wandering

FROM LAND TO SEA

servants that shall come within plantations or houses or wandering abroad, or that shall have arms, clubs or other unlawful weapons or instruments ...[17]

The bulk of the evidence suggests, however, that most runaway slaves were concerned more with establishing reliable contacts on the various estates for food, shelter, information and social interaction, than with raising additional recruits who might, in fact, jeopardise their rather tenuous and uncomfortable 'semi-freedom'.

The case of runaway servants was somewhat more complicated. Primarily because of the small size of the servant population, runaway servants were always more visible. They could not easily disappear within either the urban or rural white communities. As a result, runaway servants commonly confronted the law in groups, sometimes demanding their freedom by threatening to create internal strife. They were aware that they constituted, in the final instance, an important part of white society's anti-slave military vanguard, and this allowed them to appear more openly aggressive than their slave counterparts. This was particularly the case with the Irish Catholic servants, whose rejection of their servitude was reinforced by anti-English and anti-Protestant ideological attitudes. As most Irish ex-servants suffered severe discrimination on the English controlled labour market they were generally seen wandering about the estates, and being described as vagrant, criminal and rebellious.

The attempts of rebellious ex-servants to encourage plantation servants into their ranks for the organisation of armed rebellion and other forms of hostile anti-planter activities caused much concern to successive administrations. In 1657, for example, Governor Searle, while addressing the assembly on the matter, stated that

> it hath been taken notice that several of the Irish nation, freemen and women, who have no certain place of residence, and others of them do wander up and down from plantation to plantation, as vagabonds refusing to labour ... and endeavouring by their example and persuasion to draw servants unto them of the said nation to the same ... wicked courses. ... Some are now forth in rebellion, and refuse to come in, by all which it appears that could they be in a condition of power, or had opportunity, they would soon put some wicked and malicious design into execution.[18]

In order to counter these runaways and potential runaways, Governor Searle implemented a pass system. All servants were to be issued with 'a ticket under ye hand of his or her master, mistress or overseer'[19] which would enable them to travel legitimately off their estates. Any servant found off his or her plantation without such a pass was to be judged a runaway,

84　　　　　　　　　　　　　　　OUT OF THE HOUSE OF BONDAGE

arrested by any constable and firmly whipped. The constable conducting
the arrest was then to convey the said servant 'to the next constable, and so
from constable to constable, until he or she be returned to his or her master,
mistress or overseer'. In addition, if that servant should again refuse to
labour according to contract, 'but absent and runaway, in that case as often
as they shall absent and runaway, being found, to be again whipt and
ordered to service, as before mentioned'.[20] These provisions did not lead to
an immediate reduction in the number of servants who ran away from their
estates. Governor Searle was soon informed that runaway Irish servants

> that are in rebellion do pass up and down from plantation to plantation
> with counterfeit and forged testimonials, [pretending] that they are
> freemen, or that they have liberty so to pass, and, by that means have
> opportunity to accomplish their wicked purposes.[21]

The Governor was forced once again to instruct

> all persons ... to be very circumspect in their inquiries into such
> tickets and testimonials, as shall be produced unto them; and if they
> shall appear to be counterfeit or forged, that they cause such persons
> having ye same to be conveyed before the next Justice of ye Peace, to
> be proceeded against according to Law.[22]

Governor Stede had noted in August 1687 that the number of runaway
slaves and servants had continued to increase and had become a major
problem for his administration. He noted that 'most of the white servants
sent here being taken from the gaols, and being men whose lives have taught
them all kinds of villanies', cannot be kept 'in due order and obedience as is
required by their masters and by the safety of the island unless there be
severe laws to punish any insolence towards their masters'.[23] Later that year
he was informed by the Provost Marshal that the 'Bridgetown cage', a
prison constructed specifically to harbour recaptured runaway servants and
slaves, was filled and that the construction of a new facility was required.[24]

Stede's requests for tougher laws to control runaway servants did not
materialise. Laws penalising runaway servants in Barbados were probably
the mildest in the English New World. In Maryland, runaway servants
under a 1639 law could be executed. In Virginia, under a 1642 law, captured
runaways were liable to have their time doubled for the first offence and
branded on the shoulder or cheek with the letter R for the second offence.[25]
In Pennsylvania, captured runaway servants were sometimes made to wear
iron collars which generally carried the initials of their master.[26] Under
the 1652 Barbados Masters and Servant Law, captured runaways were
sentenced to one extra month service for every two hours of absence. In
1661, when the Barbadians collected all the existing rulings and constructed
the first comprehensive Masters and Servants Statute in the English West

FROM LAND TO SEA 85

Indies, the punishment was reduced to one extra day service for every two hours absent, and the maximum extension was not to exceed three years.[27] The reduction of the penalty was part of the overall Barbadian attempt to make their indenture system a more attractive package in Europe. There was, in addition, also a reduction in the length of indenture contracts offered by custom from five or seven years to between two to four years. Under the 1662 Jamaica Servant Code, which was a minimally modified version of that of Barbados, captured runaways were sentenced to one extra month service for every 24 hours absent.[28]

The Barbados servant laws were rarely fully applied. Efforts to attract servants to the island placed the responsibility upon successive Governors to be lenient, in spite of the occasional insistence by planters that the full force of the law be applied. The Minutes of Council contain instances of Governors reprieving runaway servants after they had been punished at law by freeholders' courts. For instance, in August 1654, Thomas Carter, servant of John Colleton, assemblyman, absented himself from his estate one day longer than he was given permission. Colleton insisted that, according to the 1652 Law, Carter was to serve him one extra year. Governor Searle reprieved the servant on the grounds that since he was overtaken with drink, it could not be established that he intended to run away 'upon any pretence of freedom'.[29]

Runaway slaves, however, did not receive such generosity at law. They were generally executed and their masters compensated at their estimated market value by the public treasurer. In December 1684, for example, the runaway slave of Sir Timothy Thornhill was re-captured and legally executed. Thornhill was paid £20. 17s. 6d by the Treasurer for his financial loss.[30] Likewise, in 1701, George Harper was paid £25 compensation for the execution of his runaway slave woman 'who had escaped and hid for one whole year' before being caught;[31] likewise, Henry Applewhaite was also paid £25 in the same year following the execution of his captured runaway slave.[32]

Loyal servants and ex-servants were commonly employed by plantation owners to retrieve runaway servants and slaves. In the case of servants, it was merely part of their work description as defined by their masters. Ex-servants were paid a fee for their service. During the 1680s, for example, Robert Frument was a servant on Othoniell Hagges' plantation, where he continued as a paid labourer after his contract had expired. Among his many tasks was the retrieving of runaway servants and slaves. Eventually he suffered the loss of an arm from a blow administered by a runaway slave. The slave was finally caught and executed but Frument, not receiving any compensation from his master, was forced to petition the Council pleading for some financial consideration.[33] In the same year, another servant, Peter Leare, also lost an arm pursuing a runaway slave. He received £15 con-

86 OUT OF THE HOUSE OF BONDAGE

sideration from the Council.[34] In 1701, however, when a servant of Colonel Frere was murdered by one of his rebel slaves, he received £6 from the Treasurer for the loss of the servant, and £22 for the slave who was executed at law.[35] Runaway slaves seem to have had little fear of such individual servants, though they dreaded the organised hunts of militia regiments.

Posing substantial problems for the expansionist Barbadian plantocracy and Imperial government were the 'maritime maroons'. For slaves, their best chance of successful long term marronage was in escaping to the frontier of the Carib inhabited Windward Islands of St Lucia, St Vincent, Tobago and Dominica. Servants who escaped to sea, on the other hand, tended to be attracted to activities ranging from piracy to – in the case of Irish Catholics – settling in the French colonies in the Leewards and Windwards. Some also attempted to join army and navy operations in the region. By taking to the high seas, most runaway slaves and servants proposed to reject totally and irrevocably their respective enslavement and indentureships. The number of such escapes cannot be quantified, even crudely, but it was sufficiently problematic to engage the island's legal and political administrators continuously throughout the second half of the century.

During the early 1660s, assemblymen became quite disturbed about the number of servants escaping the island. The 1661 code for the governing of servants had provided that

> whatsoever servant ... shall be found or apprehended in the act of running away upon board of any ship, bark, or boat, upon departure of this island, whereby it may be justly presumed that the said servant intended and prepared to escape and runaway unlawfully from the island ... such servant so taken ... shall upon conviction thereof be condemned for the full space and term of three years.[36]

These servants escaped the island in several ways. They stowed away on vessels plying the region; some collectively seized boats at night and sailed towards the Windward Islands; others disguised themselves as sailors, seamen, or soldiers and got aboard military vessels. Ironically, seamen wanted to trade their lifestyles for those of the servants on the estates, while the servants envied the seamen for their apparent freedom and adventurous lifestyles. In 1667, the Council heard how seamen, not wanting to fight against the Dutch, when their ships docked at Barbados ran away and hid on the estates, offering themselves as servants. Two provisions were made to correct this situation by the Council. First, it was ordered that 'inhabitants of the island who presume to harbour or hide any seaman in any of their houses or plantations' would be liable to prosecution. Second, 'whatsoever servant or slave ... shall be found on board any vessel who have absented themselves from their masters, be there publicly lashed by order

FROM LAND TO SEA   87

of the Commander of the said ship and sent ashore ... to the common gaol till their masters may have notice thereof'.[37]

In 1675, the Council ordered that an act be 'drawn up to prevent the running away of christian servants and their getting off by the negligence of such as keep boats and other vessels'.[38] Those who owned vessels were ordered under penalty to give security that servants would not be allowed to escape with their vessels. In addition, an act was considered to give encouragement to all persons who assist in the retrieval of such servants. Governor Stede noted in 1687 that the number of servants running off the island had increased during the previous years. He noted that they frequently got together and seized fishing boats, after having 'stolen what they can from the estates', and on some occasions after having 'beaten their overseers and masters'.[39]

Such complaints continued throughout the century, and in 1699 the owners of vessels were required to hire servant tenants (who were specially imported by the Assembly for the control of slaves and rebel servants) to police their vessels. In 1701, another Act was passed 'to prevent freemen, white servants and slaves running from the island in shallops, boats and other vessels'. Under this law, it was a felony to steal vessels, and runaway servants found guilty of such thefts were liable to capital punishment. The Attorney General, however, informed the Council that this measure was prejudicial to His Majesty's prerogative since it also embraced freemen whose categorisation with servants and slaves was not acceptable.[40]

The unstable nature of international relations in the region during the century provided conditions conducive to servant marronage. The many expeditions outfitted to wage war upon the French, Dutch and Spanish, generally docked at Barbados for water, supplies and men. Throughout the century, planters complained of their servants being taken up by these military commandos.[41] Large numbers disappeared from the island in 1654 when Generals Penn and Venables arrived there to outfit their fleet for the attack upon the Spanish at Hispaniola. One planter, Gyles Sylvester, noted that during this time 25 of his men servants ran away to a 'man of war'. He unsuccessfully sought compensation from the Council.[42] In addition, many Barbadian servants, between 1660 and the 1680s, tried escaping the island in order to reach Jamaica – the new English colony which offered plenty of free or cheap land, and contained few sugar estates to remind them of their labour experiences in Barbados. In 1662, the Jamaica Assembly offered servants indenture contracts of four years and 30 acres of land upon the expiration of these contracts.[43] Few ex-servants could purchase land in Barbados, and this hope of being propertied was the ideal with lured most servants to the West Indies.

Barbadian planters feared that the runaway Irish servants would not only offer the French critical intelligence on the island fortification and military

88 OUT OF THE HOUSE OF BONDAGE

strength, but would physically assist in an attack upon the English interest. In 1689, for example, when the Prince and Princess of Orange were declared King and Queen of England, the Irish servants in the English portion of St Christopher 'assembled suddenly, and declared themselves for King James', and then proceeded to 'kill, burn and destroy all that belong to the Protestant interest' before going over to the French section of the island.[44] Governor Stede of Barbados was concerned that the behaviour of these 'bloody Papists' would affect the balance of European power within the region – especially since several 'mulattos, mustees and negroes were with the Irish', and all of them in league with the French.[45]

In 1693, the assembly discussed at great length a bill to prevent the servants fleeing to the enemy in case of an invasion, but soon discovered that many servants ran away also because of the severity of militia duties. The bill was enacted and servants were legally eligible to attain freedom by order of council if it was believed that they fought manfully against the enemy. On such occasions, their masters would be reimbursed from the public treasury.[46] By 1694, many captured runaway servants and slaves were imprisoned in the Bridgetown cage accused of giving the French intelligence on the island's fortification.[47]

No specific legal arrangements were made for the retrieval of servants or slaves who managed to flee the island successfully. The general English planter policy was that any servant or slave who fled to another English island would be returned if recognised and captured. This was administratively possible and legally enforceable as Lord Willoughby's proprietorship had initially united the islands under one jurisdiction.[48] During the period 1649–51, when royalist Barbadian planters threatened to declare the island a republic, breaking away from Cromwell's Commonwealth, one argument which was made against the decision was that the republican status would assist servants and slaves to escape fully from island to island, as planters would then be unable to legally demand the return of their property.

The relationship between runaway Barbadian slaves and what Colonel Codrington referred to in 1699 as 'the amelioration of the French interest' in the Windward Islands, was also a subject of much concern to both the Barbados planters and the Imperial government. Colonel Codrington noted that many slaves fled to the French islands because of the many holy days the French allowed their slaves. But many also hoped to trade their freedom in French colonial society for both military information and service. These runaways, Codrington noted, were not 'handed over, notwithstanding frequent demands' made to the French, who saw their guests as useful allies against the English.[49] The extent of this fear in Barbados must not be underestimated. It was widely believed that the French would use these runaways to infiltrate Barbados' society in order to collect military intelligence. For example, in the early 1680s, three free-born Catholic

FROM LAND TO SEA 89

blacks from Portuguese Brazil arrived at Barbados. They were enslaved on arrival but subsequently imprisoned on the charge that they were emissaries of the French, 'or some other Catholic interest'. When, however, they rejected the charge of being spies, but 'openly profess themselves Roman Catholicks' the Governor ordered that they 'be forthwith transported and sent off this island to be sold accordingly'.[50]

Following the 1692 aborted slave uprising, in which six Irish Catholic servants were centrally involved, Governor Kendal informed his Council of the necessity of preventing 'the negroes ... and the white servants and poorer sorts ... from fleeing to the enemy'.[51] At the 31 July 1695 sitting of the Council, one Josiah Jackson was rewarded for

> taking up at sea [six leagues off land] a wherry with 11 negroes which in all probability might have arrived at some of the French Islands and give intelligence of the fleet here then ready to saile ...[52]

Jackson had seen the slaves taking the boat, and quickly assembled a party of nine white men and seven slaves to pursue the rebels. Jackson was awarded £40, each of his nine white men £5, and each slave £1.[53]

Large numbers of slaves also fled to the Carib controlled island of St Vincent. Pere Labat who visited the island in 1700 noted that it was 'the military ... head-quarters of the Caribs' in the Windwards. Labat noted:

> Besides the Indians ... the island is also populated by negroes, most of whom have escaped from Barbados. Barbados being to windward of St. Vincent makes it an easy matter for the slaves to escape from their masters in canoes or rafts and join the savages.[54]

These Maroons had a noticeable impact upon the nature of European and Amerindian rivalry for dominance in the Windward Islands. Prior to the 1660s, when attempts by England and France to colonise these islands were spasmodic and not well organised, the Caribs 'brought the runaway slaves back to their masters, or sold them to the French and Spanish'.[55] During the latter part of the century, however, more serious attempts were made by the Barbadian planters to establish settlements at St Vincent, St Lucia and Tobago. In addition, during the 1680s, the French colonists at Martinique began a colonisation drive into Grenada and St Lucia. These developments affected the political evaluations of the Caribs, who now under greatly intensified military pressure, began to regard Barbados 'runaways as an addition to their nation'.[56]

As the information filtered through Barbados' slave communities that the policy of the Caribs toward runaways had changed, it seems to have given added impetus to the flight of slaves. The Maroons soon outnumbered the Caribs on the island, and in addition, according to Labat, 'compelled the latter to give them the windward side of the island'.[57] This was the first

90   OUT OF THE HOUSE OF BONDAGE

Barbadian Maroon community to be established. According to Labat, the
Maroons soon asserted their dominance over the island, and the Caribs were
forced to 'suffer impatiently their outrages'.[58] The Caribs had changed
their policy towards the runaways in order to win an ally in their anti-
European resistance, but were soon forced to reconsider their strategy.
Black domination threatened not only their independence but also their
survival on the island. Labat noted:

> what annoys the Indians more than the loss of half their island is that
> the negroes continually steal their women and girls. It is not possible
> for the Caribs to rescue them, as the negroes, who are a much braver
> race and in far superior numbers, only laugh at them, ill-treat them,
> and possibly will one day make them work as their slaves.[59]

The Caribs re-appraised the situation and invited both the English and
French to invade the island so as to 'rid them of their unwanted guests'.
Subsequently, a minor English invasion was defeated by the Maroons. In
1719, the Caribs convinced M. de Chevalier de Frenquières, Commander
General of the French Islands, to launch a large scale attack. The plan
was approved by the Council of Martinique, and Messieurs Poulain de
Guerville, Major of Martinique, and M. de Buc, Lt. Col. of the Windward
militia, were commissioned to raise 500 men and to lead the expedition.[60]
The Caribs promised them every assistance.

The Maroons, however, were expecting the invasion, and devised their
defence strategem. First, they painted themselves 'red like Indians', and
hid at various points about the island. Second, the bulk of them 'withdrew
to the mountains and inaccessible places, only coming down at night to lie in
ambush for [the French soldiers] and surprise them'.[61] Labat noted that
'this method of carrying on the war was successful; not a single negro was
captured, while they killed a number of [soldiers]', including Poulain de
Guerville, Major of Martinique. It was soon realised that a much larger
force was necessary, but calls for reinforcement were not fruitful. The
Council tried to force the free negroes of Martinique to assist, 'but they
flatly refused'. Meanwhile, the troops were taken with dysentery and M. de
Buc was forced to withdraw. The Caribs, according to Labat, 'merely
looked on and did not join in the game, and though it was as important for
them as it was for the French, they made not the slightest move in the
matter. This wrecked the scheme'.[63] Defeat of the troops by the Maroons
weakened the defence of the French settlement at Grenada and St Lucia,
and was accompanied by outcries from those colonists. It was anticipated
that the English would take advantage of this defeat and invade St Lucia or
Grenada. During the first half of the eighteenth century, this island continued to represent what the mountains of Jamaica and the forest of Guiana
meant for some slaves – an alternative to plantation bondage.

FROM LAND TO SEA

Occasionally, servants were arrested for assisting slaves who had escaped from their masters. This was part of the wider relationship between rebel slaves and servants, one which the planters feared throughout the century would gain dangerously rebellious proportions. For example, at the end of March 1693, the Council was informed that a servant 'belonging to Mr. Thomas Holland had ... counterfeited and set Mr. Walker Colleton's hand to a ticket for a negro woman belonging to the said Mr. Colleton, now wandring and passing from place to place without being molested'.[64] The servant was then said to have 'absconded himself and could not be found to answer his crime'.[65] It was suspected that the servant had escaped the island.

Slaves also collaborated in organising the flight of servants from Barbados. On 24 December 1693 the Council ordered that the

> negro man belonging to Ann Parker, widow, who was committed to gaole by James Cortes for enticing and contriving the sending off some white servants belonging to the estate of Mr. Peter Leare be at the next Quarter Session to be held for the precinct of St. Michael there be tried for his crime aforesaid.[66]

During the trial it was revealed that the accused had organised on many previous occasions the 'sending off the island severall white servants belonging to severall inhabitants'.[67] He was found guilty and committed to gaol on 5 April 1684. It is not clear whether it was in some way an expression of intimate personal relations which transcended the formidable race barriers which structured slave society.

For both slaves and servants, then, there was a movement from land to sea in the pattern of Barbadian Maroon activity, as plantation agriculture spread throughout the entirety of the islands by the 1660s. The economic impact of the loss of servant labour upon particular estates was probably more substantial than in the case of slaves. Servant labour in the second half of the seventeenth century was not easily obtainable. After 1660 it became both scarce and expensive. During this period, servants were the skilled labour component of estates, and their flight could have jeopardised production processes. After the 1660s, slaves were cheaper and more easily replaceable. These runaways, however, posed problems for the Barbadian plantocracy which transcended mere local production or capital accumulation considerations. The Maroon slaves in the Windward islands contributed to the hindrance of their easy colonisation, particularly St Vincent where they created a complex political and military situation. The runaway Irish servants, on the other hand, in their commitment to Catholic solidarity, posed at times major problems for the English planters in the region. The magnitude of 'maritime' flight, therefore, can be appreciated within the context of regional politics rather than in the traditional terms of plantation social structure. Furthermore, it illustrates the degree to which slaves and servants sought to self-terminate their bondage.

NOTES

1. Most of this literature has been collected into an excellent symposium by Richard Price (ed.), *Maroon Societies: Rebel Slave Communities in the Americas*, Johns Hopkins University Press 1979, Baltimore. Essays on Maroons and rebel communities in the Spanish, French, English and Dutch Caribbean are presented with a detailed introduction by the editor. See also, R. Price, 'The Guiana Maroons: Changing Perspectives in "Bush Negro Studies" ': review article, *Caribbean Studies*, vol. 11, 1971/72, pp. 81–105. B. Kopytoff, 'The Early Political Development of Jamaican Maroon Societies', *William and Mary Quarterly*, April 1978, pp. 287–307.

    R. Hart, 'Formation of the Caribbean Working Class: Part One: Sugar, Slavery and the Plantation Economy', *The Black Liberator*, vol. 2, No. 2, May 1974 (for an analysis of the Maroon wars of Jamaica, 1729–1739 and 1795–96). Michael Mullin, 'Jamaica Maroon Women: and the Cultural Dimension of American Negro Slavery': Paper presented at the 12th Conference of Caribbean Historians, University of the West Indies, Trinidad, 1980. Jerome Handler, 'Runaway Slaves in Barbados', seminar paper No. 3, Dept.of History, University of the West Indies, Cave Hill, Barbados, 1983. R.B. Sheridan, 'From Jamaican Slavery to Haitian Freedom: The Case of the Black Crew on the Pilot Boat, Deep Nine', *Journal of Negro History*, vol. LXVII, No. 4, Winter 1982, pp. 328–39.

2. The concept of 'maritime marronage' was first used by N. A. T. Hall, in an excellent paper on slave runaways in the Danish West Indies. In this paper, Hall used the term 'grand marronage' to refer to overseas flight, and 'petit marronage' as internal flight. Because of the small size of the island and the extensive agricultural use of terrain long term marronage was feasible only in the externalisation of flight. Here this distinction and phraseology is used for Barbados and the Eastern Caribbean islands. See N. A. T. Hall, 'Maritime Maroons: Grand Marronage from the Danish West Indies': Paper presented at the 16th Conference of Caribbean Historians, University of the West Indies, Barbados, 1984.

3. For some useful studies on Barbados indentured servitude see three publications by Hilary Beckles. 'Sugar and White Servitude: An analysis of Indentured Labour during the Sugar Revolution of Barbados, 1643–1655', *Journal of the Barbados Museum and Historical Society*, vol. 36, No. 3, 1981, pp. 236–47 (*J.B.M.H.S.*). 'English Parliamentary Debate on "White Slavery" in Barbados, 1659' *J.B.M.H.S.* vol. 36, No. 4, 1982, pp. 344–53. On servant rebelliousness see 'Rebels and Reactionaries: The Political Responses of White Labourers to Planter-Class Hegemony in Seventeenth Century Barbados', *Journal of Caribbean History*, vol. 15, 1981, pp. 1–20.

4. See Jerome Handler, 'Slave Insurrectionary Attempts in Seventeenth Century Barbados', Paper presented at the 13th Annual Conference of Caribbean Historians, Guadeloupe, April 1981. Also 'The Barbados Slave Conspiracies of 1675 and 1692', *J.B.M.H.S.*, vol. 36, No. 4, 1982, pp. 312–33; and 'Slave Revolts and Conspiracies in Seventeenth Century Barbados', *New West Indian Guide*, vol. 56, Nos. 1 and 2, 1982, pp. 5–43. Also Hilary Beckles, 'The Struggle of African Slaves and European Workers Against Planter Rule, 1627–1680' in *Politics, Society and Culture in the Caribbean* ed. Blanca Silvestrini (University of Puerto Rico Press, San Juan 1983), pp. 223–39.

5. C. Herrick, *White Servitude in Pennsylvania* (Philadelphia, 1926), p. 231.

6. A. E. Smith, *Colonists in Bondage: White Servitude and Convict Labor in America, 1607–1776* (Chapel Hill, North Carolina University Press 1947), p. 270.

7. Ibid., p. 234.

8. In 1680, Governor Atkins noted that the early sugar industry depended largely upon the servants, but soon, all that was left for them was hard work for small wages. The general movement was from servants to proletariat rather than to small farmer or peasantry. Gov. Atkins to Lords of Trade and Plantations, 26 Oct. 1680, *Calendar of State Papers, Colonial Series (C.S.P.C.)* 1677–1680, No. 1558.

    Some observations on the Island of Barbados, 1667, CO. 1/21, No. 170. P.R.O. Francis Barrington to Sir John Barrington, 5 June 1655, Historical Manuscripts Commission Report, vii, 572a, cited in F. W. Pitman, *The Development of the British West Indies, 1700–1763* (London 1967), pp. 45–6.

FROM LAND TO SEA

9. V.T. Harlow, ed., *Colonising Expeditions to the West Indies and Guiana 1623–1667* (London, Hakluyt Society 1925). Colt's diary, pp. 54–102. See also, R. Dunn, *Sugar and Slaves: The Rise of the Planter Class in the English West Indies, 1627–1713* (New York, Norton Press 1973), p. 6.
10. Minutes of Council, 6 Nov. 1655, Jan. 1656–Dec. 1659, Davis MSS. Box 12, No. I. Royal Commonwealth Society, London. See also Hilary Beckles, 'Rebels and Reactionaries', op. cit.
11. Minutes of Council, 3 June 1655, ibid.
12. Minutes of Council, 8 June 1657, ibid.
13. Minutes of Council, 2 Sept. 1657, ibid.
14. Minutes of Council, 15 Jan. 1656, ibid.
15. Minutes of Council, 6 Aug. 1656, ibid.
16. Minutes of Council and Assembly, C.O. 31/2, No. 21, f. P.R.O. (London).
17. Minutes of Council, Sept. 1657, Davis MSS, Box 12, No. 1.
18. Ibid.
19. Ibid.
20. Ibid.
21. Ibid.
22. Ibid.
23. Gov. Stede, to Lords of Plantations, Aug. 1687, *C.S.P.C.* 1685–88, p. 17.
24. See H. Beckles, 'Rebels and Reactionaries', op. cit., p. 17.
25. A.E. Smith, op. cit., p. 265.
26. C.A. Herrick, op. cit., p. 231.
27. An Act for the Ordaining of Rights between Masters and Servants' 1661, R. Hall, MSS Laws of Barbados, C.O. 31/1.
28. Minutes of the Jamaica Council, 10 Oct. 1662, Bol. 1, IB/5/3, f. 59–60. Spanish Town Archives, Jamaica.
29. See, A.E. Smith, op. cit., p. 269.
30. Minutes of Council, Dec. 1684, *C.S.P.C.*, 1681–85, p. 747.
31. Minutes of Assembly, 27 Oct. 1701, C.O. 31/6, f. 292.
32. Minutes of Council, *C.S.P.C.*, 1701, p. 737.
33. Minutes of Council, 1682, Lucas MSS. Reel 2, ff. 31, 77. Bridgetown Public Library, Barbados.
34. H. Beckles, 'Rebels and Reactionaries', op. cit., p. 11.
35. Minutes of Council, 1701, *C.S.P.C.*, 1701, p. 731.
36. An Act for the Good Governing of Servants, op. cit., C.O. 30/1, f. 41.
37. Minutes of Council, 1 March 1667, C.O. 31/1, ff. 102, 118.
38. Minutes of Council, 1675, *C.S.P.C.*, 1675–76, p. 255.
39. Lt. Gov. Stede to Lords of Trade and Plantations, 30 Aug. *C.S.P.C.*, 1685–88, p. 584.
40. Minutes, *C.S.P.C.*, 1699, p. 517; 34, 'An Act to prevent freemen, white servants, and slaves running from this island in Shallops, boats and other vessels', *C.S.P.C.*, 1702–3, p. 754. Also, Journal of Assembly, 14 April, 1702, *C.S.P.C.*, 1702, p. 221.
41. Information on servants escaping the island by joining Cromwell's fleet in Barbados can be found in Thurloe Papers: see Edward Winslow to Secretary Thurloe 16 March, 1655, Barbados, Thurloe Papers. B.M.
42. Gyles Sylvester to Mr Sylvester, 9 June 1655, Davis MSS. Box 1.
43. Whitehall to Lord Windsor, Governor, 21 March 1662, *C.S.P.C.*, 1661–68, p. 82.
44. Lt. Gov. Stede to Earl of Shrewsbury, 16 July 1689, *C.S.P.C.*, 1689–92, p. 95.
45. Ibid.
46. See A.E. Smith, op. cit. p. 236. See also, MSS Laws of Barbados, C.O. 30/1, f. 149. For good fighting the slaves were given 'a livery coat and a hat per year'.
47. Minutes of Council, May 1689, Lucas MSS. Reel 2, f. 584.
48. Minutes of Council, *C.S.P.C.*, 1661–68, p. 512.
49. See Col. Codrington to Council of Trade and Plantations, 30 June, *C.S.P.C.*, 1699, p. 308.
50. Minutes of Council, c. 1684, Lucas MSS. Reel 2, ff. 383–497.
51. Minutes of Council, 29 Aug. 1683, Colonial Office Microfilm, f. 324.

52. Minutes of Council, 31 July 1695; ibid., f. 513.
53. Ibid.
54. Ibid.
55. Ibid.
56. Ibid.
57. Ibid.
58. Ibid.
59. Ibid., pp. 137–8.
60. Ibid.
61. Ibid., p. 139.
62. Ibid.
63. Ibid.
64. Minutes of Council, 2 March 1693, Colonial Office Microfilm, f. 368.
65. Ibid.
66. Minutes of Council, 24 Dec. 1693, ibid., f. 378.
67. Minutes of Council, 5 April 1694, ibid., f. 374.

Runaway Slaves in Nineteenth-Century Barbados*

Gad Heuman

I

Runaway slaves in nineteenth-century Barbados were a significant aspect of the slave society. Little research has thus far been done on runaways in Barbados, in part because it is surprising that slaves managed to run away at all. Barbadian slaves did not have the possibilities of *grand marronage* which Richard Price, Silvia de Groot, and others have documented for Jamaica and Surinam.[1] By the nineteenth century, there was no scope for the establishment of communities of runaways. Barbados was a relatively small and settled colony; the forests and caves which may have helped earlier generations of slaves to escape no longer existed. In addition, the proportionately high ratio of whites to blacks which characterised Barbados must have made running away a distinctly difficult enterprise.

Yet the slave advertisements in the Barbadian press indicate that running away was hardly uncommon. It is impossible to quantify precisely the numbers of such slaves; but scarcely an issue of a Barbadian newspaper in the first two decades of the nineteenth century is without an advertisement for a runaway slave or a report of a slave being discovered or lodged in gaol.

Whatever their numbers, Barbadian runaways did not generally pose a threat to the slave system. Yet running away was a form of resistance to their enslavement. At the very least, it was a denial of labour to a particular master. At the other extreme, running away was an attempt to escape the system altogether. We therefore need to know about runaways – who they were, where they went, and who harboured them. But the evidence on running away is not just important in describing individuals; it is also suggestive about the nature of slavery in Barbados during this period. This paper will seek to address both points: the runaways themselves and some of the wider issues which they raise.

---

*I am grateful to Iain Liddell of the Computer Unit at the University of Warwick for guiding me through the labyrinth of SPSS and to Seymour Drescher, Stanley L. Engerman, Barry Higman, and James Walvin for their helpful comments on this essay. It is a revised version of a paper originally given at the 16th Annual Conference of Caribbean Historians, Cave Hill, Barbados in April 1984 and subsequently at the History Workshop Conference on 'Slavery' in Oxford in 1985. Delegates to these conferences also made useful suggestions. The research for this paper was funded by the Nuffield Foundation.

BARBADOS: PARISH BOUNDARIES
Kindly supplied by Jerome S. Handler.

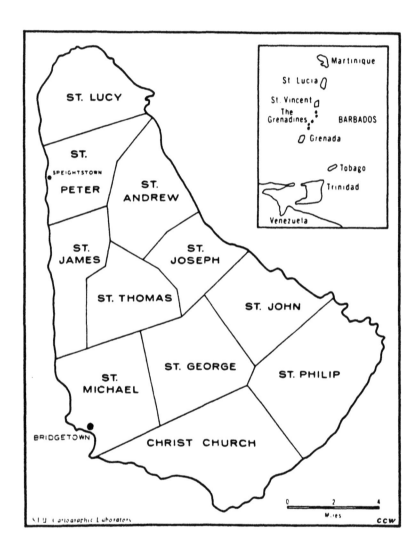

II

The statistical evidence on runaways was collected from advertisements in the Barbadian press at roughly five-year intervals from 1805 to 1830. As certain runs of newspapers were unavailable in the Barbados Archives, the years included in the survey were 1805, 1810, 1815, 1819, 1824 and 1830. Two newspapers, *The Barbados Mercury and Bridgetown Gazette* and *The Barbadian*, were the sources of the advertisements. Where it was possible, the press was also examined for other years during this period for general information on the runaways. The statistical material was coded and run through a computer, using the programme, SPSS.[2]

There are obvious hazards in using data of this kind. The information is often sketchy. It is usually possible to ascertain the name, the sex, and the date first advertised of any slave. Colour, country of birth, occupation, and age are to varying degrees less available. For the years after 1817, it was possible to examine the Slave Registers for additional data, especially for the slaves' occupation, colour, and age.[3] But this only added significant material for 1819. The most revealing information in the advertisements was often the description of the slaves rather than their age or sex; in many cases, however, there were no such data at all.

Other problems also arose with the material. In some cases, the country of birth was cited, especially when the slave was African. When this information was not cited, it was assumed that the slave was Barbadian. The evidence of origin in the Slave Registers reinforced this supposition. A more insoluble problem concerns the length of absence of any slave. All that is generally known is the elapsed time of the advertisements, although in some cases, the owner indicated the period the slave had already been away before the advertisement appeared in the press. The time that advertised slaves were away is therefore seriously understated, although the data do provide an indication of this important variable. As in the case of the Jamaican material, slaves who were caught had rarely been sought in advertisements, thus making it impossible to make use of this information to ascertain length of absence.[4] It is also likely that owners would have been more eager to get back their most valuable slaves; as a result, the sample includes more skilled and elite slaves than in the general population of runaways.

It could be argued that the descriptive material in the advertisements is itself not very reliable. In many cases, owners were guessing where their runaway slaves might be. Information must also have come from other slaves, some of whom may have sought to mislead their masters. Yet, as Michael Mullin has suggested, this data was unbiased; it was not intended for use by propagandists, let alone historians. With all its faults, the evidence from slave advertisements may therefore be 'more appropriate for the study of a people who could not or were not inclined to write things down'.[5]

98 OUT OF THE HOUSE OF BONDAGE

The sample consisted of 368 slaves, a large proportion of whom were male (see Table 1).[6] Since the sex ratio of the Barbadian slave population had become balanced by the early nineteenth century, it is clear that males were disproportionately represented among the cohort of runaways. Similarly, creoles (who were slaves born on the island) made up the overwhelming majority of runaways. For those slaves for whom there are data on origins, over 90 per cent were creole while about 9 per cent were African. These figures are not very different from the proportions of creoles and Africans in the slave population generally in 1817; if anything, the proportion of African runaways is slightly larger than in the general population (see Table 1).

TABLE 1
RUNAWAYS IN THE SLAVE POPULATION

	(%) RUNAWAYS	(%) TOTAL SLAVE POPULATION
SEX		
Males	63.5	45.6
Females	36.5	54.4
NATION		
African	9.2	7.1
Creole	90.8	92.9
COLOUR		
Black	46.8	85.1
Coloured	53.2	14.9
Population	360	77,493

Sources: B.W. Higman, *Slave Populations of the British Caribbean, 1807–1834* (Baltimore, 1984), pp. 413, 116; Sample Survey.

Most of the runaways were relatively young, if young is defined to include those under 30 years of age. Nearly three-fourths of all runaways were in this age-range. When the age ranges were broken down by sex, it was found that male and female runaways were represented roughly in proportion to their respective percentages in the overall sample of runaways.

RUNAWAY SLAVES IN 19TH CENTURY BARBADOS

Not surprisingly, the percentage of coloured runaways was high:[7] 53 per cent of slaves for whom there is such evidence were of mixed colour while 47 per cent were black (see Table 1). Since the percentage of brown slaves in the Barbadian slave population was about 15, the large proportion of coloured runaways is immediately evident.[8]

The data for Jamaica provide an interesting contrast with some of these figures. While the male/female ratios in the Jamaican case are roughly similar to those of Barbados, the origins of the runaway slaves in the two colonies differ widely. Pat Bishop calculated that nearly 70 per cent of runaways in Jamaica had been born in Africa. Allowing for the longer time span of her study and the greater proportion of Africans in the Jamaican slave population, the evidence nonetheless suggests very different origins for runaways in Jamaica and Barbados.[9]

Owners were often very clear about the type of slaves who escaped. They were generally creoles or behaved like creoles. For instance, Chloe was an African woman who had gone out to sell some glassware one day but had not been heard of since. Her owner, E. S. Bascom, could think of no reason for her disappearance; moreover, he noted that 'by her appearance and speech, she may be taken for a Barbadian'. Many slaves sought to pass as free people; this meant that they could usually act the part. Words like 'plausible' and 'artful' appear quite frequently in the advertisements to describe such slaves. Thomas 'is a very artful fellow, and may undertake to pass himself as a free man'.[10] The owner of the slave, Hamlet, put it another way: Hamlet 'has a [good] deal to say for himself, [and] may easily pass for a free man'. These were generally highly assimilated and often skilled slaves who could merge into the black and brown free community.

Skilled slaves were far more likely to escape. An analysis of 92 occupations listed in the advertisements reveals that the overwhelming number were skilled or semi-skilled. Just over 20 per cent were carpenters, 12 per cent sold goods of one kind or another, and nearly 9 per cent were tailors or domestic slaves. Other occupations represented in significant proportions included shoemakers, masons, and sailors; there were also smaller proportions of a wide range of other skilled workers. On the other hand, field slaves formed less than 5 per cent of this occupational cohort. The slave elite – and particularly the artisan elite – were therefore heavily represented in the occupations of the runaways, far more than their proportion of the total slave population.

A breakdown of the sex of the runaways for whom there are data on occupations is quite revealing. The only categories cited for female occupations were hucksters, house servants, and field slaves. Approximately three-fourths of those runaways who sold goods were women while just over 60 per cent of house servants were females. Only one-quarter of the runaway field slaves were females. In every other occupational category – most of which were skilled – no women were listed at all. The dominance of male runaways in the skilled occupations and in the slave elite reinforces what is known about the respective position of men and women in Caribbean slave society.

The colour of these slaves is also interesting. All of the field slaves were black as were three-fourths of the domestics. Women whose occupations are known were more likely to be black than brown. By virtue of their colour and their occupations, women generally would have had a more difficult time merging into the free community. The exception to this was runaway hucksters, nearly 70 per cent of whom were coloured.

As expected, most skilled runaways were coloureds: there were usually two skilled coloured to each one skilled black. This was the case for carpenters, cooks, masons, and tailors. Porters and fishermen violated this rule, as both categories included only blacks. Nearly all the runaway slaves for whom occupations were known were creoles: almost 95 per cent were in this category.

But where did the runaways go? In many cases, the owners did not know, but in a large number of instances, they were able to be quite specific about their slaves' possible destinations. One of the obvious places was a town, especially Bridgetown or Speightstown. For skilled slaves, towns probably offered greater possibilities of employment. The relatively large free black and brown communities there must have made it easier for a runaway to pass as a free person. Of those runaways whose destinations are known, more than a quarter of them were said to be in a town.

What is perhaps surprising is that a similar proportion – over 25 per cent of the runaways – found refuge in the country, presumably on other plantations. Roughly 6 per cent of runaways were either abroad or on a ship and a similar percentage were attempting to pass as free, most probably in a town. Owners knew nothing about the destination of another quarter of their slaves, and the remaining 8 per cent were thought to be employed either in a town or in the country. These categories clearly overlap, and many slaves were in more than one grouping. The figures suggest that running away to the country was a more significant destination than might have been expected.

It is also interesting to examine the destinations of slaves by sex. Table 2 demonstrates that more female runaways went to the country than to the town, while males favoured the towns. This correlates with earlier data about the occupations and colour of female and male runaways. Since the women were more likely to be in less skilled occupations than the men, female runaways seem to have escaped more frequently to the country where they may have had kin to harbour them. On the other hand, skilled males more often attempted to blend into the free urban community, looking for employment and trying to pass as free. Male runaways also sought to get abroad: 90 per cent of this cohort were male.

There are tantalising suggestions about slaves who fled abroad and who may have formed an earlier generation of 'boat-people'. In 1805, a slave was picked up in a boat by a Mr Todd near St Vincent. Since the runaway claimed to have a Barbadian master, Todd, who was from St Vincent, was prepared to have the slave returned on proof of ownership. Fourteen years later, a seaman slave named James Cuttery absconded from a mail boat. He stole a smaller boat, a bucket, and a sail and probably also headed for St Vincent. Cuttery had a good reason for getting to St Vincent: he had formerly lived there. As the island was to the windward of Barbados, it is quite plausible that other slaves sought to escape in the same way.[11]

St Vincent was not the only foreign destination of Barbadian runaways. Nancy Efey was the mother of two mulatto children and perhaps therefore had a better chance of obtaining 'spurious papers'. Her owner reported that Nancy intended to go to Demerara, where she had a sister. Another owner thought that her slave, Jane Frances, would leave Barbados, but did not make any specific suggestions about where she might go. Jane 'endeavours to pass as a free woman, and, in all probability, will wish to quit the Island. All masters and owners of vessels are hereby cautioned not to take her off the Country, and other persons from harbouring or employing her'.[12]

This was a frequent warning, but it is unclear what effect it had. Jacob was a well known slave who worked on board English ships, and whose professional name was Samson. 'He went down the river on the 15th inst. on board the ship FAIRY, Capt. Francis, and has not since been heard of'.[13] Another slave, identified in the Slave Registers as John Maycock, was a 15-year-old butler. He seems to have 'imposed himself on the master of either the ship Constantine or Tiger, as a free man ... [and] quitted the island'.[14] Ships' captains may have found it in their interest to have runaways on board. Runaways were potential extra hands, they could be sold at another

TABLE 2
DESTINATION OF RUNAWAYS BY SEX

		TOWN	COUNTRY	PASS AS FREE	ABROAD
M	No.	68	55	17	10
	%	71.6	60.4	77.3	90.9
F	No.	27	36	5	1
	%	28.4	39.6	22.7	9.1

Source: Sample Survey

port, or they could possibly pay for their passage. The constant warnings about the complicity of captains not only suggest that this was one of the possible escape routes for runaways but also that it was of considerable concern to Barbadian slaveholders.

Whether they fled abroad or remained in Barbados, runaway slaves seem to have been quite consistent in the month or the season they chose to escape (see figure 1). Based on the month the owners first advertised for their runaways, the data reveal that slaves most frequently left in July and August. The least popular month for running away was February. One possible explanation for these various months, at least for plantation slaves, is related to the plantation cycle. Slaves may have escaped after the crop had been harvested in the early summer, partly because supervision was more lax or because the dead season meant fewer extra perks for slaves. Barry Higman's research adds weight to this view: he found that food supplies from the plantations as well as from the slaves' provision grounds were most stretched in this season. Since Barbadian slaves knew this time of year as the 'hungry-time' or 'hard-time', seasonal nutritional stress could have been an additional factor in increasing the number of runaways in July and August.[15] It is also important to note that owners may have been less concerned by slaves running away in the slow season. This view is supported by

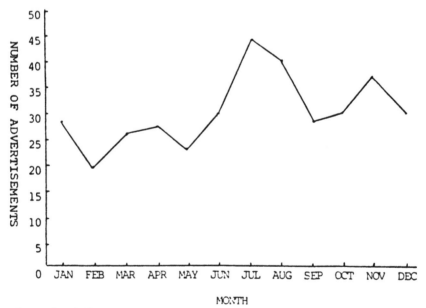

FIGURE 1
RUNAWAYS BY MONTH FIRST ADVERTISED

Source: Sample Survey

RUNAWAY SLAVES IN 19TH CENTURY BARBADOS 103

the unpopularity of February as a time to escape; at that point, sugar was being harvested and the planters would have needed all their labour.

There are other data to support this interpretation. It is possible to examine the date each slave was first advertised and how long the advertisements continued. In this way, it can be shown in which months slaves were absent for the longest and the shortest periods of time. The analysis reveals that slaves were away for the greatest average time in December, January, and February and for the least number of days in August. July is in the middle range of this cohort. This evidence would suggest that planters may have been quite desperate to get back their labour for crop-time and therefore advertised heavily for their slaves during these winter months. Similarly, it adds weight to the belief that owners generally were less concerned about slaves' running away after the crop was over. Another possibility for the relative popularity of staying away during the winter months was the Christmas festivities and the importance of slave families and friends being together then. It may also be that slaves may have sought to avoid returning to the most difficult work of all: harvesting the crop.

Data on the slaves' length of absence are revealing in other areas as well, especially if the time elapsed is broken down into the following categories: short (under two weeks), medium (two weeks to three months), and long (over three months). In this case, a slightly higher proportion of female runaways is among the short stayers than their proportion in the overall runaway sample. Male runaways were more heavily represented in the medium and long categories. These figures reinforce the possibility that women may have escaped more often for relatively short periods to visit family or friends. On the other hand, males were more likely to have escaped for longer periods – seeking more frequently, as we have seen, to merge into the free community or to escape abroad. The data may also reflect the differential importance owners placed on male and female runaways. Males were usually more valuable economically, and this may have been reflected in the number of advertisements placed for them.

Other categories for the elapsed time slaves were gone are perhaps more predictable. The average figure for creoles' length of absence was twice as high as for Africans and that for coloured three times the figure for blacks. Slaves aged between 18 and 29 years of age were away considerably longer than those in the younger and older age ranges. According to the data, slaves over 40 were gone the least amount of time. For those slaves whose occupations are known, field slaves were away for among the shortest periods of time, while domestics and shoemakers were gone for twice the average of this occupational cohort. Carpenters, fishermen, hucksters, and tailors were all near the average length of absence. Again, it is clear that runaways who were creole, coloured, and skilled had a far greater chance of escaping for a longer duration than those who were African, black, and unskilled.

104   OUT OF THE HOUSE OF BONDAGE

The evidence also suggests that the overwhelming majority of slaves were gone for a relatively short time. Nearly 65 per cent of runaways were in this category. It would be fair to assume that many of these slaves had left their owners temporarily and intended to return. But what of the 35 per cent of slave runaways who were gone for a longer period, and within that grouping, the 8 per cent who had escaped for at least three months?

It may be instructive to examine some cases of slaves who stayed away for a very long time, even within the confines of Barbados. One of the most striking examples involved a slave named Johnny Beckles, who was caught in 1805 on the Pool Plantation in St John. Beckles was about 45 years old, and the man who discovered him reported that 'from the best information I can collect, [Beckles] has been living in the Pool Negro-yard for many years before the storm of 1780'. This would mean that Beckles had run away at least 25 years previously. Another long-term runaway was a shoemaker named Sam, who was about 20 years old. Sam had been harboured by his father 'for nearly 16 years when by accident he was discovered to be a slave; and it was fairly proved that he was stolen by his parents when the mother was leased on Haymond's Plantation, and he a child'. For all those years, Sam had successfully passed as free, but was now possibly harboured with his mother.[16]

An even more curious case involved an African man named Buffy, who was discovered at Lancaster Plantation in St James in 1806. According to Buffy, his owner was a Frenchman in Jamaica who had died about six years previously. At that point and somewhat mysteriously, Buffy 'came over as a cook on board a vessel, and ... has remained on the island ever since'. The advertiser pointed out that Buffy spoke broken English 'but plain enough to be understood by any person' and 'has his country marks on both cheeks'.[17] Buffy was hardly an assimilated slave, although he did have a profession. Yet he had been able to live for six years in Barbados before being discovered as a slave.

Even an unacculturated African slave was able to escape for nearly two months. Betsy 'can speak little or no English, having been purchased from a Guinea ship about 10 months ago'. The first advertisement for her appeared on 5 October 1805 and she was not caught until 23 November of that year. This is one of the few cases where an advertised slave was caught and for whom there was an additional advertisement. Betsy's experience suggests that slaves appearing in the advertisements were probably away a minimum of two months and perhaps longer.[18]

One of the interesting questions to ask is whether the pattern of running away altered in any way during the period 1805 to 1830. It is immediately clear that the highest number of advertisements, 105, appeared in 1815, with 101 advertisements in 1805 and 91 in 1810 (see Table 3). There were far fewer advertisements in the years after 1815. Although it is not possible

RUNAWAY SLAVES IN 19TH CENTURY BARBADOS

TABLE 3
NUMBER OF RUNAWAYS ADVERTISED AND THEIR MEAN NUMBER OF DAYS GONE BY YEAR

	1805	1810	1815	1819	1824	1830
No. Runaways Advertised	101	91	105	48	6	12
Mean Length of Stay in Days	32.3	10	52	41	18	?

Source: Sample Survey

to account for the significant drop in the number of advertisements after 1815, one of the consequences of the 1816 slave rebellion may have been an alteration in the system of dealing with runaways. The law may have changed, or the apprehension of slaves may have become more rigorous. It seems unlikely that the actual number of runaways would have dropped significantly in the period after the rebellion.

The year 1815 did not just experience the largest number of advertisements; it also witnessed the highest average length of stay for runaways, apart from 1830 which was distorted statistically (see Table 3). When absence is examined as previously by short, medium, and long stays, 1815 is the year with the largest number of slaves who were absent for the longest period of time. The destination of runaways in 1815 is also suggestive: far more than the statistical average went to the country than to the towns. Nearly 43 per cent of all the slaves escaping to the country in the sample went there in 1815, contrasted with only 31 per cent of slaves going to the towns. The 1816 Rebellion was not an urban phenomenon: it broke out in St Philip. The evidence about the number of runaways in 1815, their length of stay, and their destinations points to the conclusion that runaways were not simply merging into the free community or temporarily visiting kin. Although runaways did not normally pose a threat to the system, they apparently could do so. It would be unwise to correlate runaways with rebellion; however, the increase in the number of runaways in 1815 may have been symptomatic of the heightened tension in Barbados which ultimately resulted in the 1816 Rebellion.[19]

Owners were very aware of the dangers posed by runaways. The year after Bussa's Rebellion in 1816, the master of a female slave named Massey sought to warn planters about runaways generally and his escaped slave in particular. Massey probably had a forged pass and was working as a laundress. Her owner believed that 'gentleman proprietors and managers are not aware of the evil in suffering absent slaves about their property, as they certainly will imbibe pernicious maxims, and afterwards afford a ready

106   OUT OF THE HOUSE OF BONDAGE

asylum to such of their slaves as may abscond'.[20] One problem, then, was the potential example of successful runaways. But there were also more serious cases to worry about.

Appea was a tall, 50-year-old man with a

> surly countenance, has several scars about his head occasioned by fighting, and a piece off one of his ears, bit out by the same cause; he has been absent upwards of 12 months, and has eluded every vigilant attempt to take him. He is perhaps one of the most notorious villains the Country ever possessed; and a dangerous person to be at large amongst Plantation Negroes.

Yet this dangerous runaway – whose advertisement appeared in the middle of 1815 – was able to survive by 'drawing the figure of negroes on paper, by which means he gets a subsistence, going from one Estate to another; although he seldom stays long on any'.[21]

A final example reveals the potential danger of trying to arrest runaways as well as an important aspect of the system of apprehending escaped slaves. In October, 1815, the driver of Mount Wilton Plantation, Primus, was sent to search for a runaway and given a pass for ten days. 'Primus not returning home since, though invited to do so through his connections. it became necessary to seek him; he has a Wife at Mr. Searles' in St. Joseph'. The owner of Primus, Reynold Ellcock, hired Frank, the ranger of Pickering Plantation, and two other men in January 1816 to find the runaways.

> As they were returning at midnight, on Saturday the 20th instant, without finding the Runaways, they were suddenly attacked in the public road, not far from the buildings at Mount Wilton, and Frank, who seemed to be the sole object of their vengeance, was barbarously murdered by 5 or 6 men who had concealed themselves in a corn-field near the road. The subscriber offers a reward of £25 to any person or persons who will give evidence to convict the perpetrators of this horrid murder, it being natural to suppose Prince [the first runaway] and Primus had gotten notice of this search, and had waylaid the men sent after them.[22]

This murder followed a particularly difficult year in Barbados. Michael Craton has documented the economic problems as well as the political ferment in the island in 1815 over the act for slave registration.[23] These developments may have given Primus as well as Appea more determination to flee in the first instance and subsequently to resist arrest.

One other interesting point is worth noting about this case. Primus had been sent out to catch a runaway and then Frank had been sent to get him. Indeed, the system depended on drivers and other elite slaves helping to apprehend escaped slaves. But slaves often used this system to their own

RUNAWAY SLAVES IN 19TH CENTURY BARBADOS 107

advantage: when running away themselves and when challenged, they claimed to be searching for escaped slaves.

Like many slaves, Primus had run away to kin; in his case, it was to his wife. More than twice as many slaves in the sample were supposedly harboured by family as by non-family members. While a significant proportion of runaways were harboured either by a wife or by a husband, it is interesting that a greater percentage of this cohort were thought to be with their parents. Siblings played a slightly lesser role than husbands and wives, but they too were not insignificant.

If these data are examined by length of absence, parents emerge as the kin who harboured runaways for the longest average time. Parents are above the mean time for the cohort of all families as harbourers (28 days) as are husbands, while wives are just below this figure. Siblings, grandparents and children are well below the mean figure for families generally.

Families were an obvious destination for runaways. But the evidence goes further than this: it points to the strength of family ties and to that of the extended family. Betty Beck was a mulatto slave who was 'supposed to be harboured in the Plantation of Richard Cobham, Esq called Stepney, where she was born, and many of her family belong'. Jack Charles was also well connected: he had numerous family in St Philip, St George and St Michael. His owner knew that Jack had already spent time with his wife in St Philip, but there was a mother and an uncle to worry about as well. Families not only hid their escaped kin; they sometimes put them to work. Bob was a carpenter who had 'been seen at work with his father, by the name of Johnny Gittens, living in Milk Market'. Bob's sister also lived in the same district.[24]

The data are also suggestive in other ways about the family relationships of escaped slaves. Nearly a third of all the slaves who were harboured by wives had more than one of them; in several cases, owners mentioned three wives for their runaways. It is also interesting that the harbouring family members were not necessarily all slaves; many slaves had free kin. Clarissa, who was about 20 years old, had a free black mother 'living under the green trees in the Roebuck; and her father a black man belonging to James Holligan, Esq. called Mingo – by either of whom it is supposed she may be harboured'. It was obviously a considerable help to have free kin: Sanco 'passes as a free man, having family of that description in town'. Mimbah was doing even better. She had been a retailer of dry goods and had a house where she lived with her free black husband.[25] These harbourers suggest a complex pattern of relationships. They provide evidence of the existence of the slave family and should redirect efforts to examine the intricate and connected world of slave and free people.

Many slaves were not harboured by kin, but by friends, by employers, or by the soldiers of the West India Regiment. Judged by the length of their

108   OUT OF THE HOUSE OF BONDAGE

absence, those runaways harboured by non-family may have been able to stay away longer than those hidden by families. In part, this was because of the relative success of the runaways harboured by whites.

Although there were not many slaves in this cohort, planters were concerned about the implications of whites harbouring runaways. Sarah Jane was thought to be harboured by her mother 'or by some evil-disposed white person or other in behalf of her mother'. April 'had been harboured at [Codrington] College and at a white man's house' in St John, although on a previous escape, he had been hidden by slaves. More important was the type of advertisement for Jacob: 'a further £10 to any person who will give information of any free subject who has employed him'.[26] The implication here is that whites may have often hired runaways; alternatively, that escaped slaves may have sought particular whites as employers. These slaves were not threatening the slave system generally but were making choices about their owners. White collusion with runaway slaves was not uncommon elsewhere as well; discussing runaways in the United States, Mullin concluded that a large number of runaway slaves were successful 'because for a variety of reasons, many whites who "harboured" them were willing to challenge the slave code at its weakest point'.[27]

It was not only whites who employed runaways; slaves did so as well. Ceafor was a mason who was 'supposed to be harboured by black masons employed upon the King's Works'. Another escaped slave named James was a fisherman who had lost his right leg and used crutches; nonetheless, he was thought 'to be employed and harboured by some of the fishermen about Fontabelle, particularly by a man belonging to Isaac Green'.[28] Slaves working for other slaves are indicative of a more elaborate structure of employment and harbouring than has previously been recognised.

Slaves were also harboured in and around the Castle, the home of the West India Regiment. Runaways could more easily pass as free among the black soldiers and among the free community which served them. There were some amusing cases in this group. For instance, Marissa 'had been repeatedly seen at St. Ann's [the Castle], and was once taken from there, and rescued by some soldiers, before she could be delivered up to her owner'. This was despite her being 'remarkably stout'. Fortune had escaped once before as well and 'by virtue of a certificate given by some evil-disposed person of his freedom, he enlisted in the black corps under the name of Thomas Panton, a native of Jamaica'. The Castle also offered a refuge for two Africans who had several countrymen there but who spoke little English.[29] For a variety of reasons, then, white West Indians may have been right to worry about the effects of free black soldiers on a slave society.[30]

RUNAWAY SLAVES IN 19TH CENTURY BARBADOS 109

IV

It is clear from the evidence that the majority of advertised runaways were male, creole, coloured, and skilled slaves. Runaways escaped to the country as well as to the towns, with males apparently preferring the towns where they were more likely to pass as free men, gain employment, or try to get abroad. Women, on the other hand, opted more often for the country where they sought refuge among kin. Runaways more frequently chose to leave in the dead season, after the crop had been harvested. The majority seem to have stayed away a relatively short time, although a significant percentage of runaways were gone for over three months. There were also some prominent examples of slaves who managed to hide for several years, even within Barbados. More slaves in the sample left in 1815 than any other year and those slaves stayed away the longest period of time. This suggests a possible link to the 1816 slave rebellion and to the political ferment in Barbados in 1815. Slaves were harboured by both family and non-family; interestingly enough, whites as well as slaves were among the harbourers who hid and sometimes employed runaways. These are some of the conclusions of the study, but there are a number of other points worth emphasising.

On the one hand, it was sometimes in the masters' interest to allow slaves to run away. As we have seen, planters may well have regarded the July/ August period as a more convenient time for slaves to be absent. Owners undoubtedly wanted to get rid of some of their runaways, and some runaways who were caught were apparently never claimed. Joe and William were two such runaways; they were arrested, put in gaol, and first advertised in January, 1830. Almost a year later, they were still unclaimed and unsold.[31]

Other masters had specific reasons to get rid of their slaves. The owner of Nelly reported that she had escaped along with £104 worth of dry goods. He was prepared to 'dispose of her for £100, and her child, and give the goods into the bargain to the purchaser'. Another case involved Betty Phyllis: she 'was well known ... to be the object who set on fire the bed and curtains of her former owner, Mrs. Griffith'. The owner of Ben reported he would probably try to pass as a free man and get employed, but she had clearly had enough and would 'be glad to dispose of the said Man'.[32]

On the other hand, there were many masters who were quite determined to get their slaves back. The owner of two runaways who were brothers offered the extraordinary reward of £50 for them. He also made it clear that 'if they will both or either of them return to their business of their own accord, I will freely pardon them, and inflict no kind of punishment upon them whatsoever, nor ask any questions where they may have been harboured'. John H. P. King was another anxious owner. His slave,

110 OUT OF THE HOUSE OF BONDAGE

Richard, had run away and was probably harboured by his father or mother. Richard's father had 'lately expressed a great wish that [Richard] be also sold to his present owners, the Messrs Cumberbatch'. However, King was not about to sell, 'it being the subscribers unalterable determination not to dispose of him'. King placed 16 advertisements in the press for Richard without apparent success.[33]

Richard's case suggests that some slaves ran away to put pressure on their owners to sell them. In some instances, masters promised that their runaways would be able to choose new owners on their return. Phill had run away, and was now offered for sale, but 'should he voluntarily return, the privilege of choosing an owner will be granted to him'. Similarly for Hamlet, 'if he will return of his own accord in 8 days from this date, he shall have a paper to look for another owner'. Or in the case of Charlotte, should she 'return home accompanied by a ready money purchaser, she will be pardoned, and sold reasonably'.[34]

Running away, then, could serve a variety of purposes. Some slaves managed to escape altogether; others used it to change their owners while most probably sought to make life more bearable for a while. In the process, runaways revealed the strength of family and personal ties in Barbadian slave society as well as the collusion of free people in their escape. While runaway slaves were clearly resisting aspects of the slave society, they were also testimony to 'the role of the powerless in affecting, and even controlling important parts of the lives of the masters'.[35]

NOTES

1. Richard Price, ed., *Maroon Societies* (Garden City, N.Y., 1973) and Silvia W. de Groot, *From Isolation Towards Integration: The Surinam Maroons and their Descendants, 1845–1863* (The Hague, 1963). See also Alvin O. Thompson, 'Some Problems of Slave Desertion in Guayana, c. 1750–1814', Occasional Paper No. 4, *ISER* (1976) and David Barry Gaspar, 'Runaways in Seventeenth-Century Antigua, West Indies', *Boletin de Estudios Latinoamericanos y del Caribe 26* (June 1979): 3–13.
2. For a useful introduction, see Marija J. Norusis, *SPSS, An Introductory Guide* (New York, 1982).
3. T71/520–33; T71/540–46.
4. P. A. Bishop, 'Runaway Slaves in Jamaica, 1740–1807' (unpublished M.A. thesis, University of the West Indies, 1970), p. 151.
5. Gerald W. Mullin, *Flight and Rebellion: Slave Resistance in Eighteenth-Century Virginia* (London, 1972), p. x.
6. The statistical material in the paper is derived from the sample survey and from an SPSS analysis of this data.
7. *Coloured* is used here to mean slaves of mixed colour. Synonyms include browns and mulattoes.
8. B. W. Higman, *Slave Populations of the British Caribbean* (Baltimore, 1984), p. 116.
9. Bishop, 'Runaway Slaves', p. 22.
10. *The Barbados Mercury and Bridgetown Gazette* (hereafter BM): 4 March, 24 June 1817; 19

RUNAWAY SLAVES IN 19TH CENTURY BARBADOS

Aug. 1815.

11. BM: 8 June 1805; 6 Nov. 1819; see also Michael Craton, *Testing the Chains: Resistance to Slavery in the British West Indies* (Ithaca, 1982), p. 147.
12. BM: 6 April 1819; 14 Oct. 1817.
13. BM: 20 Aug. 1805.
14. T71/520, f. 456; T71/524, f. 271; BM, 24 April 1819.
15. Higman, *Slave Populations*, p. 215.
16. BM: 11 June 1805; 24 Oct. 1818.
17. BM: 19 July 1806.
18. BM: 5 Oct., 23 Nov. 1805.
19. For a further discussion of this argument, see Hilary Beckles, 'Emancipation by War or Law? Wilberforce and the 1816 Barbados Slave Rebellion' in David Richardson, ed., *Abolition and its Aftermath: The Historical Context 1790–1916*, London, Frank Cass 1985, pp. 80–104.
20. BM: 4 Oct. 1817.
21. BM: 15 July 1815.
22. BM: 27 Jan. 1816.
23. Craton, *Testing the Chains*, pp. 259–60.
24. BM: 30 Dec., 8 Aug. 1815; 19 Oct. 1805.
25. BM: 23 Feb. 1819; 3 June 1815; 17 Dec. 1805.
26. BM: 10 Nov. 1810; 21 Jan. 1815; 10 Nov. 1810.
27. Mullin, *Flight and Rebellion*, p. 106.
28. BM: 18 June 1805; 24 July 1816.
29. BM: 27 April, 16 Nov., 9 Nov. 1805.
30. For further information on these regiments, see Roger Norman Buckley, *Slaves in Red Coats: The British West India Regiments, 1795–1815* (New Haven, 1979).
31. *The Barbadian*: 19 Jan., 18 Dec. 1830.
32. BM: 9 Oct. 1810; 28 Nov. 1815; 24 Nov. 1810.
33. BM: 22 Dec. 1810; 6 Aug. 1805.
34. BM: 29 Nov. 1817; 1 Sept. 1810; 11 Feb. 1809.
35. Sidney W. Mintz and Richard Price, 'An Anthropological Approach to the Afro-American Past: A Caribbean Perspective', *ISHI Occasional Papers in Social Change* (1976), p. 16.

On the Eve of the Haitian Revolution: Slave Runaways in Saint Domingue in the year 1790

David Geggus

Marronage has enjoyed a particularly controversial position in the historiography of Saint Domingue. Some scholars accord it a fundamental role in the genesis of both the voodoo religion and the 1791 slave revolt. Others see no such connection. In some interpretations, runaways are presented as a serious threat to the slave regime. In others, marronage is seen merely as a safety-valve within the system. The debate has divided not only white and black historians who disagree as to how stable slavery was in Saint Domingue but also the *noiriste* and *mulâtre* 'schools' of Haitian history. Here the underlying issue has been the relative contributions of the black masses and free coloured elite to resisting French colonialism.[1] The statue of *Le Marron Inconnu*, erected by the Duvalier regime in Port au Prince, testifies to the continuing presence of the fugitive slave in the national sentiment and political ideology of modern Haiti.

While the source material for studying Saint Domingue runaways is extremely rich, quantitative work on the subject has been limited to three short articles and Jean Fouchard's *Les Marrons de la Liberté*, a work more descriptive than analytic. Gabriel Debien and Jean Fouchard analysed three small samples of fugitives from the periods February–August 1764 and October 1790–August 1791, the largest of which totalled 560 and derived mainly from Saint Domingue's North Province.[2] Fouchard's *Marrons*, on the other hand, covers the whole colonial press from 1764 to 1793 but provides only rough annual totals of the runaways mentioned.[3]

Sources

This article examines data drawn from the main colonial newspaper, the *Affiches Américaines* and its various supplements, during the year 1790. The data are of two types. The first category is that of advertisements for fugitives placed by colonists at their own expense. These were almost always grouped under the rubric 'Esclaves en Marronage,' though a few appeared as separate 'small ads'. Much the largest category is formed by the 'Esclaves Marrons entrés à la géole,' the lists of captured runaways lodged in the colony's dozen or so prisons, drawn up by the local recorders for publication. When most complete, the data can be very detailed, giving the

ON THE EVE OF THE HAITIAN REVOLUTION

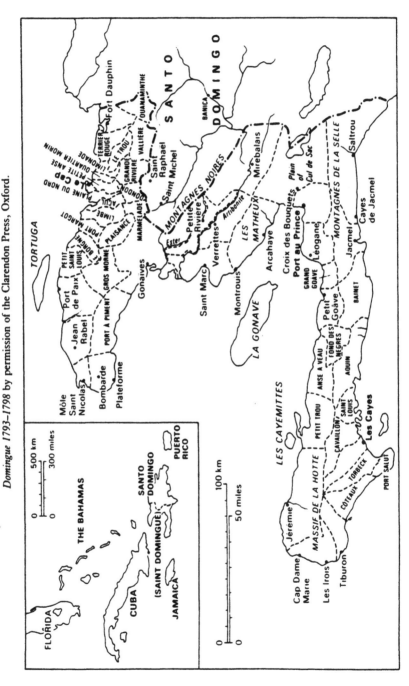

SAINT DOMINGUE: PARISH BOUNDARIES AND TOWNS

Reproduced from D. Geggus: *Slavery, War, and Revolution: The British Occupation of Saint Domingue 1793–1798* by permission of the Clarendon Press, Oxford.

114   OUT OF THE HOUSE OF BONDAGE

slave's name and that of his owner, his age, sex, ethnic identity, personality traits, height and other physical characteristics (especially brands and scarification), sometimes the place where the slave was caught or his presumed whereabouts, and the length of time he had been absent.

As separate editions of the *Affiches Américaines* were published in the towns of Cap Français and Port au Prince, the runaway data is divided by region. It is thus possible to distinguish the North Province, where the great uprising was soon to take place, from the West and South Provinces, where the slave revolution would develop much more slowly. I have also divided part of the data by month, and the whole into six-month segments, the January–June period corresponding to the sugar harvest.

Care was taken to avoid counting duplicate entries. Lists from the various town jails were generally printed only once, but a few were repeated at different dates. Advertisements for fugitives were usually repeated in three different issues of the *Affiches*. As the second and third entries were so marked, it is not difficult to eliminate them. However, I have noted that some entries were not marked. Others may have escaped detection. A few advertisements refer to slaves who escaped in previous years and were still missing. These cases tend to inflate slightly the number of 1790 fugitives for whom adverts were placed.

Numbers

In 1790, when the slave population numbered more than 500,000, 2,020 runaways were jailed and 632 were advertised as missing. These figures can be compared to Jean Fouchard's 'environ 3,500 signalements de marrons' for this year.[4] In his pioneer work, Fouchard conflated not only runaway adverts and prison lists but also the published lists of *épaves*, those runaways who were not reclaimed from the jail and after two months were advertised for sale. This technique in itself ensured that some fugitives were counted three times over. In addition, Fouchard used data from other newspapers which duplicated that in the *Affiches Américaines*. He also stated he had not always identified duplicate advertisements within the same newspaper. As he rightly observed, the task requires a whole team of researchers.[5] It is hoped that more detailed studies such as this one will help bring into closer focus Fouchard's broad outline.

The number of fugitives advertised or jailed of course bears no certain relation to the number who actually fled or were caught, still less to the total number at large. As the number 'jailed' was here three times as great as the number 'fled', it seems that only a minority of runaways were the subject of advertisements. The likelihood that a planter would advertise for a fugitive depended probably on the slave's value, the varying demands of the agricultural cycle and the plantation's proximity to Cap Français or Port au

TABLE 1

SAINT DOMINGUE RUNAWAYS, 1790

North

	Total	Female	% African	Creole		Total	Female	% African	Creole
Jailed					**'Fled'**				
Jan.–June	429	13	84	13	Jan.–June	152	14	75	17
July–Dec.	577	13	88	11	June–Dec.	157	11	74	23

West/South

	Total	Female	% African	Creole		Total	Female	% African	Creole
Jailed					**'Fled'**				
Jan.–June	461	10	84	14	Jan.–June	184	12	75	18
July–Dec.	553	9	85	12	June–Dec.	139	17	76	17
	2,020					632			

The discrepancy between the African/Creole total and 100 per cent is accounted for by Foreign Creoles ('Portugais', 'Hollandais', etc.).

116   OUT OF THE HOUSE OF BONDAGE

Prince. Hence, fugitives from mountain coffee plantations, mainly African males, are doubtless underrepresented in the 'fled' category. Planters also tended to wait a few weeks before advertising, during which period unknown numbers of runaways must have returned or been caught.

The number jailed depended on the vigilance and activity of the *maréchaussée*, the mainly free coloured rural police force. Its zeal was probably not constant, especially during these revolutionary years. Moreover, a great many fugitives captured close to home (or far from a jail) were returned directly to their plantations without being lodged in prison. Some also returned voluntarily. Others died. On the other hand, the rural police were known to capriciously arrest slaves who were away from their plantation, even tearing up their passes, so as to demand the standardised reward for recapture. The accounts of one sugar plantation, studied by Debien, record a remarkable one in four recaptures as being bogus, though it is true not many of these passed via the prison.[6]

In theory, one could go a long way towards estimating the total number of runaways in a given year by discovering what proportion of those advertised missing were later jailed. Unfortunately, the vagueness of many of the published descriptions renders this approach probably impossible. Allowing for the difficulties mentioned above, the number of runaways jailed is the best guide we have to the extent of marronage in Saint Domingue. The jail statistics were subject to fewer external influences than the runaway advertisements, which doubtless grew in number with the circulation of a newspaper. They should therefore be the preferred source in tracing the evolution of marronage through time. In the absence of any indications that Maroon activity was notably increasing, the prison lists probably corresponded most closely to the number of slaves who fled in a given year. The problem is to know how closely.

Fouchard hypothesized that only one in four runaways passed through a jail. This was a quite arbitrary guess, and he assumed that the other 75% remained free.[7] However, important data published by Debien drawn from the accounts of a coffee and two sugar plantations shows that some five-sixths of their runaways who were recaptured were returned directly to the estates.[8] This is excluding the bogus recaptures mentioned above. Were they included, the proportion of recaptured fugitives who were imprisoned would shrink to 15%. If these were not atypical cases, then the prison list totals will have to be multiplied by six simply to know the number of runaways recaptured in a given year. Furthermore, only 3% of these fugitives appear to have been advertised for in a newspaper. Most probably, these cases were unusual; they are certainly distorted by the largest and most extreme example. But they do suggest that more extensive research into plantation accounts will assist in the interpretation of the runaway statistics in the colonial press.

ON THE EVE OF THE HAITIAN REVOLUTION 117

This is also true of plantation slave lists, which should indicate the proportion of slaves missing at a given moment. Lists drawn up annually by a manager for an absentee owner doubtless minimise the extent of marronage and probably mention only those runaways who have been missing for some time. Even so, we have found some such lists which probably exaggerate the phenomenon by listing fugitives who disappeared 30, 40 or even more years before and had most likely died. At the same time, inventories drawn up by resident planters or for legal purposes can be expected to include all runaways whose return or recapture was considered possible.

A sample of over 4,000 slaves living on Saint Domingue sugar plantations and listed on inventories of these different types included only 0.5% runaways.[9] In an earlier period in southern Saint Domingue Arlette Gautier found a much larger percentage, 4.4%,[10] but this would seem rather unusual. A major study of Guadeloupe notarial papers from the 1780s reveals only 1.5% fugitives in a sample of nearly 9,000 slaves.[11] In similar material from eighteenth century rural Bahia, Stuart Schwartz found 0.7%.[12] Vestry returns from north-west Jamaica during the crisis of 1798 suggest a figure certainly no larger.[13] Even in rugged and undeveloped Dominica following several years of mounting desertions and conflict the census of 1813 put runaways at only 2.4% of the slave population.[14]

In trying to make projections from this sort of material with a slave population of half a million, the scope for error would obviously be very great. One would also need to calculate the average length of absence per fugitive. Nevertheless, it may be hoped that in time sufficient data can be accumulated from plantation accounts, correspondence and inventories, so one can attempt by a process of triangulation with the newspaper data finally to rescue the problem of runaway numbers from the realm of naked guesswork.

Men and Women

Marronage in Saint Domingue was heavily dominated by males. Females accounted for only 12% of this sample, as in the case of Arlette Gautier. In the three quantitative studies mentioned above[15] females represented 22%, 10% and 13% of the runaways counted. Fouchard's estimate that women made up 15–20% of Saint Domingue runaways may therefore be slightly exaggerated.[16]

As elsewhere, family ties, biology and gender role socialisation no doubt account for most of this differential. However, the unusual degree of imbalance between male and female fugitives in Saint Domingue must be attributed to other factors. It was apparently not due to an exceptionally high sex ratio in the slave population. According to the 1790 census, the sex ratio in the North was 130:100, and 115:100 in the West and South, and

118   OUT OF THE HOUSE OF BONDAGE

these ratios were probably exaggerated.[17] One potentially important factor could have been the very high level of slave imports, which averaged over 30,000 p.a. in the years 1785–90,[18] coupled with the usual prominence of new arrivals among runaways.[19] New arrivals were always heavily male, and particularly so in Saint Domingue, it seems.[20] However, it will be shown that newcomers bulked just as large among female fugitives as among the males. The likeliest explanation of the imbalance, therefore, is that marronage in the colony was directed to a large degree towards the mountains and forests, rather than the towns and slave quarters of nearby plantations, and that this increased the predominance of males.

Among the slaves advertised as missing, women were slightly more numerous in the West and South (14%) than in the North (13%). This accords with their distribution in the population as a whole. However, among those jailed a notable difference emerges. Women constituted 13% of those in the North but only 9% of those in the West/South. There, it would seem, a woman's chances of escape were significantly better, but in fact ethnic differences were the cause of this contrast.

Creoles

The apparent success of women in the West/South in evading capture was almost exclusively enjoyed by local-born creoles, and especially by those of mixed descent (*mulâtresses, griffonnes, quarteronnes*).

Table 2, which compares the numbers of jailed and 'fled', provides a crude guide to the failure rate as runaways of different groups. It is not entirely reliable, as, for the reasons stated above, it probably favours the most valuable slaves and prejudices those from mountain plantations. This means that the relative success in marronage of creoles as opposed to Africans cannot be deduced with certainty from the table, particularly when black creole males were recaptured so frequently. However, there seems no reason why the table should not accurately reflect gender differences in marronage, and it probably does not distort too much relevant differences between blacks and coloureds. If, for example, slaves identified as skilled were omitted from consideration, the findings that follow would not be altered.

In their ability to escape from slavery, light-skinned females were obviously in a class by themselves. With a ready market for their sexual favours and domestic skills, they may easily have found white patrons or at least merged into the large free coloured population, two-thirds of which were of mixed descent. Coloured males, too, proved difficult to recapture, whether they were born in Saint Domingue or not. In fact, coloured creole men from outside Saint Domingue were only slightly less successful as runaways than local coloured women and significantly more so than local coloured men, who nonetheless ranked next in order. Curiously, even the black creole males from foreign colonies did much better than local black creole males, though not quite as well as local black creole females. Only two coloured creole women from foreign colonies were listed, both *en marronage*.

Insofar as the jailed: 'fled' ratio indicates success in marronage, it is clear that three factors were of paramount importance. Chief among these was a light skin, presumably because of the employment skills this implied, and because of the greater plausibility with which coloured slaves could pass for free (most free coloureds being of mixed descent). Next in importance was being female, followed surprisingly by being a foreign creole. Having been sold abroad probably meant that these slaves already had experience of running away: their reputation with Saint Domingue planters was not good.[21] Foreign creoles had the advantage of speaking foreign languages and at least some familiarity with shipping and the waterfront. Some were sailors. Of all the slaves, they were the best equipped to escape off the island. Good linguists with a wider knowledge of the outside world, they were possibly also better able to assume different identities. And to the extent that they were newcomers, they were less likely to be recognised than were local creoles. Taking these three factors into account, it is not surprising that we find no foreign coloured female in jail.

Of 83 foreign creoles, 30 came from British colonies; Jamaica, Bermuda and Dominica being mentioned once each. Another four were from the US and two were termed '*Mississippienne*'. Only 14 were from French colonies, primarily Martinique but also Guadeloupe, and Ile de France and Ile de Bourbon in the Indian Ocean as well. Twelve were '*Portugais*' presumably from Brazil, perhaps imported via Angola. Two were Danish, four Spanish, and 14 Dutch mainly from Curaçao. Some were probably creolised Africans. Wherever they were born, they certainly do not represent the full total of runaways who had arrived via the foreign slave trade. Slaves described in terms such as '*Barba Anglois*' or '*Mesurade parlant Anglois*' I have counted as Africans.

What of the propensity to run away? Creole slaves as a whole were clearly underrepresented in marronage. They constituted about one-third of the adult slaves in Saint Domingue but less than one-fifth of the adults in this sample. Coloured slaves were not particularly prone to flight either, accounting for around 2% of both this sample and the adult population. They enjoyed relative advantages not only as runaways but within the system, too. The foreign creoles, on the other hand, exhibited a marked propensity to 'pull foot'. The 3% of the adult sample they represent was at least four or five times the proportion one would have expected.

Africans

Africans, both male and female, were far more likely to flee than any other group (excepting foreign creoles). This appears to have been the case in all American slave societies. Africans were probably also the most prone to recapture, though here gender was a significant factor, the experience of Africans and creole men contrasting sharply with that of creole women (Table 2).

TABLE 2

RATIO JAILED: 'FLED'

		Ratio per 100 'Fled'
Local black creole males	193:56	345
Local black creole females	30:21	143
Local coloured males	23:18	128
Local coloured females	1:12	8
Foreign creole males*	39:32	122
Foreign creole females	9:3	300
African males	1,492:400	373
African females	175:46	380
Unidentified males	48:42	114
Unidentified females	10:2	500
Total sample	2,020:632	320

* Within this group the coloureds had a ratio of 20 (2:10) and the blacks 168 (37:22). No foreign coloured female was jailed. The one '*Mulâtre Indien*' was assumed to be a local creole. Other '*Indiens*' were counted as Africans, probably coming from Madagascar or Mauritius, though they may have been from Louisiana.

While Africans make up 83% of this sample, fully 21% were '*nègres nouveaux*' who had yet to acquire competence in creole and were assumed to have spent less than a year in Saint Domingue. Assuming that such new arrivals represented about 7% of the slave population in 1790, a rough estimate would suggest they were three times as likely to run away as were

ON THE EVE OF THE HAITIAN REVOLUTION 121

'established' Africans, who were themselves twice as likely to flee as were adult creoles. As new arrivals account for a quarter of both male and female African fugitives, the newcomers' increased propensity to flee was evidently shared by both sexes. In part, of course, this propensity simply reflected the youthfulness of the new arrivals. It is not clear if planters would be more, or less, likely to advertise for newcomers (who could be only vaguely described, especially if not yet branded), but their jailed: 'fled' ratio was predictably higher than that of other groups, 393:100.

Debien and Fouchard in their studies of fugitives in the Cap region at this time found broadly similar proportions of *nègres nouveaux*, 15% and 20%.[22] Debien's later statement that newcomers were 'les plus nombreux' is therefore difficult to understand. The prominence of new arrivals as fugitives no doubt depended on the rate of importation. As this was probably very near its height in the year 1790, the peak year of slave imports, it appears unlikely that new arrivals ever accounted for much more than one-fifth of the colony's runaways. However, it should be interesting to see how prominent they were in previous decades, for the following reason. An intriguing and unexplained aspect of the annual totals Jean Fouchard produced, is the marked fall in the number of runaways during the American War of Independence. These years also saw slave imports drastically curtailed, except that they briefly recovered in 1781, in which year the annual total of runaways also temporarily rose.[24] Comparing the years 1774–8 and 1779–83, we find that the average annual total fell by exactly 21%.

Which ethnic groups were most prominent among these runaways? If one compares the general distribution of *'nations'* in the sample with that among the fugitives designated as newcomers, two factors should be highlighted – the greater propensity of certain groups to flee on arrival in the colony, together with the trend the slave trade was taking in the years 1789–90. In this respect, one group stands out sharply, the 'Mozambiques'. They represent 10% of the African sample but 18% of the new arrivals.[25] By breaking down the figures into regional and seasonal components, it appears that this prominence was entirely due to a massive upswing in imports from South-East Africa into the North Province during the second half of 1790. This helps solve a minor mystery created by the Debien and Fouchard studies of the period October 1790–August 1791, which showed the Mozambiques to be very prominent as fugitives in the North, although on surviving plantation lists from the region they are all but non-existent.[26] Their arrival in large numbers in the North was therefore confined to the very last months before the slave insurrection.

Also disproportionately represented among the *nègres nouveaux* were the 'Ibo' and 'Bibi' from Biafra, and the 'Canga' from the Cape Mesurado region. They were purchased to a large extent from British contraband

122   OUT OF THE HOUSE OF BONDAGE

traders, whose activity in this period was evidently increasing, as other evidence besides these figures also suggests. One ethnic group notably underrepresented among the new arrivals were the 'Congos'. They formed by far the largest component of both the African sample (45%) and the newcomers (31%), but it would seem that their propensity to flee during their first year was lower than average. This is a valuable indication, because till now it has been difficult to reconcile their enormous preponderance in marronage with their reputation for adapting well to slavery.

As Congos constituted 45% of both the jailed and 'fled' Africans, it would seem that they enjoyed no particular success in escaping. One might have thought that their numerical dominance within the slave population would have made Congo fugitives less easy to detect and more likely to receive shelter and assistance. In fact, no such correlation shows up between the numerically prominent ethnic groups and apparent success in marronage. Clearly the most unsuccessful of the large groups were the tall, slow-moving[27] 'Bambara', followed by the 'Senegal', 'Hausa' and 'Nago'. None of these groups were disadvantaged by an above-average proportion of newly-arrived slaves, and the Bambara and Hausa were actually favoured by extremely high sex ratios, since African men were less likely to be recaptured than African women. The high proportion of females among the Nago (Yoruba) may explain their lack of success. The groups best able to avoid recapture were the 'Côte d'Or' and 'Mina', followed by the 'Mandingues', 'Mondongues' and 'Arada'. Interestingly, in eighteenth century South Carolina the Bambara and Gold Coast slaves had similarly divergent experiences as runaways.[28]

Given the present state of knowledge about the ethnic make-up of Saint Domingue's slave population, the question of whether some ethnic groups were more prone to marronage than others remains elusive. While it has been shown that the mix of ethnic groups varied considerably between different regions of Saint Domingue and between different plantation types,[29] the data available is not yet sufficient for putting together a composite picture. In this sample, for example, some 'nations' were more prominent in the North than in the South/West, such as the Congo (49%/41%) and Mozambique (13%/8%). Biafran slaves, as expected, were more prominent in the South/West, which obviously had closer links with the British interlope trade. Some peoples associated with the British slave trade do not show up in the North at all, including the Moco, Bibi, Cap Lao and Caramenty.[30] This is also true of the Canga, but only because they were known as 'Mesurades' in the North, where they were even so noticeably less common.[31]

With the figures available, and taking into account distortions caused by sex ratio and newcomers, it would seem difficult to say that any ethnic group was particularly prone to marronage, not even the Congo. Their

ON THE EVE OF THE HAITIAN REVOLUTION

paradoxical reputation as runaways was probably based simply on their numerical prominence in the colony and their high sex ratio. The Mozambiques do appear overrepresented among the runaways, but this could have been a function of their age. The vast majority of them had arrived in the colony in the previous few years and they were therefore in the prime age-group for running away. Of the groups apparently *not* prone to marronage, the evidence is unequivocal with regard only to one, the Bambara. This accords well with the finding that they were the least successful of runaways.

Seasonal Variation

One of the most striking aspects of these figures is the large increase in the number of fugitives imprisoned between the first and second halves of the year. While the number of 'fled' held steady in the North and fell in the South/West, the number jailed rose by 20% in the South/West and by 34% in the North.

It might be tempting to see in this a harbinger of the 1791 uprising, a sign of increasing militancy. Were this a correct interpretation, however, the number of 'fled' would surely have risen along with the number jailed. It could be that the *maréchaussée* became more active in this period, responding to public alarm, but this also seems unlikely. Fear of a slave rebellion appears to have been decreasing at this time. This was also the period of the free coloured revolt led by Vincent Ogé, which probably disrupted *maréchaussée* activity, and led to the disarming of free coloureds in the North. One might expect that the revolt itself inspired a wave of marronage, but the number of runaways both 'fled' and jailed in the North actually fell in the months following the rebellion.

Another possible explanation of this increase is that it was caused by seasonal variation in the slave trade and by an influx of new Africans imported towards the end of the hurricane season. This could account for a rise in numbers jailed without an increase in numbers 'fled'. Disoriented new arrivals speaking no creole were probably quickly recaptured. However, Table 3 shows that there was no overall correlation between numbers jailed and the proportion of new arrivals among fugitives. Newly imported *bossales* may have accounted for one-third of the seasonal increase in the North but evidently they had no impact at all in the South/West.

I would suggest that two factors best explain the seasonal variation observed. One is the agricultural cycle, whose influence on Barbados runaways Gad Heuman has perceptively delineated,[32] revealing a monthly pattern very similar to that found in Saint Domingue. For a period when slave imports were almost non-existent, Heuman shows an increase in marronage of over 33% in the second half of the year with a peak in the summer months after cropover. This was also the case in Saint Domingue in 1790. In both Saint Domingue and Barbados February appears to have been the low-point for runaways, while April witnessed an increase (albeit much larger in Saint Domingue) doubtless associated with Easter. Studies of other years before 1790 should easily reveal if such a seasonal pattern was general.

The second factor accounting for the upsurge in the number of runaways imprisoned was more specific. This was the terrible drought that hit Saint Domingue in 1790. It appears to have been at its worst in the North and to have reached its height in early October. While many slaves died of hunger, some plantation managers gave up making sugar and let their workforces scavenge for themselves, or take off for Cap Français to live by their wits.[33] In so doing, many must have been arrested as runaways.

Regional Variation

In addition to these seasonal differences and the varying mix of African ethnicities in the two areas studied, other contrasts may be noted between the North and the South/West. Although the proportion of Africans and creoles in the runaway populations of the two regions were almost identical, creole females bulked much larger in that of the South/West. This may well explain why in that region females were notably more successful in evading capture. Recapture rates for males were approximately the same in both areas. For reasons that are not clear, newly-arrived slaves were much more common among fugitives outside the North, particularly in the first half of the year (Table 3). Part of this difference may reflect the fact that shipments from Africa were concentrated on the port of Cap Français. Arriving in the autumn, many *bossales* must have been transshipped to the West and South early in the new year. Finally, while the two regional samples are nearly equal in number, that from the North is, in proportion to the regional slave population, more than half as large again as that from the South/West. It could be that in the latter, much larger and less compact, region, the newspaper was simply less used by the colonists. Or it is possible that marronage was substantially more common in the North Province.

Age

From a 90-year-old Fulani man to babies carried off by their mothers, slaves of all ages became fugitives. However, the great majority of runaways were young adults. Two-thirds were thought to be in their twenties and a fifth to be adolescents. As the ages of new arrivals were rarely given, both these proportions can be considered underestimates.

ON THE EVE OF THE HAITIAN REVOLUTION

Specialists

Details of fugitives' occupations were recorded only in advertisements *en marronage*, where 31 slaves (5%) were listed as being skilled. Sixteen were artisans, and eight domestics. The seven others included four sailors, a slave-driver and a female peddler. Most of the major occupational categories are represented with the exception of sugar-boiler, perhaps the most common of all. Boilermen no doubt did flee, but there was no point in their owners identifying them as such, since they could not use their skills as free labourers. The sample is probably skewed by seven African carpenters who ran off together from an urban enterprise. Nevertheless, the presence of a dozen carpenters and joiners suggests that this was the occupational group most prone to marronage. Carpenters could command good wages in the colony and were much needed in both town and countryside. As in the runaway population in general, women were underrepresented (6%) and Africans and foreign creoles were exceptionally prominent.

TABLE 3

NEWLY ARRIVED SLAVES* AS A PERCENTAGE OF THOSE JAILED

	North	South/West	Whole Colony
Jan.-June	7	31	20
July-Dec.	19	27	23

*Defined as those who had spent 12 months or less in the colony, or who could not speak creole.

Individuals

As Jean Fouchard has demonstrated, Saint Domingue's slaves come to life nowhere more vividly than in these *signalements de marrons*. Covered in brand-marks or sores, dragging heavy weights, missing teeth, fingers or toes, the worst cases document slavery's brutality in dramatic fashion. Among the slaves who ran away twice in 1790 was Pierre, a creole of about 48 'having two unreadable brand-marks on each side of his chest, a large burn on his lower stomach, a very considerable hernia, and both ears cut off'. He was arrested at Haut-du-Cap in both July and December.[34]

One occasionally gets intriguing glimpses of runaway life, as with a 28-year-old Mozambique recorded in January as being missing since 1788. He was known to buy rum at the gates of sugar estates in the West and then sell

126 OUT OF THE HOUSE OF BONDAGE

it in the mountains of Matheux, receiving stolen goods in exchange. The slave regime itself appears in rich diversity. Venus, the female peddler mentioned above, had a pass from her owner 'to go wherever she liked in order to sell'. In June, her owner advertised her as missing. She was a 40-year-old Ibo and had decamped with her three children, the two eldest being mulattoes. Among the captured runaways a couple (out of how many?) were caught giving false identities to their captors. It is interesting that both claimed to be slaves of free coloureds, which suggests they had been either helped or covertly employed by them.[35]

Running away was overwhelmingly a solitary activity. Slaves who ran away in pairs or in groups of four, five or six tended to be new arrivals, usually of the same '*nation*'. Two heterogeneous groups of eleven show up, both from estates that had recently been sold or leased out. A change of owner or overseer was known to be often a cause of disruption. Three-quarters of those *en marronage* had fled alone. Some seem to have been remarkable linguists. It is perhaps not surprising that a Danish creole sailor should 'speak foreign languages and creole well', but more curious is the case of Jean-Louis, a local creole of Le Cap who spoke 'Spanish, Dutch, English and the creole jargon'. Polylingualism in African languages of course went unnoticed.

Only five slaves appear to have fled with firearms. Four were newly arrived Makwa from Mozambique. The other was a young Arada. All were from the West Province. However, an oblique reminder of the approaching revolution can be found in the following advertisement, which refers to the young voodoo priest Hyacinthe, soon to become famous in the plain of Cul de Sac. The missing slave was

> Magdelaine, creole, about 29 years old, extremely black, skinny, tall and pock-marked. Has been missing about three months, presumed to have been lured away by the negro Hyacinthe of Monsieur Ducoudray with whom she has relations. She has free relatives in Port au Prince and Petit Goâve, where she is from. She is in the habit of dressing up as a man and passing herself off as free.[36]

Within a year, other female slaves in the colony would be both dressing as men and also carrying guns.

The only other famous name to crop up among these runaways is that of the Congo, Goman, whose exploits as a Maroon leader in the South spanned both the Revolution and the first two decades of Haiti's independence. There is no way of knowing if the 28-year-old with this name jailed in Port au Prince in July, 'unable to say the name of his master', was indeed the same person, but the entry may mark the beginning of a long career in marronage.[37] Perhaps the most surprising advertisement, however, is one which tantalisingly resurrects a lost reputation and challenges notions of the

ON THE EVE OF THE HAITIAN REVOLUTION

individual slave's anonymity within the system: 'Isidore, creole, 36, well known in the colony ...'.[38]

Conclusion

None of the findings in this paper can be called more than tentative until earlier runs of the *Affiches Américaines* are subjected to similar scrutiny. Only then will a clear picture emerge of the ethnic, sexual, regional and seasonal variations outlined here. The source material is very rich and provides important data on subjects besides marronage, such as the height of slaves, Islamisation, language use and scarification. Covering a full thirty years and deriving from one of the richest of all slave societies at its apogee, the *Affiches Américaines* deserve more attention.

NOTES

1. For conflicting views, see E. Paul, *Questions d'Histoire*, Port au Prince, 1955, pp. 5–6, 12–20; E. Brutus, *Révolution dans Saint-Domingue* (np, nd), vol. 1, p. 70; J. Fouchard, *Les Marrons de la Liberté*, Paris, 1972; L. Manigat, 'The Relationship between Marronage and ... Revolution in Saint Domingue–Haiti', *Annals of the New York Academy of Sciences*, 292 (1977); and Y. Debbasch, 'Le Marronage', *Année Sociologique* (1961, 1962); T. Ott, *The Haitian Revolution*, Knoxville, 1973, p. 18; G. Debien, *Les Esclaves aux Antilles Françaises*, Basse Terre, 1974, pp. 411–69. The question is reviewed in D. Geggus, *Slave Resistance Studies and the Saint Domingue Slave Revolt: Some Preliminary Considerations*, Miami, 1983, 2nd imp., pp. 4–10.
2. G. Debien, 'Les Marrons autour du Cap', *Bulletin de l'Institut Français d'Afrique Noire*, 27, série B (1965), 755–99; G. Debien and J. Fouchard, 'Le Petit Marronage autour du Cap', *Cahiers des Amériques Latines*, (1969); G. Debien, 'Les Esclaves Marrons à Saint-Domingue en 1764', *Jamaican Historical Review*, 6 (1969).
3. Fouchard, *Marrons*, pp. 197–222.
4. Ibid., p. 218.
5. Ibid., p. 198.
6. Debien, *Les Esclaves*, pp. 440–1.
7. Fouchard, *Les Marrons*, pp. 439–41. In Fouchard and Debien, 'Petit Marronage', p. 55, it is suggested that those jailed represented half or one-third of all runaways.
8. Debien, *Les Esclaves*, pp. 437, 439–41.
9. D. Geggus, 'Les esclaves de la plaine du Nord à la veille de la Révolution Française: partie 4', *Revue de la Société Haitienne d'Histoire*, forthcoming.
10. A. Gautier, 'Les femmes esclaves aux Antilles françaises', *Social Reflections*, forthcoming.
11. N. Vanony-Frisch, 'Les esclaves de la Guadeloupe à la fin de l'Ancien Régime', thèse 3me cycle, 1981, Univ. Paris I.
12. S. Schwartz, *Sugar Plantations and the Formation of Brazilian Society (Bahia, 1550–1830)*, Cambridge, 1985, ch. 18, n. 2.
13. Jamaica Archives, Spanish Town, Council Minutes, 11 June 1798. To estimate the parish populations, I extrapolated backwards from the 1817 census.
14. See M. Craton, *Testing the Chains*, Ithaca, 1982, pp. 231–2, 368. Craton suggests that there may have been 1,000 more Maroons than the 490 counted. This seems unlikely, as only 578 were killed or captured before the Maroon War ended more than a year later.
15. See note 2.
16. Fouchard, *Les Marrons*, p. 289.

128   OUT OF THE HOUSE OF BONDAGE

17. S. Ducoeurjoly, *Manuel des Habitants de Saint-Domingue*, Paris, 1802, vol. 1, p.clxxiv; D. Geggus, 'The Slaves of British-Occupied Saint Domingue', *Caribbean Studies*, 18 (1978), 7.
18. D. Geggus, *Slavery, War and Revolution*, Oxford, 1982, p. 405.
19. In Jamaica, females represented 14% of runaways imprisoned in 1794, following the peak year of importations, but 24% in 1813, after the end of the slave trade: H. O. Patterson, *Sociology of Slavery*, London, 1967, p. 262.
20. In 1788, the only year for which data appears available, males outnumbered females 213:100 among imported slaves. By contrast, the sex ratio in the Jamaican slave trade was a remarkably consistent 162:100 between 1760 and 1800: D. Geggus, 'Ethnicity and Sex Ratio in the Atlantic Slave Trade', forthcoming.
21. Geggus, *Slavery*, pp. 40–1.
22. Debien, 'Marrons autour du Cap', p. 794; Debien and Fouchard, 'Petit Marronage', p. 55. The proportion was 14% in 1764: Debien, 'Esclaves Marrons', p. 8.
23. Debien, *Les Esclaves*, p. 449.
24. See Fouchard, *Marrons*, pp. 207–12.
25. This is excluding those listed simply as *'Africains'* or *'Nègres Nouveaux'*.
26. A sample of 1,267 Africans of identified origin taken from northern sugar estates in the period 1780–91 revealed not a single 'Mozambique': Geggus, 'Plaine du Nord: partie 4'.
27. M. L. E. Moreau de Saint-Méry, *Description de Saint-Domingue*, Paris, 1957 ed., vol. 1, p. 48.
28. D. Littlefield, *Rice and Slaves: Ethnicity and the Slave Trade in Colonial South Carolina*, Baton Rouge, 1981, p. 129.
29. Geggus, 'British-Occupied Saint Domingue'; Geggus, 'Plaine du Nord: partie 4'.
30. Nor do they appear in the sample mentioned in note 26.
31. They have yet to be identified with a modern ethnic group: Geggus, 'Plaine du Nord'.
32. See Gad Heuman, 'Runaway Slaves in 19th Century Barbados', pp. 95–111. However, it should be noted that Heuman used advertisements rather than jail lists, that in Saint Domingue, unlike Barbados, only a minority of slaves worked on sugar estates, and that the timing of the sugar harvest may have varied between different regions of Saint Domingue (as in Jamaica).
33. Archives Nationales, Paris, T 561, Vaudreuil Papers.
34. *Affiches*, Cap Français, nos. 60 and 100.
35. *Affiches*, Cap Français, nos. 72, 84 and 93.
36. *Affiches*, Port au Prince, no. 91.
37. *Affiches*, Port au Prince, no. 58.
38. *Affiches*, Cap Français, no. 53.

PART THREE

MARRONAGE

Cimarrones *and* Palenques: *Runaways and Resistance in Colonial Colombia*

Anthony McFarlane

During the eighteenth century, the Spanish colony of New Granada – a territory roughly coterminous with that of modern Colombia – held one of the largest populations of slaves in mainland Spanish America.[1] Its major port, that of Cartagena de Indias, on the Caribbean coast, had long been a leading centre for the slave trade, not only supplying New Granada's markets for servile labour, but also acting as a major entrepot for the traffic in slaves to the whole of Spanish South America.[2] Within the colony itself, slaves were put to various uses in both urban and rural areas, but were used mainly in the gold-mining and agriculture of those regions where Spanish occupation had decimated the indigenous population.[3] Thus, by the eighteenth century, slavery had become firmly established in some regions of colonial Colombia and it continued, throughout the late colonial period, to play an important part in their economic and social development.

Late colonial Colombia was not, of course, a slave society comparable to that of the Brazilian coastal regions, the American South, or the Caribbean islands. While in absolute terms the number of slaves was high – it was estimated to be almost 65,000 in the censuses of 1778–80 – slaves constituted only about 7.6% of a population in New Granada of some 855,000 people composed chiefly of people of mixed race (44%), whites (31%), and Indians (18%).[4] The slave population was, however, unevenly distributed among the different regions of the colony, and the ratio of slaves to free people varied considerably from area to area. In the relatively densely-populated temperate and highland zones of the eastern and southern Andes, where substantial Indian communities had survived and where miscegenation had created large mestizo populations, there were correspondingly small numbers of slaves. In the province of Santa Fe de Bogotá, for instance, slaves were only 1.5% of the population; in the neighbouring province of Tunja, only 2%; in the southern Andean province of Pasto, a mere 0.7%. In the Caribbean coastal provinces, the ratio was rather higher: about 10% in the province of Santa Marta, and about 8% in the province of Cartagena. Most of the latter were urban slaves, concentrated in the city of Cartagena which held nearly one-half of the province's slaves; the remainder were scattered over the length and breadth of the province and were employed mainly on haciendas which combined

132 OUT OF THE HOUSE OF BONDAGE

sugar cultivation with cattle-raising. But the highest proportions of slaves to free people were found in the southern and western provinces of New Granada, where gold-mining played a more significant role in local economic life. In the provinces of Popayán and Antioquia, slaves formed about 20% of the regional populations, and were used in both agriculture and mining. In the specialised mining zones, slaves were a still higher proportion of local populations, coming close to equalling, sometimes surpassing the size of the free population. In the Chocó, for example, they formed about 39% of the region's people; in Iscuandé, another mining zone, 33%; in Tumaco, 63%, and in Raposo, an extraordinary 70%. It must be remembered, however, that even in these areas, with their relatively large concentrations of slaves, the slave population tended to be rather dispersed. Due to the character of the economy in which they were involved, they were scattered over large and inhospitable areas, working gold-bearing streams amidst the luxuriant tropical forests of the Pacific lowlands, and largely sealed off from contact with the outside.[5]

In these areas, as in other regions of slavery in the Americas, the institution of servitude and bondage engendered its opposite: the resistance of its victims and their struggle for freedom. From the early days of slavery in New Granada, Africans responded to their captivity by rebellion, either in open insurrection against their oppressors or by seeking to escape from their control. By the late sixteenth century, runaway slaves or *cimarrones* had become a serious problem for Spanish society on the Caribbean coast. They not only deprived slaveowners of their property but, by forming fugitive communities or *palenques*, posed a threat to the stability of slave society itself. This form of resistance persisted throughout the colonial period. Indeed, Jaramillo Uribe has argued that during the eighteenth century the *palenques* became part of a pattern of slave resistance which took on the characteristics of a civil war and became so widespread that it seemed that there was 'an agreement between the different nuclei of slaves to carry out a general rebellion'.[6] In his view, these conditions of conflict – when combined with a contracting slave trade and the inability of entrepreneurs to finance new imports of slaves – helped create a climate propitious to the abolition of slavery following the foundation of the republic of Colombia in the early nineteenth century.[7]

Whether slave resistance spread and intensified during the eighteenth century remains a problematical issue which cannot be systematically analysed here. For the moment, suffice to say that, being impressionistic and general rather than quantitative and precise, Jaramillo's conclusions on this point remain open to question. The present concern is, rather, with the nature of marronage in late colonial Colombia, its various forms, and the motives, aims and organisation which lie behind it. The aim is not to calculate its frequency, but to consider its manifestations, to examine its

POPULATION OF NEW GRANADA (1778–1780), SHOWING DISTRIBUTION OF SLAVES

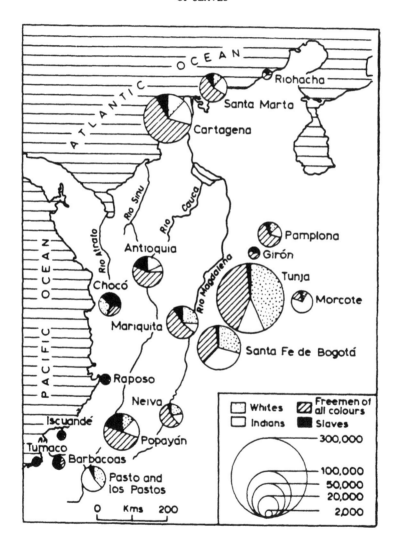

Reproduced from Carey Robinson: *The Fighting Maroons of Jamaica*, by permission of William Collins.

134 OUT OF THE HOUSE OF BONDAGE

dynamics, and to illuminate the social and mental world of slaves who sought, successfully or unsuccessfully, to change their lives by flight from bondage.

The Maroon Tradition

Large-scale marronage, involving runaways who joined together to create their own communities on the margins of Hispanic settlement, first appeared in New Granada at an early stage in its history. A Spanish expedition against such fugitive communities took place in the province of Cartagena in the 1570s and by the late 1590s draconian legislation was enacted in an effort to curtail the flow of runaways from the city of Cartagena and to combat the depredations of fugitive bands in its vicinity.[8] At the turn of the century, renewed efforts were made to extirpate the *palenques* in the province until, disillusioned by their failure, the Spanish authorities granted some privileges and a measure of autonomy to one powerful group of fugitives, which later came to form the famous *palenque* of San Basilio.[9] Such conciliation did not, however, provide an enduring solution to the problem of *palenques* in the province of Cartagena. Indeed, communities of Maroons appear not only to have survived, but to have multiplied. At the end of the seventeenth century, the government and municipal authorities of Cartagena decided once again to embark on a major campaign against the *cimarrones* and their communities. In the end this campaign proved largely unsuccessful for, although it destroyed some of the *palenques*, its main effect was simply to displace their inhabitants towards the south of the province, where they reestablished their settlements.[10]

Information on these *palenques* is sparse, but it is clear that, by the end of the seventeenth century, there were several well-established Maroon communities in the backlands of the neighbouring provinces of Cartagena and Santa Marta. Based on agriculture, they were organised in stable settlements under well-defined political and military leadership and were sometimes aligned according to African ethnic or tribal origins. Equipped with bows and arrows and firearms, the people of the *palenques* protected their settlements with palisades and hidden ditches, and seem generally to have inspired fear rather than friendship with local Indian villagers. In 1680, one such group of *palenques*, located in the forested and difficult terrain of the Sierra de Santa María, sought to come to terms with the Spanish authorities through the intercession of a missionary who was exploring the region. This priest told of his meeting with their 'governor', who informed him that 'he had at his command six hundred men who were ruled by four captains, each of his "nation" '.[11] After long negotiations with the priest, the governor stated that his people, together with other fugitives in the backlands, were ready to acknowledge Spanish authority and to collaborate with it in return-

CIMARRONES AND PALENQUES   135

ing fresh runaways, in return for a grant of freedom to themselves and their descendants, the provision of a priest to minister to them, and the allocation of cultivable lands sufficient to meet their needs.[12]

In the event, though the Crown was ready to accept these terms, opposition from Cartagena slaveowners aborted negotiation, and the Maroons were forced to withstand repeated attack before the prospect of conciliation was reopened in the early eighteenth century. Then, between 1713 and 1717, the bishop of Cartagena, backed by the provincial authorities, organised a treaty with black communities in the Sierra de María, granting them freedom and a general pardon on condition that they would refuse to permit new runaways to live amongst them.[13]

This community, which came to be known as San Basilio, is the best-known example of official compromise with Maroons in colonial Colombia, but it is not the only instance in which Maroons sought to come to terms with the authorities in New Granada. Such, for example, was the case of the *palenque* of El Castigo in the province of Popayán, whose one hundred inhabitants had created two villages, built a church for each, and tried in the early 1730s to negotiate for a priest to be assigned to them. In this case, however, the fugitives roundly refused entry to colonial magistrates and continued to accept new runaways into their communities.[14] On the whole, formal compromise between *palenques* and the state was rare in colonial Colombia, and there is no extant evidence to suggest that Maroon communities became an instrument for policing slave society, as they did in Jamaica. Instead, the Caribbean coastal *palenques* discussed above seem to represent a first stage in the experience of collective escape by blacks sold into slavery in New Granada. They were the survivors of a first great cycle in the formation of fugitive communities, born in the flight of newly-arrived Africans and the formation of runaway bands, leading to the creation of stable agricultural communities, and ending in the consolidation of permanent free communities which could coexist with the dominant society. But they were, in turn, succeeded by further attempts to break out of bondage and, throughout the eighteenth century, the tradition which they had created was constantly renewed by the attempts of slaves to escape their masters and to shape their own destinies. In order to explore the motives, organisation and ideology which underpinned these efforts, we will now turn to a closer examination of episodes involving fugitive slaves in eighteenth-century New Granada. For, through the reports and testimonies arising from such cases, we may catch glimpses of the motives and aspirations of slave runaways, the character of their lives and culture, and their adaptions to different conditions and circumstances.

All runaways, in the very act of flight, registered a protest against slavery, a rebellion against its constraints and conditions. Such protest was, of course, far from uniform. At its most fundamental level, each act of flight

136 OUT OF THE HOUSE OF BONDAGE

was ultimately unique and irreducible, in that it involved different individuals and occurred at particular times in highly specific circumstances. At a more general level, however, there are some broadly discernible patterns of runaway behaviour. As we shall see, slaves might be pushed to escape by fear and mistreatment, or by the need to protect customary rights; they might be pulled towards flight by the dream of freedom beyond the bounds of the slave regime; they might escape individually or collectively; they might seek some temporary refuge or strike out towards a permanent respite from servitude. Whatever their choice, runaways in eighteenth-century Colombia all expressed some degree of resistance to their condition of enslavement.

Individual escape

At its simplest level, escape from slavery might be undertaken by individuals acting alone, for a variety of motives. Flight might be a spontaneous act, spurred by the threat of punishment, either by the master or because of some infringement of the law. In 1749, two slaves who worked on a sugar hacienda in Tocaima, in central Colombia, ran away to the hills, each for one of these reasons. The incident stemmed from the slaveowner's decision to punish a mulatto slave accused of systematically mistreating his wife and of beating her so savagely that she became unfit for work. When the slaveowner duly ordered the slave captain, himself a black slave, to seek out the offender for punishment, the latter made off on a stolen mule. When the slave captain went after him, accompanied by two other slaves, one of these turned on the captain, murdered him, and then escaped himself. To avoid the law, the assassin went into hiding, joining forces with another runaway who was already on the run from magistrates seeking to arrest him for a previous murder on the same hacienda.[15]

In other circumstances, slaves might flee, not to evade punishment or to elude the law, but to escape from bad conditions and to appeal to the law. In 1802, a slaveowner of Popayán lost six slaves in just such an escape. Four of them simply attempted to go into hiding in other areas, but two of the runaways took a distinctive course of action. They travelled to the viceregal capital in Bogotá, a long and arduous journey, to petition the *protector de negros*, the state attorney for slaves. Complaining that they had been starved by their master, they protested that his influence in Popayán deprived them of the chance of a fair hearing there, and they appealed to the Bogotá authorities to order their transfer to a new owner.[16] In this, as in other such cases, slave flight was an element in the wider practice of slaves who sought to take advantage of paternalistic legislation designed to protect slaves from abuse, to ensure minimal standards of material and spiritual welfare, to guarantee legal rights and to provide channels through which the slaves might exercise these rights.[17]

CIMARRONES AND PALENQUES

The extent of flight by individuals evading punishment, attempting to change their owners or seeking redress of grievances is unknown: no systematic records were kept, nor were all cases necessarily reported to the authorities. For the same reasons, it is difficult to say how often individuals sought permanent escape from slavery through flight. An incident that occurred in the city of Cartagena in 1776, involving a slave brought before the Inquisition, does, however, illustrate some of the opportunities and difficulties facing an individual slave who tried to escape to freedom.

This case involved Felix Fernando Martinez, a young mulatto in his early twenties, who was arrested when trying to sell various ornaments stolen from a church in the city. When it was discovered that these included a vessel holding a consecrated Host, he was brought before the Inquisition and charged with the crime of sacrilege.[18] Initially, Martinez gave an assumed name, claimed that he was a free man from the town of Girón in the interior, and denied the charges against him. Eventually, however, prolonged questioning revealed that he was an escaped slave who had fled from his master when about twelve years old and had since passed himself off as a free mulatto.

In his confessions to the inquisitors, cumulatively and convincingly built up over several months, some salient points emerge. First, though very young when he left his master, he had already had unusually wide experience of the world. On reaching the age of ten or eleven, he had accompanied his master on several long journeys around the country, including a visit to Cartagena, where they had lodged in the houses of prominent aristocratic families. These travels seem to have made the boy confident that he could survive on his own, and attracted him to the idea of striking out for freedom in the city of Cartagena. This he did within a year or so of returning from the city to his master's home in the interior province of Tunja.

Another striking feature of his experience is that he seems to have had relatively little difficulty in evading recapture. After briefly attaching himself to a Jesuit priest in Pamplona, a couple of hundred miles from where he had lived, he assumed a new name and then journeyed up the River Magdalena en route to Cartagena. There was a risk in small towns: once he was arrested as a suspected fugitive, travelling without licence from his owner, and jailed in the small settlement of Tenerife. But he managed to go free again, and to journey on to the city. Once there, the risk of detection diminished, and he was able to find work with several different employers before falling into a demi-monde of petty thieves. Even when this led to his arrest for theft, he still sustained his new identity and, after serving a term of forced labour, he went back to seek a living in the city.

Increasingly, however, his life was plagued with problems. Fearful of exposure, he decided to raise money in order to purchase manumission from his erstwhile master, and became a cabin-boy with the coastguard

138   OUT OF THE HOUSE OF BONDAGE

which patrolled neighbouring Caribbean waters. But, after three years' service, he deserted with only three months' pay, and fell back into a life of petty thieving until he was apprehended as a deserter, severely flogged and thrown into prison. He escaped, signed on a ship leaving the port, but was returned to Cartagena shortly after when the ship foundered off Maracaibo. Thrust back into the city, he slipped into vagabondage and theft, until finally arrested for stealing from the church. For this crime, with its taint of blasphemy, he was to pay with his life on a public scaffold.

This was, by any account, an extraordinary story, and it vividly illustrates the difficulties and anxieties of life for a fugitive slave. In a large city like Cartagena, with its substantial population of free coloureds, an unknown runaway from another area could evidently merge into the urban milieu, particularly if he was mulatto like Felix Martinez. But even in this relatively favourable environment, the problems of life on the run were formidable, for, without secure employment, the fugitive was forced into poverty and insecurity, constantly fearing exposure. It would be hardly surprising if few slaves took this difficult choice to seek freedom alone and unaided in an environment where, without property or a stable livelihood, they faced suspicion, hardship and indigence. For even the bravest, this must have been a harsh option to confront and a high risk to take. Because their colour implied slavery, wandering blacks and mulattoes were treated with suspicion, especially in villages and small towns where any stranger would arouse curiosity and enquiry. Small wonder, then, that when slaves dreamed of freedom, they sought to find it in the company of their fellows, either by seeking out runaway communities or by trying to escape in groups which might establish their own self-sustaining communities, away from the threatening context of a white-dominated society.

Runaways and *palenques*

At its most dramatic, slave flight stemmed from the collective rebellion of a group of slaves and led to the foundation of a fugitive community, or *palenque*. The first element did not, however, always lead to the second. At times, rebellion and the threat of flight was used to bring pressure on the slaveowner, while stopping short of actual escape to a *palenque*. Such, for example, was an incident of rebellion recorded in the Caribbean coastal province of Santa Marta in 1768. In this case, a small group of slaves on a cattle-raising hacienda attacked and wounded their foreman and, when a force was sent to subdue them, killed a white man.[19] Faced with their defiance, the slaveowner took up his slaves' demand for negotiation, and came to terms with them. The slaves stated that they had not intended to escape from his service, but had attacked the foreman because he treated them badly. They agreed to return to work if the owner swore on the Holy

CIMARRONES AND PALENQUES 139

Sacrament to pardon them and to agree that, if he wished to sell any of them, he must sell all, together with their women and children. If he failed to agree, they threatened to fire the hacienda, to slaughter its livestock, and to run off to join the 'wild Indians'. They added that if there was any further mistreatment or any recriminations for their action, they would rebel again. When the owner agreed to their demands, the slaves emerged from their defensive positions, firing off a salute and praising God. They then surrendered the arms which they had captured, while insisting that they retain those belonging to the hacienda. After the owner had distributed tobacco and *aguardiente* (brandy) among them, they returned to work.[20]

Here, then, rebellion did not lead to flight or the formation of a *palenque*; instead, insurgent slaves used violence and the threat of escape as a means of winning redress of their grievances. In this frontier area, freedom in the wilds among the 'wild Indians' to whom the slaves referred was a path open to the rebels, but it was also, for that very reason, a strong bargaining counter which the slaves could use to protect certain basic freedoms within the economy of slavery.

At other times, slaves went further, going beyond the protection of basic rights within slavery to attempt collectively to break from its regime and to exercise a more untrammelled freedom. The pursuit of this more ambitious purpose might arise from a reaction against mistreatment, in circumstances akin to those which prompted the Santa Marta slaves to rise, but led beyond compromise to the formation of a runaway community out of the master's reach. The origins and development of such a movement can be illustrated through the history of a small group of fugitive slaves who were recaptured in 1753 near the old mining town of Los Remedios in the province of Antioquia after about a decade of freedom.

In this instance, a group of slaves had rebelled against their owners, seized arms, and made off into the backlands. Although the reasons for their rebellion and flight were never stated, their subsequent attacks on the property of their former masters suggest that they harboured a deep resentment against them, born in mistreatment. Whatever the reason for their flight, the fugitives saw no ground for compromise. They headed off into the wilds and founded a *palenque* which survived for many years, and became a thorn in the side of the slaveowners. Hidden deep in the bush, their tiny community remained undetected until some fishermen, wandering in a swampy area far from the nearest settlement, heard the sounds of nocturnal drumming and singing. The slaveowners were not slow to take advantage of this accidental discovery and, within a short time, the fugitives' community was located and destroyed.[21]

The reports of the expedition sent against the slaves reveal that, protected by their isolation, the runaways had managed to create a community which not only survived, but had begun to reproduce itself. When it was taken, the *palenque* housed sixteen adults – ten men and six women – and eight children, some of whom had been born in freedom. Furthermore, descriptions of the *palenque* show that, despite their small number, the runaways had created an ordered settlement in the wilderness. The raiders found a hamlet consisting of ten huts, each with its own cooking place and storehouse, plentifully stocked with vegetables, fruit, maize and small livestock. It also had, at its centre, a place of worship, presided over by an old man who was both the community's leader and its priest. This 'church' seems to have fused elements of Christianity with other, possibly African beliefs. The old man, the runaways said, was in contact with 'saints who came down from Heaven, some by day and some by night, with thunder'.[22] He made them worship in the church and they said they all believed, though they did not know in whom. Certainly the slaves' captors saw nothing which they recognised as Christian and they destroyed what they took to be the work of idolaters.

In their years of creating this settlement, the runaways had not simply isolated themselves from all contact with the outside world. On the contrary, they had used their hiding-place as a base from which to launch periodic attacks on local *estancias*, settlements and merchants travelling in the area. These attacks arose in part from material needs: the slaves took arms and gunpowder, tools, clothing, jewels and money, as well as a couple of females. But they also seem to have been inspired by hatred for their owners, and defiance of the local society. Not only did they prey on the property of a former master, whom they also attempted to kill, but the fugitives sometimes challenged the local authorities with calculated gestures of abuse. Thus, on one occasion, they burst into the village of San Bartolomé, playing musical instruments, and warned its *alcalde* that, if he did not provide them with food, they would eat one another. As a sequel to this bizarre threat, they broke into a strong-box of valuables belonging to their former owner, stole the contents, and sent word to the *alcaldes* of Los Remedios to make ready to receive them for dinner on Christmas night.[23] This, and other acts of defiance were ultimately to prove their downfall, for as soon as their whereabouts were revealed, the local authorities moved swiftly to organise their recapture.

In this case, rebellion clearly involved more than simply a test of wills between the slaves and their masters within the slave economy. Starting from a group of seven slaves working in a gold-mining gang, it bore the mark of a conscious effort to escape from slavery and to establish a free community. Having found a suitable place to set up a community, the slaves then attracted new recruits – mostly young males – and raided local *estancias* for women. At least three of the women were slaves seized in this way, while the presence of two *zambo* (Indian/black) children indicates that the slaves also had contacts with Indians in the area. Thus, though the *palenque* seems

CIMARRONES AND PALENQUES 141

to have achieved a high degree of self-sufficiency – reflecting the slaves' skills in subsistence agriculture – the slaves did not completely disengage from local society. Indeed, the inventory of goods found in the *palenque* shows that the runaways felt a need to acquire a whole range of goods from colonial society, including many kinds of cloth and clothing, tools for mining, weapons and munitions. They not only stole merchandise and valuables but, by prospecting for gold, also sought to acquire them through trade.[24] While the fugitives defied colonial society, they also managed, on their own terms, to sustain relations with it.

Another episode which involved a project for collective escape with the intention of establishing a runaway community, but which carried clearer overtones of a desire to combat slavery itself, was recorded in 1785, again in one of the colony's mining regions, at the southern town of Cartago. Set in the Cauca Valley region, where slaves were commonly employed in agriculture and mining, this incident involved an attempt by a small group of slaves to escape from haciendas near the city and to take refuge in the backcountry of the neighbouring Quindío mountains. Despite careful planning, the slaves' intentions were soon frustrated. Acting on information received from the *alcalde* of an Indian village in the hills, an expedition mounted by the slaveowners searched out and recaptured the fugitives within a short time of their escape. Nevertheless, the accounts left by the participants in this expedition, combined with the statements taken from the captured slaves, offer an insight into the project of flight and the commitments and goals which it might involve.[25]

The escape brought together a small group: it included five male slaves, one with his wife, son and nephew, two others with their free *mulata* concubines, and a slave widow together with her son, making up a total complement of fourteen people. Their flight evidently involved much forethought and preparation, not because they were tightly controlled in their movements, but because they were fully aware of the conditions essential to their survival in the wilderness. Thus, when the posse, led by Indian guides, tracked down the fugitives, it found that the slaves had chosen an ideal site for their hideaway. It was located in a heavily wooded area, near a river, where a steeply embanked hillside provided such natural defences that, as one of the pursuers commented, the terrain would soon have enabled the fugitives to create a *palenque* from which not even 'a thousand men' could have removed them. In the event, they were surprised while scattered and, though some mounted a valiant resistance, they were soon overcome.[26]

In the subsequent interrogation of the slaves, it transpired that this site had been chosen well in advance and that some cultivation had already begun before the escape. Indian guides had been contacted, to provide the runaways with help when they arrived in the area, while arms for defence

OUT OF THE HOUSE OF BONDAGE

and hunting, as well as tools for agriculture and mining, had also been gathered prior to departure. The core of the runaway band had formed among seven slaves who lived and worked on the sugar hacienda of the same master; to this core were added four other slaves of different owners, together with the two free *mulatas*. The leader was a 28-year old mulatto slave, Prudencio, who was the captain at his master's sugar mill. He gave the orders, and all were expected to obey without question, or to leave. Prudencio also planned the escape and shaped its purpose.[27]

Each individual had his or her own reason for flight. Prudencio and his wife said that they left because they no longer wished to serve their owner, but had failed, despite two attempts, to find another owner; others said that they had been mistreated, or had escaped to evade punishment for some misdemeanour. But the intention which lay behind the enterprise was not simply to run *from* intolerable or objectionable circumstances; it was to run *to* a new future, establishing a free community in the wilds of the Otún river in the Quindío. There the fugitives planned to live together, plant crops, fish, hunt, prospect for gold, and befriend the 'savage Indians' whom they expected to encounter.

The immediate goal of the runaways was, then, to isolate themselves from white society. But they also discussed more radical proposals. Under questioning, several slaves said that they had discussed plans for allying with the 'savage Indians' to attack Cartago, to kill all the whites, to free their slaves, and to take control of the whole area. They also recalled a more modest proposal for returning to the town in time of fiestas, to bring out the slaves of the *sargento mayor* Gregorio Simon del Campo, some of whose slaves clearly knew of, and had taken part in, the planning of the escape.

Given that the slaves' testimonies were taken under duress, it is difficult clearly to establish the runaways' aims and intentions. Their evidence was recorded in harsh conditions of imprisonment and under the shadow of severe punishment; it may have been distorted by threats, even torture. In these circumstances, the statements given by the slaves may have been manipulated by their interrogators, revealing more about white fears and attitudes than about the slaves' real plans. It is, however, also possible that their testimonies signal the slaves' continued defiance of their captors, revealing not only a commitment to escape from bondage, but also a deep hatred of whites and a belief that it was possible to overcome the system of slavery itself.

In practice, however, it is unlikely that the fugitives were primarily inspired by the hope of raising a general rebellion against slavery in the area. While they may have harboured subversive visions of a society entirely free of slavery, the practical economic opportunities available in a frontier area were, no doubt, a more immediate and important incentive to escape. The slaves were well aware that the mountains and forests of the backlands

CIMARRONES AND PALENQUES 143

offered a space in which they could sustain themselves as free peasants, cultivating their own food crops to sustain their family groups and searching for gold. The prospect of finding gold was, perhaps, a particularly strong inducement to seek a free life on the frontier. Not only was the gold prospector, panning alluvial streams in the wilderness, a clear image of freedom and independence, but slaves in mining areas also knew that gold could buy freedom, through self-purchase. Indeed, some of the fugitives testified that they had hoped to find gold which would permit them to pay their masters for their freedom.[28] Evidently, the slaves' conception of freedom went beyond simple withdrawal from Hispanic society; the economic opportunities available on the frontier encouraged them to see a future in which they would take their place as free people in the wider society, as part of the mainly free population of mestizo and mulatto peasants and prospectors in the region.[29]

Evidence collected in the course of the investigation in Cartago also shows how slaves had developed a subterranean form of social and political organisation which existed within slavery, but which might also harbour subversion and foster a vision of an alternative society, free of white control. It seems that slaves in Cartago had created their own informal and autonomous political system which was at once an imitation, perhaps a burlesque of Hispanic government, and an alternative to it. The captured runaways made repeated reference to the existence of *cabildos* among the slaves of Cartago. Imitating and adapting the institutions of the dominant society, these *cabildos* met annually, at New Year, in the houses of different slaves. They elected a viceroy, a governor, a lieutenant-governor, as well as all the officers of a kind of shadow municipal government. These included an *alférez real*, an *alcalde provincial*, *alguacil mayor*, *depositario general*, two *regidores*, two *alcaldes ordinarios*, two *alcaldes de la Hermandad*, and two *alcaldes pedáneos*. The viceroy and the governor were, it seems, elected for two-year periods, and were, in the words of a slave witness, 'given the corresponding insignia of wooden staffs', with which they displayed their authority to their subjects.[30] The others were elected annually.

The elections were carried out in a festive atmosphere: when the viceroy had been selected, he was received into office, with appropriate celebrations, in the house where he had been elected. The remaining officers each organised entertainments in their own houses, and paid for the costs of refreshment. But the organisation created by the elections also had a serious political purpose. The elected officers had to be obeyed by their fellow slaves, and they maintained a hidden prison, with stocks made from cane, for punishing transgressors.[31]

That the slaves had created a quasi-independent world, which had absorbed elements of the prevailing Hispanic culture, is also apparent in the field of religion. Indeed, the fugitives from Cartago fortified and

144   OUT OF THE HOUSE OF BONDAGE

disciplined, perhaps even legitimated, their escape by recourse to the symbols and practices of Christianity. They took images of Christ and various saints with them on their flight and stated that they had carried these images on their flight for praying and for 'commending themselves to God'.[32] And this was an organised matter: the runaways prayed together every night, around these images, led in the rosary by their leader Prudencio or by one of the other slaves, with the rest forming the 'chorus'.[33] The images also had a part in the slaves' dream of an independent future, for, as two of the fugitives testified, they planned, once established, to build a chapel and to bring a priest from Cartago.[34]

This commitment to the forms of Christian religious practice, like the mimesis of Hispanic political institutions, indicates the extent to which slaves had absorbed and adapted the practices of the dominant culture to meet their own needs, and reflects the existence of a creole, or American slave culture which had developed beyond the African heritage. Evidently, the penetration of Christian beliefs had not necessarily promoted accommodation or fatalistic acceptance of slavery. Instead, as Genovese has observed, adherence to the religion of the slaveowners could become a 'most powerful defence against the dehumanisation implicit in slavery' whereby the slaves, by 'drawing on a religion that was supposed to ensure their compliance and docility, rejected the essence of slavery by projecting their own rights and values as human beings'.[35] While the runaways from Cartago did not claim that Christian beliefs had inspired their escape, their observation of Christian practices and their vision of a future community with its own chapel and priest suggests that, far from being an unalloyed instrument for domination and control, the slaveowners' religion contributed to both the slaves' notion of freedom and their image of life in a free community.

The concatenation of motives and aims found among the Cartago runaways – to escape from bondage, to create a permanent, autonomous community based on subsistence agriculture and mining – may also be discerned in another slave conspiracy uncovered in the city of Cali in 1761.[36] Here, again, the testimonies of imprisoned slaves reveal the formation of a project for collective flight which also envisaged the establishment of an autonomous community. After a long period of planning and persuasion, of clandestine meetings and exchanges of promises, it was ultimately betrayed by a slave informer who overheard discussions of the project.[37]

The conspiracy was originated and led by one Pablo, a mulatto slave who, as a mason and bricklayer, was able to move around the city and neighbouring haciendas and thus to canvass support. Two black brothers, both shadowy figures who appear only indirectly in the investigation, were also said to have been prime movers in the organisation of the escape, until they were sent by their owner to work in the mines of Chocó. Between them, these three men managed, by a combination of cajolery and threats, to

CIMARRONES AND PALENQUES

muster about twenty recruits, all males, for their plan. The conspiracy brought together slaves in the town with slaves in the surrounding rural area, and some attended meetings convened to plan the escape, to choose captains and to discuss their future in freedom.

Their avowed aim was, first, to flee from Cali, taking arms from their masters on a feast day, either that of the Immaculate Conception (December 8) or during Christmas, when their owners would be at church. They then intended to take refuge in the mountains behind Cali and to set up a free community, cultivating its own crops and prospecting for gold. There is, however, also a clear echo of that same hatred for the system of slavery found among the fugitives in Cartago. This time there was no mention of any plan to kill whites, but the mulatto Pablo recalled that he and his co-conspirators had discussed the possibility of raising the blacks in the mines of the Yuramangui river and elsewhere on the Pacific coast in a general rebellion, and seizing all the arms of the mines.[38]

In the end, the plan came to nothing, as those recruited proved reluctant to participate. Some were deterred by sickness (there was an outbreak of 'peste heraya' at the time planned for the escape); some said that they had uncollected debts; others apparently lost confidence in the venture after Pablo's two co-conspirators had been dispatched to the mines.[39] Thus, when the scheme was betrayed by careless talk, it had already been postponed and was probably dissolving. Nonetheless, like the Cartago escape which was also aborted, the Cali plan does reveal something of the attitudes, organisation and aspirations which shaped the project of collective flight.

First, it seems that slaves did not necessarily have to be goaded into flight by bad treatment. In both these episodes, the plans for escape responded to opportunities for becoming independent peasants and prospectors on an open frontier. And, while the runaways aimed to withdraw from slavery, they were evidently concerned with more than simply isolating themselves in an archaic social order, reminiscent of a lost African past. Instead, they thought of becoming gold miners, thereby engaging in an activity which would provide them with the currency required for dealing with, and maintaining independence from, colonial society. In this, the slaves showed their absorption of the economic values of the larger society, and their awareness of how its rules might be used for their own purposes. At the same time, interacting with these practical intentions, there was also the presence of a more profound ideal of freedom: the notion of allying with others, Indians and fellow-slaves, to attack white society and to set free the slaves of an entire region. Here, then, individual notions of freedom as the pursuit of an independent life away from slavery overlapped with a wider, collective conception of freedom that envisaged the elimination of slavery as a system.

Fugitives to Justice

Apart from the type of collective rebellion and group escape considered above, there was another strategy of collective slave protest which also involved flight, but on a more limited scale and with more limited objectives. This arose, as the following examples will show, when slaves ran off in order to achieve group objectives by formal appeal to colonial justice.

This resort to escape as a tactic in a campaign of collective protest is graphically illustrated by the behaviour of slaves who worked on the cattle hacienda of Villavieja, in the province of Neiva, in 1773. This estate – which had a slave population of 89 persons at this time[40] – had belonged to the Jesuits until their expulsion in 1767, when it passed into the hands of an administrator appointed by the royal authorities. With this change of ownership came attempts to alter the work regime of the hacienda which provoked resentment and antagonism from its slaves, and led, in 1773, to the flight of four of them to Bogotá, where they petitioned the viceroy.[41]

The reasons for their flight were plainly stated by the slaves in the petition which they presented to the viceroy. They protested, as 'slaves of His Majesty', that the crown administrator had deprived them of their feast-days, ordered them to cease cultivating their own crops, and defaulted on their customary rations of meat and clothing. Consequently, they called for a change in administrator, or whatever other reform the viceroy might think appropriate to redress their grievances.[42] Despite the ingratiating tone of the petition, the slaves were clearly claiming what they saw to be the rights of their community, invoking custom to denounce change in a campaign of action which had begun with non-cooperation on the hacienda and now culminated in the pursuit of justice from a paternalistic government.

It is also clear that the escape was not a random action by a few individuals, but part of a structured campaign to preserve concessions made within the slave economy, backed by the authority of a recognised group of 'principales', the leaders of an informal slave hierarchy which preceded and paralleled that of the new hacienda administration. In fact, the administrator stated that, in his efforts to control the slaves, he had tried to win over these leaders, allowing them to manage some of the ranches on the hacienda and permitting them the unsupervised use of mules and a horse which they claimed to need for their work.[43] This internal leadership was buttressed by kin relations within the slave community, as several of the leaders were related by family ties.

Thus, in Villavieja the slaves behaved like peasants seeking to protect traditional labour relations rather than as slaves who acknowledged an owner's unquestioned dominion. Their attitude was, moreover, strengthened by the hacienda's free mulatto tenants, who rented land on the estate in return for seasonal labour and who supported the slaves' pre-

CIMARRONES AND PALENQUES

tensions.[44] Though formally enslaved, the slaves evidently did not regard themselves as disposable chattels at the whim of their master. Indeed, the local priest alleged that they were convinced that only the Jesuits were their rightful masters, and that the Jesuits would return 'even from Hell' to restore their just position.[45]

The readiness of slaves to defend concessions which they enjoyed within the slave economy was also at the root of a similar incident which occurred, also on an ex-Jesuit hacienda, in the hot country near Cucutá in 1780.[46] This also involved the flight of a small group of slaves, led by their slave foreman, to Bogotá to petition the viceroy. Their complaint was against the new owner of the hacienda, who had recently bought it from the crown, and who, they claimed, was violating their customary rights and mistreating them with 'excessive' punishments. They did not deny their new master's right to own them, but proffered a series of economic grievances arising from his introduction of new practices to the hacienda. They alleged that he had prevented them from working their own plots of land – of which they said that they were the 'owners' – by depriving them of the free day traditionally reserved for such work. They also complained that the new owner did not pay them for the cacao which they produced on these plots, or paid them at prices lower than the going market rates, and they asked that they be allowed to sell their produce on the open market, or that the owner should pay them fair prices.[47] Evidently, some kind of sharecropping arrangement had developed on the hacienda during the time of Jesuit ownership, which the new owner was now seeking to modify for his own profit. The slaves also complained about the new owner's disciplinary regime. They did not challenge his right to administer corporal punishment, but sought to regulate it by demanding that it should be justified. Finally, after airing their grievances in Bogotá, the slaves returned to the hacienda with an agreement that their case be heard – as it subsequently was – before a group of local citizens commissioned by the viceroy to ensure a fair trial.

Both these episodes indicate that slave runaways were not always concerned with seeking freedom outside of slavery. What they wanted was to preserve a species of freedom within slavery, enabling them to work without mistreatment, to be adequately clothed and fed, to have some freedom of movement, and even to be able to participate in the market economy. This did not necessarily mean that they were uninterested in freedom from their servile status. Indeed, the assertion of the right to work their own plots of land may have arisen from a desire to accumulate money in order to take advantage of the paternalistic legislation of the colonial state in another way, by the purchase of manumission, for themselves or their children. In the short term, however, the goal was not to challenge the system of slavery, but to protect their position within it by collective and concerted action,

148   OUT OF THE HOUSE OF BONDAGE

tenaciously clinging to hard-won, practical privileges which, though they did not amount to freedom, at least provided a meaningful substitute grounded in the needs of everyday existence.

From these brief reconstructions of episodes of slave flight in eighteenth-century Colombia, some general observations and conclusions may be drawn. The cases presented above suggest, first, that slave runaways may be grouped into two broad categories. One of these consisted of slaves who ran off – individually or collectively – in order to ameliorate, to change, or to regulate their treatment within slavery. This includes cases of flight which arose from slave infractions of disciplinary or legal codes, and where slaves escaped to avoid punishment from either their masters or the law. This category also includes episodes in which slaves ran off, not because they had transgressed rules, but because they believed that their masters had done so. Rather than flight *from* the justice of slaveowners or the state, this was flight *to* justice, embodied in legislation which regulated slave–master relations and guaranteed minimal rights for slaves. Thus, while the corpus of Hispanic legislation concerning slaves included harsh provisions for punishing runaways, it also incorporated paternalist measures which might act as an inducement to, and a justification for flight.

The second broad category of runaways was made up of those slaves who, individually and in groups, sought to rebel against slavery by permanently escaping to freedom. This form of action represented a more direct resistance to the system of slavery. Not only did it envisage a total break with bondage, but, when undertaken by groups of slaves, it also enshrined a dream of free life in autonomous communities living beyond the reach of the slaveowners and their state. This kind of marronage was, in a general sense, heir to the *cimarrones* and *palenques* of the early colonial period, first constituted by Africans who rebelled against slavery on their arrival and established the original Maroon communities on Colombia's Caribbean coast. Basically, the slaves who planned or participated in the establishment of runaway communities were moved by motives similar to those of their predecessors. They sought freedom by creating autonomous communities in isolation from and in opposition to the demands of servitude. In this sense, the *palenque* of Los Remedios, described above, was the lineal descendant of the *palenques* of sixteenth-century Cartagena. The project and practice of *palenques* in the eighteenth century, however, also differed in some important respects from those of their predecessors, in both their organisation and aims.

First, they were much less likely to seek to recreate the African traditions of social and economic organisation found in the early Maroon communities of the province of Cartagena. The plans of the Cali and Cartago slaves suggest, instead, the presence of different models, nurtured in an American

CIMARRONES AND PALENQUES

rather than an African experience. These slaves built their plans for freedom, not on the memory of an African past, but on the experience of a colonial present. Rather than isolating themselves in self-sustaining agricultural communities based on African ethnic groupings, they sought to become free peasants and gold prospectors, exploiting the economic opportunities which mining and agricultural frontiers offered to the majority population of mestizos and mulattoes. And, if the slaves' testimonies are to be believed, both these conspiracies, small though they were, also incorporated a more formidable ideal. Realising, perhaps, that the only ultimate guarantee of freedom was an end to slavery, they envisioned alliance with other slaves in regional insurrections which would overturn the power of local slaveowners. In this sense, the eighteenth-century plots presented here may point to an underlying change in slave consciousness, signalling an advance from a notion of freedom that was 'restorationist' towards a broader conception that imagined, even if it could not achieve, an attack on the structure of slave society itself.

It is difficult, however, to detect the stirrings of any general or substantial movement of slave rebellion in late colonial Colombia. Large-scale rebellions were extremely rare and, with due respect to Jaramillo's opposite view, *palenques* were small, transient and few in number. Several factors inhibited slave rebelliousness. First, the very dispersion of the slave population, both between and within regions, was undoubtedly an impediment to rebellion. Slaves in the Pacific mining areas, for instance, were not only separated from those of other provinces by vast distances of difficult, mountainous terrain, but their distribution in small communities scattered over large areas hindered any systematic effort to build fugitive communities or to overturn slavery.[48] Linked with this dispersion of the slave population over the expanses of diversified regional economies, there were also other elements of the colonial environment which inhibited rebellion. Most slaves lived in areas where they were considerably outnumbered by whites and '*libres de todos colores*' (free people of all colours), and therefore faced very uneven odds in any conflict with slaveowners. And, given the decline of slave imports in this period, the proportion of Africans to local-born slaves was steadily diminishing.[49] More slaves were, therefore, born into bondage and socialised in its ways.

This did not efface the vision of freedom, but made its pursuit more complex and variegated. As we have seen, some runaways sought to break with slavery completely. Others had more limited goals, which suggests that slaves had learned to come to terms with the system in different ways, concentrating their resources on building a life within slavery, protecting the concessions which they had gained from it, and using paternalist legislation both to defend their position within it and, at times, to purchase their manumission from it. Between these extremes, recourse to flight was, in all

150 OUT OF THE HOUSE OF BONDAGE

dignity, claim their rights and, in the widest sense, to construct the world in which they lived.

NOTES

1. Leslie B. Rout, *The African Experience in Spanish America* (Cambridge University Press 1976), p.95.
2. On the slave trade through Cartagena, see Jorge Palacios Preciado, *La Trata de Negros por Cartagena de Indias, 1650–1750* (Tunja 1973), *passim*; Colin Palmer, *Human Cargoes: The British Slave Trade to Spanish America, 1700–1739* (Chicago, University of Illinois Press 1981), pp.97–111.
3. German Colmenares, *Historia económica y social de Colombia, 1537–1719* (Cali, Universidad del Valle 1973), pp.203–16; Robert C. West, *Colonial Placer Mining in Colombia* (Baton Rouge, Louisiana State University Press 1953), pp.9–51, 78–101.
4. These and subsequent calculations of the slave population in colonial Colombia are based on the 'Padrón General del Virreinato del Nuevo Reino de Granada (1778–1780)', reproduced in J. M. Pérez Ayala, *Antonio Caballero y Góngora, Virrey y arzobispo de Santa Fe, 1723–1796* (Bogotá, 1951), Cuadro A.
5. On the use of slaves in agriculture, see Hermes Tovar Pinzón, *Grandes empresas agrícolas y ganaderas* (Bogotá, Ediciones CEIC 1980), pp.41–63; German Colmenares, *Historia económica y social de Colombia, II: Popayán, una sociedad esclavista, 1680–1810* (Bogotá, 1979) *passim*; on slaves in a mining economy, see W. F. Sharp, *Slavery on the Spanish Frontier: The Colombian Chocó, 1680–1810* (Oklahoma University Press, 1976), *passim*.
6. Jaime Jaramillo Uribe, 'Esclavos y señores en la sociedad colombiana del siglo XVIII' in his *Ensayos sobre Historia Social Colombiana* (Bogotá, Universidad Nacional de Colombia 1969), p.60.
7. Ibid., p.77.
8. Roberto Arrozola, *Palenque, primer pueblo libre de America: Historia de las sublevaciones de las esclavos de Cartagena* (Cartagena, 1970), pp.11–29; Richard Price (ed.), *Maroon Societies: Rebel Slave Communities in the Americas* (New York, 1973), pp.74–5.
9. Jaime Jaramillo Uribe, *Ensayos*, pp.61–2.
10. María del Carmen Borrego Pla, *Palenques de negros en Cartagena de Indias a fines del siglo XVII* (Seville, 1973), *passim*.
11. Ibid., pp.123–4.
12. Ibid., pp.44–55; 121–7.
13. Richard Price (ed.), *Maroon Societies*, p.79.
14. German Colmenares, *Historia económica y social de Colombia, II*, pp.104–5.
15. Archivo Histórico Nacional de Colombia (hereinafter AHNC), Negros y Esclavos (Cundinamarca), tomo 4, folios 342–53.
16. AHNC, Negros y Esclavos (Cauca), tomo 3, fo. 997–1000.
17. On the recourse of slaves to such legislation, see David L. Chandler, 'Slave over Master in Colonial Colombia and Ecuador', *The Americas*, vol. 38, 1981–1982, pp.315–26.
18. Archivo Histórico Nacional (Madrid), Inquisición, legajo 1623 (1), no. 12.
19. AHNC, Negros y Esclavos (Magdalena) tomo 3, fo. 911–31.
20. Ibid., fo. 921–5.
21. AHNC, Negros y Esclavos (Cauca), tomo 3, fo. 603–85.
22. Ibid., fo. 635.
23. Ibid., fo. 680.
24. Ibid., fo. 647–8.
25. AHNC, Negros y Esclavos (Cauca), tomo 3, fo. 1–265.
26. Ibid., fo. 5–13.
27. Ibid., fo. 13–36.
28. Ibid., fo. 33, 37.

CIMARRONES AND PALENQUES

29. The population of Cartago in 1778 was as follows: 1,169 whites, 134 Indians, 2,257 freemen of all colours, 763 slaves. AHNC, Censos de varios departamentos, tomo 6, fo. 375.
30. AHNC, Negros y Esclavos (Cauca), tomo 3, fo. 27.
31. Ibid., fo. 24, 27.
32. Ibid., fo. 23, 25, 28, 31, 37.
33. Ibid., fo. 23.
34. Ibid., fo. 23, 33.
35. Eugene Genovese, *Roll, Jordan, Roll: The World the Slaves Made* (New York, Vintage Books 1976), p. 7.
36. The population of Cali in 1778 was as follows: 934 whites; 330 Indians; 7,120 freemen of all colours, 2,606 slaves. AHNC, Censos de varios departamentos, tomo 6, fo. 375.
37. AHNC, Negros y Esclavos (Cauca), tomo 2, fo. 489–503.
38. Ibid., fo. 498.
39. Ibid., fo. 500.
40. German Colmenares, *Las Haciendas de los Jesuitas en el Nuevo Reino de Granada* (Bogotá, Universidad Nacional de Colombia 1969), p. 96.
41. AHNC, Negros y Esclavos (Tolima), tomo 3, fo. 996–1048.
42. Ibid., fo. 998–9.
43. Ibid., fo. 1008–9.
44. Ibid., fo. 1011.
45. Ibid., fo. 1009–10.
46. AHNC, Negros y Esclavos (Santander), tomo 3, fo. 880–935.
47. Ibid., fo. 880, 893–914.
48. William F. Sharp, *Slavery on the Spanish Frontier*, pp. 155–60.
49. German Colmenares, *Historia económica y social*, II, p. 227; Adolfo Meisel R., 'Esclavitud, mestizaje y haciendas en la provincia de Cartagena, 1538–1851', *Desarrollo y Sociedad*, no. 4 (Bogotá, 1980), pp. 252–3.

The author wishes to thank the British Academy for financial assistance that enabled him to undertake research in Colombia.

The Maroons of Jamaica, 1730–1830: Livelihood, Demography and Health*

Richard B. Sheridan

I

The Maroons were communities of ex-slaves who had escaped from the plantations and found refuge in the rugged interior parts of colonies. Here they lived by hunting wild game, growing food crops, and raiding plantations. Though small in number by comparison with the slaves, the Maroons were sufficiently numerous to harass and threaten the European slave-owning colonists. They raided plantations to acquire metal goods, cloth, salt, and other goods they were not able to produce themselves. Moreover, since they were predominantly male communities they raided plantations to acquire women, at the same time that they provided a refuge for runaway slaves. Colonial governments reacted to the Maroon menace by sending militia parties and European regiments into the backcountry on search and destroy missions. The Maroons, however, proved to be superb guerrilla fighters, laying ambushes and picking off the white troops as they marched through narrow passes in the mountains. The Maroons, on the other hand, were vulnerable to sustained campaigns which included the destruction of their provision grounds and the use of Amerindian guerrillas and bloodhounds. When long campaigns against the Maroons led to stalemate, the contending parties entered into treaties which accorded extra-territorial rights to the Maroons in return for their promise to return runaway slaves to their masters and join in defending the colony against foreign aggressors.[1]

It is the purpose of this article to trace by means of surviving census and other data the demographic and health experience of the Maroons of Jamaica. It will be instructive to see how this experience differed from that of plantation slaves. Both the Maroons and slaves were of African origin or descent and lived at least part of their lives in Jamaica. However, both

---

* Research for this article was supported in part by the National Institutes of Health Grant No. LM-01539 from the National Library of Medicine. I am indebted to Dr George Cumper for permission to use extracts and tables from his 'The Demographic Balance of the Maroon Communities in Jamaica, 1799–1830', unpublished paper presented at the Fourth Conference of Caribbean Historians, University of the West Indies, Mona, Kingston, Jamaica, 9–14 April 1972. I also wish to thank Ms Deborah Dandridge for help in researching this article.

JAMAICA, SHOWING THE MAIN AREAS OF MAROON SETTLEMENT
Parish Boundaries are the present ones.

Reproduced from Carey Robinson: *The Fighting Maroons of Jamaica*, by permission of William Collins.

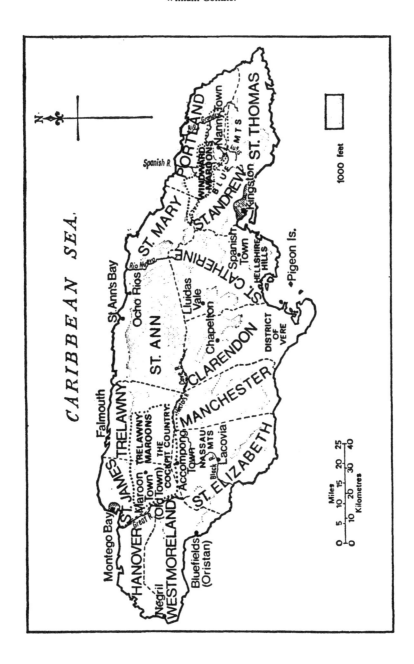

154   OUT OF THE HOUSE OF BONDAGE

groups of blacks lived in parts of the island which were markedly different in their physiographic characteristics and disease environments. Moreover, while the dominant group of blacks lived at the margin of subsistence and produced surplus agricultural staples for their masters, their brothers and sisters in the backcountry were free to roam the woods and mountains in search of game and confine their sedentary agricultural labour to the growing of foodstuffs for local consumption. It will be our task to show how these and other differences affected the health and demographic performance of the Maroons and slaves.

The Arawaks, the original inhabitants of Jamaica, were enslaved by the Spaniards who settled the island in 1609 and were totally exterminated by 1655. They were replaced by African slaves who at the time of the English conquest of 1655 numbered about fifteen hundred, and were nearly equal to the whites.[2] Before the Spaniards withdrew from the island they freed their slaves and armed them to fight the English. Some of these black guerrillas remained unconquered in the hills and mountains. Maroon settlements expanded as more and more slaves escaped from the English plantations. In the period from 1655 to 1739, writes Barbara Kopytoff,

> The English settled the valleys and flatlands, cleared them of forests, established large sugar plantations, and by the 1680s were importing thousands of African slaves each year to do the work. In the interior, those slaves who had escaped grew steadily in numbers, cleared their own planting areas, and formed settlements in the remote woods and mountains. New bands of maroons were constantly formed by runaway and rebellious slaves from the plantations; these fought with the older bands, or joined them, or tried to avoid them.[3]

In time the Maroons formed settlements in different parts of the island. Those to windward settled in the rugged Blue Mountains which rise to 6,000 to 7,000 feet, while those to leeward eventually settled in the west-central part of the island in the Cockpit Country, which consists of a succession of sinkholes, jagged rocks, and dense vegetation where alluvial soil is deposited.

As islands of freedom in a sea of slavery, the Maroons sought maximum security by establishing their communities in inaccessible areas and organizing on rigid military lines. The famous Cudjoe who commanded the Leeward Maroons was said by an anonymous Jamaican to have exercised his captains and their respective men in the use of small arms and the lance. He led 'the bold and active in Robbing the Planta[tions] of Slaves, Arms, Ammunition Etc., Hunting wild hogs, and to direct the rest with the Women in Planting Provisions – and Managing Domestic Affairs'. Moreover, the same writer said that 'In all plunderings they were Industrious in procuring Negro Women, Girls, and Female Children'. While such raiding

THE MAROONS OF JAMAICA, 1730–1830   155

may have eased the problem, it did not solve it. Kopytoff says the sexual imbalance continued. To avoid the threat to unity and to encourage reproduction, both the Windward and Leeward Maroons had rules regulating men's access to women which point to the granting and sharing of sexual rights by men.[6]

The expansion of the slave plantation economy was paralleled by the growth of Maroon settlements and growing friction between the two communities until internecine warfare culminated in what is often known as the First Maroon War in the decade of the 1730s. The Maroons, to a greater extent than formerly, took advantage of the cover of darkness to steal into frontier plantations where they set fire to cane-fields and outhouses, killed cattle, and carried off slaves and other moveables. Being highly mobile and elusive, they were adept at concealing themselves from pursuit. By 1737 the Maroons had grown very formidable in six frontier parishes of Jamaica where the whites 'greatly suffered by the frequent robberies, murders, and depredations committed by them'. They had 'large settlements among the mountains, and least accessible parts', from whence 'they plundered all around them, and caused several plantations to be thrown up and abandoned, and prevented many valuable tracts of land from being cultivated ...'.[7]

The forces marshalled against the Maroons consisted of militia companies, British regiments, Mosquito Indian guerrilla fighters, companies of black troops, together with 'baggage negroes' and dogs. Lieutenant Philip Thicknesse told of one search and destroy mission in which he participated. The military force marched towards the head of a river where a Maroon settlement was supposed to be situated. After a march of three days they came to a spot where the footprints of men and dogs were visible. Thinking they were near a Maroon settlement they camped for the night and prepared to attack early next morning by surprise. To their disappointment the town had been abandoned. Thicknesse said it was not a principal town but a temporary fishing and hunting village which was 'situated on the margin of a river, accessible every way, and consequently not tenable'. The inhabitants, who had been alerted to the approaching troops, had gone off in the night, leaving seventy-four huts and a fire burning in each. Putting the town to the torch, the soldiers followed the trail cut by the Maroons. 'At every half mile', Thicknesse wrote, 'we found *Cocoes, Yams, Plantains*, &c. left artfully by the Negroes, to induce us to believe, they were in fear of our overtaking them, and at length we found a fire, before which they had left several *grills* of wild hogs, *probably well seasoned for us*'. The military force continued the pursuit till near night, and then, hearing the dogs bark they concluded the Maroons had heard them also, and gave up all hopes of seeing or hearing anything more of them.[8]

By 1738 a stalemate had been reached in the internecine warfare. The

156 OUT OF THE HOUSE OF BONDAGE

provision grounds upon which the Maroons chiefly depended for their sustenance had been systematically destroyed by the Mosquito Indians and black troops. Captain Cudjoe, finding his refuge in the Clarendon Hills untenable, had retreated with his followers into the Cockpit Country, where wild hogs, goats, and plenty of pigeons were to be found.[9] The white inhabitants of the island wanted relief from 'the horrors of continual alarms, the hardships of military duty, and the intolerable burthen of maintaining the army'.[10] No less anxious for an accommodation were the Maroons, who, according to Edward Long, the planter-historian,

> were hemmed in and closely beset on all sides; their provisions destroyed; and themselves reduced to so miserable a condition by famine and incessant attacks, that Cudjoe (whom I conversed with many years afterwards) declared, if peace had not been offered to them, they had no choice left but either to be starved, lay violent hands on one another, or surrender to the English at discretion.[11]

Governor Edward Trelawny, by the advice of the principal whites, proposed overtures of peace to the Maroon chiefs. The treaty was concluded with Captain Cudjoe, head of the Trelawny Town or Leeward Maroons on 1 March 1738, and with Captain Quao, head of the Windward Maroons on 23 June 1739.[12]

The treaty of 1738 called for all hostilities to cease on both sides forever. The Maroons were granted lands lying between Trelawny Town and the Cockpits to the amount of 1,500 acres where they were to reside permanently. On this land they had liberty to plant

> cocoa, ginger, tobacco, and cotton, and to breed cattle, hogs, goats, or any other stock, and dispose of the produce or increase of the said commodities to the inhabitants of this island; provided always, that when they bring the said commodities to market, they shall apply first to the custos, or any other magistrate of the respective parishes where they expose their goods to sale, for a licence to vend the same.[13]

Moreover, Captain Cudjoe and his people were granted liberty to hunt where they saw fit, except within three miles of any settlement where, if they met hunters from the settlement, the hogs were to be equally divided between the two parties. Cudjoe promised military aid to colonial forces in repelling foreign invaders and putting down internal rebellion. Another clause provided that 'if any negroes shall hereafter run away from their masters or owners, and fall into Captain Cudjoe's hands, they shall immediately be sent back to the chief magistrate of the next parish where they are taken; and those that bring them are to be satisfied for their trouble, as the legislature shall appoint'. Other clauses of the treaty provided for the administration of justice, the appointment of a white superintendent to

THE MAROONS OF JAMAICA, 1730–1830   157

reside with the Maroons in order to maintain a friendly correspondence with the inhabitants of the island, and a plan of succession as commander in chief upon the death of Cudjoe. The treaty with the Windward Maroons was to much the same purport as that made with Cudjoe.[14]

The treaties brought an end to hostilities which had continued for upwards of forty years, during which time forty-four acts of the assembly had been passed and at least £240,000 expended in suppressing the Maroons.[15] In concluding his account of the First Maroon War, Robert Charles Dallas said that 'A small body of negroes defied the choicest troops of one of the greatest nations in the world, kept an extensive country in alarm, and were at length brought to surrender, only by means of a subvention still more extraordinary than their own mode of warfare'.[16]

II

Maroon population statistics point to a falling off in number in the decade following the treaties. Governor Trelawny wrote to the Duke of Newcastle that at the time of the treaties the Windward Maroons numbered 490 as they were counted 'by notches on a stick'. In the same letter the Leeward Maroons were said to have had 'about the same number' as the Windward Maroons.[17] From a total of approximately 980 in 1739, the Maroon population, as shown in Table 1, declined to 664 in 1749.

TABLE 1
MAROON POPULATION OF JAMAICA, 1749

	Men	Women	Boys	Girls	Total
Trelawny Town	112	85	40	39	276
Crawford or Charles Town	102	80	26	25	233
Accompong Town	31	25	13	16	85
Nanny or Moore Town	28	21	9	12	70
Total	273	211	88	92	664

Source: Edward Long, *The History of Jamaica* (London, 1774), II, 347.

Edward Long wrote that although they occupied more towns than at first, the Maroons were 'diminished in their numbers by deaths, and cohabitation with slaves on the plantations, instead of inter-mixing with each other'.[18] The fact that there were 62 more men than women in 1749 may go far to explain why the men cohabited with slaves on the plantations. Besides the male dominance, Table 1 shows an abnormally low proportion of children in the Maroon population. Kopytoff believes the post-treaty population decrease was no short-term phenomenon. Owing to such factors as sexual imbalance and the hardships of life in the bush during the long war with the

158   OUT OF THE HOUSE OF BONDAGE

English, it seems very likely that the Maroons were not naturally repro-
ducing during the half century prior to the treaties.[19]

TABLE 2

MAROON POPULATION OF JAMAICA, 1773

	Men	Women	('Breeding Women')	Boys[1]	Girls[2]	Children[3]	Total
Trelawny Town	121	140	n.d.	27	11	115	414
Charles Town	55	80	n.d.	14	21	49	219
Moore Town	32	52	n.d.	4	11	23	143
Accompong Town	29	39	n.d.	4	11	20	103
Scott's Hall	14	17	n.d.	4	2	12	49
Total	251	328	(289)	71	59	219	928

Notes: 1. All boys aged 9 to 14 years, except for Charles Town where they ranged from 7 to 13
years.
2. Same age ranges for girls as for boys.
3. All male and female children from 3 months to 9 years of age, except for Charles
Town where they ranged from 1 to 6 years.

Source: *Journals of the Assembly of Jamaica*, Vol. VI, 26 November 1773, pp. 464–466.

Whereas the decade following the treaties witnessed a decline in the Maroon
population, a comparison of Tables 1 and 2 shows an increase from 664 in
1749 to 928 in 1773. Presumably this was a natural increase in the population because the Maroons no longer harboured runaway slaves. On the
contrary, they were paid approximately two pounds a head by the island
government for capturing and returning runaways to their owners.[20] It is
significant that while the men decreased from 273 to 251 from 1749 to 1773,
the women increased in the same period from 211 to 328, of whom 289 were
'breeding women'. In 1749, boys and girls made up 27.1 per cent of the
Maroon population, whereas, in 1773, boys, girls and children comprised
37.6 per cent. The census of 1773 is incomplete since it omits infants aged
less than three months in four of the Maroon towns and children under one
year in Charles Town.

III

The Second Maroon War which broke out in the summer of 1795 involved
only the Trelawny Town Maroons and was concluded after a struggle of
about five months. It was caused by an accumulation of grievances, chiefly
the appointment of a white superintendent who was disliked by the
Maroons, the indignity suffered by the Maroons when two of them were
accused of hog stealing by the authorities in Montego Bay and allowed to be
publicly whipped by a runaway slave, and the Maroons' complaints that
they lacked sufficient land to sustain their growing population.

According to Michael Craton, 'the most fundamental and difficult complaint of the Trelawny Maroons concerned the shortage of land'. They were increasingly hemmed in by white settlements as the plantation frontier advanced to the perimeter of their homelands. The conflict over the use of cultivable lands involved not only the Maroons and white proprietors but also Maroon-related slaves and slaves without Maroon relatives who competed for the provision grounds on the margins of plantations. Destruction of provision grounds was carried to great lengths in the war of attrition which followed.[21]

The turbulence among the Trelawny Maroons occurred at a time when Britain and France were at war, and when the French Revolution had extended to the great French colony of Saint Domingue where the slaves had risen in massive rebellion against their masters. Fearing that French agents had infected the Maroons with their revolutionary doctrines, the governor and assembly of Jamaica reacted by using ruthless measures to intimidate and suppress the dissident Maroons and thus stamp out any troubles that could escalate into island-wide servile war.[22]

The Earl of Balcarres, who arrived in Jamaica as governor in April 1795, believed that French agents were at the bottom of the Maroon rebellion. After negotiations between a group of planters and the Trelawny Maroons broke down, a council of war was held and Balcarres was given the power of martial law. He ordered the 83rd Regiment of Foot of over one thousand men as well as smaller military units to Montego Bay. He also sent a fast boat after a group of ships carrying troops to Saint Domingue, in order to divert them to Montego Bay. To the British troops were added white militia units, black troops and baggage slaves to create a force far more numerous than the estimated 660 Maroons of all ages at Trelawny Town.[23]

Balcarres shifted his headquarters from Spanish Town to an estate near Trelawny Town to better direct the military campaign. On 16 November he described the rugged terrain his troops faced in a letter to the Duke of Portland, Secretary of State for the Colonies:

> The scene of our action is more tremendous than can possibly be described: mountains rising one above the other, almost perpendicular from the base, all covered with wood, the surface everywhere sharp and rugged, each mountain detached and only separated from the next by a narrow defile or glade, which being daily watered by the rains produces an inexhaustible supply of ground provisions. Bold as the scenery is, Nature has exerted herself in producing something still more astonishing. In the heart of this wonderful country, the mountains change their appearance. Losing nothing in their perpendicular height, they become stupendous honey-combed rocks undermined into an innumerable range of caves, some of which are near two miles

160 OUT OF THE HOUSE OF BONDAGE

in length. Immediately adjacent to these terrible retreats have the Maroons fixed and established themselves for ages.[24]

Some two decades earlier Edward Long had written that in the parish of St James the settlements reached between 13 and 14 miles back from the sea, but that behind them there were 'one hundred thousand acres, or upwards, yet uninhabited, except for the Maroon Negroes, of Furry's and Trelawny Towns'.[25]

Believing that the Maroons would be intimidated by the powerful force arrayed against them, Balcarres sent a message to the Trelawnys on 8 August ordering them to surrender not later than 12 August. He notified them that every pass to their town had been occupied and guarded and that they were surrounded by thousands of militia and regular troops. Failure to obey the summons would result in the burning of their town and putting into force his proclamation offering a reward for their heads. When only 37 elderly Maroons surrendered and the others prepared to fight, Balcarres gave orders to build a chain of blockhouses around the Cockpit Country and to send military forces on search and destroy missions. The Trelawnys took advantage of their unsurpassed knowledge of the terrain and their courage and skill as guerrilla fighters to ambush two of these forces with numerous deaths and casualties.[26]

On 26 September the speaker of the house of assembly at Spanish Town read an address from Governor Balcarres in which he stated his reasons for detaining the troops intended for Saint Domingue. He observed that the country possessed by the Trelawny Maroons was most difficult of access, that they had it in their power to concentrate with facility the smaller Maroon nations, and could also give security and protection to such slaves as might be disposed to join them in rebellion. That the Trelawnys were prepared for a long campaign is evident from Balcarres' statement that they had 'provided ground provisions in sufficient quantities for the maintenance of some thousand men, and their rear was secured by their cockpits and fastnesses'.[27]

Balcarres' plan was to hem in the Maroons by destroying their provision grounds and wait for them to be driven out by starvation. Accordingly, large numbers of slaves were employed to destroy the Trelawnys' provision grounds at the same time that the chain of posts around the Cockpit Country was strengthened in order to stop the Maroons from obtaining food from nearby plantations. Planters were compensated for destroyed provisions. For example, the assembly of Jamaica voted £190. 0. 0. on 4 November 1796 for 20 acres of corn, yams, plantains, cocoas and peas destroyed by order of Colonel Sandford on Spring-Vale Pen, the property of William Atherton.[28]

Although the Maroons were said to be in a starving condition, they gave

THE MAROONS OF JAMAICA, 1730–1830   161

no sign that they were ready to surrender. In fact, the British lost three regiments in a few months chiefly because of ambushes and surprise attacks. In desperation Balcarres and the assembly sent to Cuba for forty *chasseurs* (dog handlers) and 104 trained and partly-trained dogs. Fear of these vicious animals was sufficient to induce the Maroons to sue for peace.[29]

In the end over 590 Trelawny Maroons were transported from Jamaica to Nova Scotia in 1796. Seventeen of them died on the voyage and others perished from exposure to the cold climate. After suffering untold hardships, the survivors were transported from Nova Scotia to their ancestral home in Sierra Leone in 1800.[30]

IV

Thomas Fowell Buxton, the abolition leader, gave testimony on the progress of the Maroon population in Jamaica before the Select Committee of the House of Lords in 1832. He noted that, according to the *Jamaica Almanack*, the Maroon population increased from 893 in 1810, to 1,037 in 1818, 1,094 in 1821, 1,160 in 1824, 1,242 in 1827, and 1,452 in 1832, of whom, however, 145 were stated to be non-resident.[31] Buxton submitted an official return of the Maroons as of 1 July 1824, together with the slaves they owned. This is shown in Table 3. Buxton explained that by an act of 1792 the Maroons were prohibited from adding to the number of their slaves under a penalty of forfeiture of any slaves they might purchase and a fine of £100 on anyone who should sell them a slave. He believed that the slaves held by the Maroons in 1824 were either the same or the descendants of the same who were held in 1792.[32] According to Table 4 below, the slaves owned by the Maroons increased to 124 in 1830.

TABLE 3

MAROON POPULATION OF 1824, TOGETHER WITH
THE SLAVES WHICH THEY OWNED

Maroon Town	*Maroons*	*Slaves*
Moore Town	438	49
Accompong Town	295	14
Scott's Hall	68	1
Charles Town	365	–
Total	1,166	64

Source: Enclosed in a Dispatch from the Duke of Manchester, Governor of Jamaica, 9 Sept. 1824, *Parliamentary Paper* No. 66, 1825.

Buxton believed that the real rate of increase among the Maroons was greater than was indicated by the census returns shown in the *Jamaica*

162   OUT OF THE HOUSE OF BONDAGE

Almanack. He explained that the full enfranchisement of the free coloured class in 1830 had 'led many Maroons to renounce their Rights as Maroons, and to exchange them for these superior Rights now enjoyed by the Free People of Colour'. Moreover, Buxton believed that Protestant missionary activity among the Maroons had the effect of accelerating their change of status. He singled out the years from 1817 to 1829 as indicating the true rate of progress. During that period the Maroon population had increased from 1,031 to 1,334, or nearly 30 per cent.[33]

Buxton then summarized the demographic experience of the slaves, noting that

> During the whole of the same Period [1817 to 1829] the Slave Population was diminishing in Jamaica; increasing perhaps among certain Portions of them, as Domestics and the Slaves employed in breeding Cattle; but materially diminishing on the whole, and more especially on Sugar Estates. On the Sugar Estates in Plantain Garden River District, in St. Thomas in the East, the Decrease in Twelve Years was nearly Thirteen per Cent; while on the Coffee Estates in the same District there was an Increase, in the same Time, of a small Fraction more than One per Cent.

Had the slave population increased at the same rate as that of the Maroons from 1817 to 1829, there would have been a total of 447,782 instead of the actual number of 322,421, or a difference in the 12-year period of 125,361. 'Thus', Buxton concluded, 'there has been a Waste of Human Life, among the enslaved Negroes of Jamaica, as compared with the Rate of Increase of the lowest Class of the emancipated Negroes in that Island, which is altogether appalling, and is only credible when thus demonstrated by the infallible Rules of Arithmetical Calculation'.[34]

A more systematic analysis of Maroon population data is afforded by an unpublished paper written by economist George Cumper. He has drawn on the annual returns of the population which the superintendents of the Maroon communities were required to submit annually to the Assembly of Jamaica from 1799 to 1841. These returns covered the communities of Moore Town, Charles Town, Scott's Hall, and Accompong Town, and supply age and sex specific data on the Maroon population, the number of slaves and strangers in the towns, and the number of births and deaths since the last return. Population totals in the years 1799, 1810, 1820 and 1830 are shown in Table 4.[35]

Although the data suffer from certain defects, Cumper attempts to overcome these defects and construct a consistent and plausible set of vital rates for the Maroon communities. Since the Maroons did not regard children as members of the group until they reached an age when their survival was assured, the returns for those under five years are clearly defective and

THE MAROONS OF JAMAICA, 1730–1830

TABLE 4
MAROONS LIVING IN TOWNS AND OUTSIDE TOWNS, AND
SLAVES AND STRANGERS LIVING IN MAROON TOWNS, 1799–1830

| Year | Maroons Living in Towns | | | Outside Towns | Maroons Slaves | Strangers |
	Male	Female	Total			
1799	375	379	754	39	42	–
1810	428	426	854	85	58	–
1820	446	480	926	158	105	55
1830	551	572	1,123	157	124	111

Source: George Cumper, 'The Demographic Balance of the Maroon Communities in Jamaica, 1799–1830', unpublished paper presented at the Fourth Conference of Caribbean Historians, Mona, Jamaica, 9–14 April 1972. Data for the above table are published in *Votes, House of Assembly of Jamaica*, 1799, p. 131 and Appendix No. 5; 1810, p. 97 and Appendix No. 38; 1820, p. 113 and Appendix No. 42; 1829/30, pp. 110–111 and Appendix No. 44.

those under one year are rarely recorded. 'The returns of deaths are also fragmentary', writes Cumper; 'they imply a crude death rate of 19 per thousand, which is not impossible but cannot be taken as a satisfactory estimate'. Cumper corrects the data for the lower ages and estimates birth and death rates by various procedures, one of which is to assume that the Maroon rates for the 1799–1830 period were the same as those recorded for the entire population of Jamaica in 1881 when a similar structure obtained. Cumper's best estimate is a Maroon birth rate of about 47 per thousand and a death rate (excluding outmigration) of about 30 per thousand.[36]

V

Two Jamaican planter-historians commented at some length on the economic and social life of the Maroons, noting that their character and mode of life differed markedly from that of plantation slaves. In the 1801 edition of his *History of the British West Indies*, Bryan Edwards included an appendix entitled 'Observations on the Disposition, Character, Manners, and Habits of Life, of the Maroon Negroes of the Island of Jamaica; and a Detail of the Origin, Progress, and Termination of the late War between those People and the White Inhabitants'. Much more substantial was Robert Charles Dallas' *The History of the Maroons*, a two-volume work published in London in 1803. The author, who was a close friend of the poet Byron, was descended from an old Jamaican family and lived in the island for several years. Considering the pervasive myth of the noble savage, it may be surmised that these authors are prone to romanticize the lifestyle of the Maroons. Nevertheless, their descriptive accounts are generally consistent with those of Maroon societies in other colonial territories.[37]

164   OUT OF THE HOUSE OF BONDAGE

Maroon agriculture, according to Edwards, was practised in a slovenly manner by a people who had no inclination for the pursuit of sober industry. Those who lived in the neighbourhood of plantations belonging to whites were said to have either purchased or stolen yams, plantains, corn and other esculents. When they had no supply of this kind, Edwards said he had 'sometimes observed small patches of Indian corn and yams, and perhaps a few straggling plantain trees, near their habitations; but the ground was always in a shocking state of neglect and ruin'. He deplored the spirit of brutality which the Maroons displayed towards their wives and also in some degree towards their children. Some of the principal men had from two to six wives whose miserable situation left them neither leisure nor inclination to quarrel with each other. In fact, Edwards asserted that the Maroons regarded their wives as so many beasts of burden. The labours of the field were performed by the women, 'who had no other means of clearing the ground of the vast and heavy woods with which it is every where incumbered, than by placing fire round the trunks of the trees till they were consumed in the middle, and fall by their own weight'.[38]

Dallas sought to refute Edwards' statements that agriculture was neglected and that Maroon men mistreated their women and children. He contended that while the Maroons placed a considerable dependence on hunting and on their rewards for taking runaway slaves, they did not neglect the cultivation of land and were by no means so averse to the toil it demanded as Edwards had represented. On the contrary, their provision grounds

> produced a stock not only sufficient for their own use, but so superabundant as to enable them to supply the neighbouring settlements. Plantain, Indian corn or maize, yams, cocoas, toyaus, and in short all the nutritious roots that thrive in tropic soils, were cultivated in their grounds. In their gardens grew most of the culinary vegetables, and they were not without some fine fruits: for though to these, in general, the soil of their mountains was unfavourable, being either moist or clayey, yet they had some valuable fruit-trees, among which the Avocado, or Alligator-pear, ranked foremost. Mammees, and other wild but delicious fruits, were at their hand, and pine-apples grew in their hedges. They bred cattle and hogs, and raised a great quantity of fowls. When to this domestic provision of good and wholesome food, we add the luxuries afforded by the woods, the wild boar, ring-tail pigeons, and other wild birds, and the land-crab, which some esteem the greatest dainty in the West Indies, we may doubt whether the palate of Apicius would not have received higher gratification in Trelawny Town than at Rome.[39]

Besides the provision grounds they cultivated on the 1,500 acres of land they were ceded by the treaty of 1738, the Trelawny Maroons were said to

THE MAROONS OF JAMAICA, 1730–1830   165

have grown foodstuffs, on sufferance, on adjoining lands prior to the Second Maroon War.[40]

Furthermore, Dallas sought to refute Edwards' contention that the provision grounds were always in a shocking state of neglect and the Maroons were thus forced to trespass on the grounds of settlers in the mountains. He said he was informed the fact was otherwise, that settlers employed their slaves in growing cash crops rather than provisions and chose to purchase the superabundance of foodstuffs of the Maroons. He admitted that after the corn was cut the grounds appeared to be in a ruinous state. However, corn was interplanted with 'nutritious roots' which afforded the Maroons their surest support after a long-continued succession of dry weather. 'In the course of time their patches of land were cleared and replanted', wrote Dallas, 'and they again gradually assumed the appearance of being neglected; it is no wonder, therefore, that the eye of a casual visitor should have been deceived, and that he should have been led to declare, "that he perceived no vestige of culture" '. From the descriptions of Edwards and Dallas it seems evident that the Maroons practised slash-and-burn, or shifting, agriculture which is referred to among Jamaican peasants as 'firestick' agriculture.[41]

Like Edwards, Dallas admitted that Maroon women were chiefly employed in cultivating the provision grounds, but he denied that they considered this labour to be imposed upon them by the men. The sexual division of labour involved the women in burning trees and in tillage, while the men, besides hunting and pursuing runaway slaves, 'were employed in fencing the grounds, building and repairing houses, attending to their cattle and horses, of which they had about 200 head, and carrying on their petty commerce'. The Maroons sold livestock, 'jirked hog', and superfluous provisions. Moreover, they made a considerable profit by purchasing the leaf of tobacco plants from the estates within a distance of 20 or 30 miles which their women and children assisted them in carrying home. These leaves were dried and twisted into a kind of rope which they rolled up in balls and sold to the people on plantations.[42]

Dallas apparently visited Trelawny Town before the Second Maroon War. He said the houses in the village were disposed irregularly on sloping ground to carry off the heavy rain which cut gullies or channels and left deposits of topsoil in the valleys. 'Here and there, in patches', he wrote, 'where the sweepings of the ashes from the houses had been collected, and also on the ground below their hogsties, which were appurtenances to every house, some clumps of plantain trees, and smaller vegetables were nourished by the manure'. These productive patches, or 'kitchen gardens', together with the houses, were each surrounded by a fence made of a prickly shrub. Connecting each enclosure were small footpaths which were hardly visible to any except the inhabitants. Their houses were in general small cottages

166 OUT OF THE HOUSE OF BONDAGE

covered with thatch or long grass and having hard-packed clay floors and most probably wattle and daub exterior walls. However, the chiefs' houses were said to be roofed with shingles and several had floored rooms.[43]

Both Edwards and Dallas said the Maroons had an immense wilderness for their hunting grounds where they ranged without interruption.

> Their game was the wild boar [wrote Edwards], which abounds in the interior parts of Jamaica; and the Maroons had a method of curing the flesh without salting it. This commodity they frequently brought to market in the towns; and, with the money arising from the sale, and the rewards which they received for the delivery to their owners of runaway slaves, they purchased salted beef, spirituous liquors, tobacco, fire-arms, and ammunition, setting little or no account on clothing of any kind, and regarding as superfluous and useless most of those Things which every people, in the lowest degree of civilization, would consider as almost absolutely necessary for human existence.[44]

Lady Maria Nugent, wife of the governor of Jamaica, described a dinner on a plantation where the first course was 'entirely of fish, excepting jerked hog, in the centre, which is the way of dressing it by the Maroons'.[45]

Again, both Edwards and Dallas commented on the remarkable health, strength and vigour of the Maroons which they attributed to the cool and healthy mountain climate, active and varied life. From the accounts of hunting wild boar and raising livestock one may surmise that the Maroon diet contained ample animal protein. They spent their lives chiefly in hunting, roaming the woods in pursuit of runaway slaves, and raising provisions and livestock.

> Savage as they were in manners and disposition [wrote Edwards], their mode of living and daily pursuits undoubtedly strengthened their frame, and served to exalt them to great bodily perfection. Such fine persons as are seldom beheld among any other class of African or native blacks. Their demeanor is lofty, their walk firm, and their persons erect. Every motion displays a combination of strength and agility. The muscles (neither hidden or depressed by clothing) are very prominent, and strongly marked. Their sight withal is wonderfully acute, and their hearing remarkably quick.[46]

Dallas attributed the health of the Maroons, in part, to the mountain climate which was seldom less than 10 degrees cooler than that of the lowlands of Jamaica. Moreover, the constant exercise of their limbs in pursuit of wild boar and other activities contributed to the strength and symmetry of their bodies. Although they seldom had recourse to the aid of medicine, Maroon deaths were not more frequent than among other inhabitants of Jamaica. They readily applied to the plantation doctors if an

THE MAROONS OF JAMAICA, 1730–1830   167

opportunity offered, and sometimes they took simple herbs prescribed to them by their old women.[47]

In his novel *Tom Cringle's Log*, Michael Scott described a party of Maroons he met on a visit to a plantation near Kingston, Jamaica:

> I never saw finer men – tall, strapping fellows, dressed exactly as they should be and the climate requires; wide duck trousers, over these a loose shirt, of duck also, gathered at the waist by a broad leathern belt, through which, on one side, their short cutlass is stuck, while on the other hangs a leathern pouch for ball, and a loose thong across one shoulder, supports, on the opposite hip, a large powder-horn and haversack. This, with a straw hat, and a short gun in their hand, with a sling to be used on a march, completes their equipment – in better keeping with the climate than the padded coats, heavy caps, tight cross-belts, and ponderous muskets of our regulars.[48]

Table 5 compares the fertility and mortality of the Maroons and the slaves on 12 sample sugar plantations and Worthy Park plantation in two selected periods. It shows that while the Maroon birth rate was higher than the death rate, the plantation slaves had a higher death rate than birth rate. In other words, the Maroons increased by natural means while the slaves experienced a natural decrease. Whereas the Maroon population increased from 754 to 1,123 from 1799 to 1830, the slave population on the twelve sample plantations and Worthy Park declined from 5,616 to 5,169 from 1817 to 1829.[49] It is significant that the birth rate of the Maroons was much higher than that of the slaves. 'Their females', wrote Robert Renny, 'living in a climate congenial to their constitutions, and from the richness of the soil, and the fewness of their wants, being exempted from hard labour, were remarkably prolific'.[50]

On the other hand, the death rate of the Maroons was only slightly below that of the slaves. Other studies show that the demographic experience of the slaves was related to the crops they produced. Barry Higman finds a high rate of natural decrease for the roughly 50 per cent of total slaves of Jamaica who were attached to sugar plantations in the period 1829–1832. On the other hand, he finds that although monocultural coffee plantations did not have a particularly high rate of increase around 1829–32, the natural increase of the slaves was substantial on properties growing minor staples and raising livestock. His findings are similar to those of Thomas Fowell Buxton whose evidence has been quoted earlier in this article. George Roberts shows that there was a 10 per cent reduction in the slave population of Jamaica from 1817 to 1834. He says it was the excess of deaths over births that resulted in this decline since manumissions were relatively few in number.[51]

In his comparison of vital rates among the slaves of the antebellum United

168 OUT OF THE HOUSE OF BONDAGE

TABLE 5

ESTIMATED BIRTH RATES AND DEATH RATES OF THE MAROONS OF JAMAICA, 1799–1830,
COMPARED WITH THE CRUDE BIRTH RATES AND CRUDE DEATH RATES OF THE
SLAVES ON TWELVE SAMPLE SUGAR PLANTATIONS AND ON WORTHY PARK SUGAR
PLANTATION, 1817–1829

MAROONS

Years	*Estimated Birth Rate (per 1000)*	*Estimated Death Rate (per 1000)*
1799–1830	47	30

SLAVES

	Twelve Sample Plantations		*Worthy Park Plantation*	
Years	*Crude Birth Rate (per 1000)*	*Crude Death Rate (per 1000)*	*Crude Birth Rate (per 1000)*	*Crude Death Rate (per 1000)*
1817–1829	26.90	31.54	22.32	33.85

Source: George Cumper, 'The Demographic Balance of the Maroon Communities in Jamaica, 1799–1830', p. 11; Michael Craton, *Searching for the Invisible Man: Slaves and Plantation Life in Jamaica* (Harvard University Press, 1978), pp. 104, 112–13.

States and the British West Indies, Stanley L. Engerman finds that 'the mortality experience of creoles in the islands may not have differed as markedly from that in the United States as did the fertility rates'. In the United States, circa 1830, the crude birth-rate was about 50 per 1000 and the death-rate about 20–30 per 1000. On the other hand, the Parliamentary registration reports for Jamaica indicate birth rates of about 23 and death rates about 26. The causes of low fertility were attributed by contemporaries to 'the cultural and psychological shock of enslavement and movement to the New World, and as a response to the conditions of life: an unwillingness to bring offspring into such conditions. To accomplish this end, it has been claimed there was frequent resort to abortion and infanticide'.[52]

The harsh fact is that the planters of Jamaica valued slave women as work units to a greater degree than as breeding units. The decrease in the slave population was materially affected by the nature of the employment, and particularly the severity of work imposed upon women. Women field workers were expected to dig holes for the planting of canes and at harvest to cut canes and work a night shift in the boiling house. It is true that amelioration measures were enacted by the planter-dominated government

THE MAROONS OF JAMAICA, 1730–1830   169

to encourage family life and reproduction.[53] Yet, as Dr Lucille Mathurin Mair has written, 'No improvement in the treatment of women was discernible in the latter period of slavery: her condition in fact, may even have worsened'. Sustained manual labour proved to be 'inconsistent with the physical demands made on women by menstruation, pregnancy, lactation, infant and child care'. The slave woman came to dominate the labour force. 'She was not only a costly work-unit', writes Dr Mair, 'but she could hold the estate to ransom, by not working, or not breeding'.[54] It can be argued that by not breeding the slave women in the aggregate ensured that the birth-rate would not increase sufficiently to overtake the declining death-rate.

Robert Dallas compared the physical attributes of the Maroons and slaves, noting differences in their manner of life which affected their health and well being. Although descended from the same race of Africans, the Maroons were said to be strikingly distinct in their personal appearance, being blacker, taller, and in every respect handsomer than the slaves. 'In their person and carriage the Maroons were erect and lofty', he wrote, 'indicating a consciousness of superiority; vigour appeared upon their muscles, and their motions displayed agility. Their eyes were quick, wild, and fiery, the white of them appearing a little reddened; owing, perhaps to the greenness of the wood they burned in their houses, with the smoke of which it must have been affected. They possessed most, if not all, of the senses in a superior degree'.[55]

Plantation slaves, on the other hand, were forced to labour long hours under conditions that frequently undermined their health. Dallas railed at the planters who kept a great number of their slaves working, on a shift basis, all night during the four to six months of the sugar harvest. 'The languor with which work is undertaken after a sleepless night is evident in the eye, and in its effects: the exertions of the fresh sink to the level of those made by the wearied and sleepy whom they join, and whose labours through a long, dark night, give a dulness to those of the day'. Avarice was said to be such a powerful motive that the business of harvesting the crop was seldom suspended during heavy rains. Shortening the hours of labour would not only promote the interest of humanity, Dallas believed, but also of the planter's purse. Furthermore, absentee proprietorship and the management of plantations by attorneys and overseers was regarded by Dallas as an evil that militated against the happiness and amelioration of the state and condition of the slaves.[56]

VI

Jamaica in the period of slavery had two frontiers, an external one marked by the physical limits of the island, an internal one separating the plantations from the Maroon settlements. Friction along the internal frontier escalated into warfare between the planter government and the Maroon settlements. Maroons raided and plundered frontier plantations, carrying off slaves, firearms, ammunition, foodstuffs and other moveables. At the same time they grew provisions and hunted wild boar and other game in the rugged interior parts of the island. Down to about 1750 the Maroon population was male dominated. Raids on plantations for the chief purpose of taking females and rules regulating men's access to women suggest that births added few if any to the Maroon population which increased by the accession of runaways and captives. In the decade following the treaties when runaways were captured and returned to their owners, it is significant that the Maroon population declined substantially.

After about 1750 the Maroon population increased by natural means. Women came to outnumber men and births to exceed deaths in a population in which over half the people were in the zero to 19 age range. We have seen that Maroon death rates were only slightly under those for the slaves on 12 sample sugar plantations and Worthy Park plantation. Although markedly different in nature, the environments of both the Maroons and slaves were inhospitable so that only the most fit managed to survive. Perhaps the slaves were more susceptible to diseases associated with malnutrition, fatigue from hard labour, punishment, and unhygienic conditions, while the Maroons were more prone to suffer physical accidents, infection, smallpox, and accidental poisoning from unfamiliar leaves and herbs. The most remarkable finding is that the birth rate of the Maroons was more than double that of the slaves on Worthy Park and 74 per cent higher than the slaves on the 12 sample sugar plantations. Although the reasons for these marked differences cannot be ascertained with precision, it may be suggested that they were associated with diet, work loads, and disease environments. Compared with their sisters on the sugar plantations, Maroon women probably had a diet that was richer in animal protein, a lighter work load which did not include night work and the digging of cane holes, and a disease environment that was less enervating and more hygienic.[57]

Emancipation brought immeasurable gains to the black people of Jamaica. Health and well-being improved as the growth of a free peasantry coincided with the retreat of sugar monoculture and the establishment of a more balanced ecosystem. No doubt the greatest improvement accrued to black women who used their freedom to escape from field labour and devote their time to family life on peasant holdings. In sum, there emerged a creole society which saw the convergence of Maroon and freedmen lifestyles and improved demographic performance.

THE MAROONS OF JAMAICA, 1730–1830   171

NOTES

1. Richard Price, ed., *Maroon Societies: Rebel Slave Communities in the Americas* (Garden City, New York, Anchor Books, 1973), pp. 1–24.
2. Bryan Edwards, *The History, Civil and Commercial, of the British Colonies in the West Indies* (3 vols., London, John Stockdale, 1801), Vol. 3, p. 303.
3. Barbara Klamon Kopytoff, 'The Early Political Development of Jamaican Maroon Societies', *The William and Mary Quarterly*, 3rd ser., Vol. XXV, No. 2 (April 1978), p. 289.
4. *Ibid.*, p. 290; Mavis C. Campbell, 'Marronage in Jamaica: Its Origin in the Seventeenth Century', in *Comparative Perspectives on Slavery in New World Plantation Societies*, Vera Rubin and Arthur Tuden, eds. (New York, The New York Academy of Sciences, 1977), pp. 389–419; Michael Craton, *Testing the Chains: Resistance to Slavery in the British West Indies* (Ithaca, Cornell University Press, 1982), pp. 67–80.
5. British Library, *Additional MS.* 12,431, f. 76; [Anon.] to James Knight, n.d., in *C.E. Long Papers*; quoted in Kopytoff, *ibid.*, pp. 295–297.
6. Kopytoff, 'Jamaican Maroon Societies', pp. 294–297, 303.
7. Edwards, *History of West Indies*, Vol. 3, p. 309; Orlando Patterson, 'Slavery and Slave Revolts: A Socio-Historical Analysis of the First Maroon War, 1655–1740', *Social and Economic Studies*, Vol. 19, No. 3 (September 1970), pp. 289–301.
8. *Memoirs and Anecdotes of Philip Thicknesse, Late Lieutenant-Governor of Land Guard Fort, and Unfortunately Father to George Touchet, Baron Audley* (Dublin, 1790), pp. 58–60.
9. Carey Robinson, *The Fighting Maroons of Jamaica* (William Collins and Sangster (Jamaica) Ltd., 1969), pp. 40–43.
10. Edwards, *History of West Indies*, Vol. 3, p. 311.
11. Edward Long, *The History of Jamaica* (3 vols., London, 1774), Vol. II, p. 344.
12. R.C. Dallas, *History of the Maroons, From their Origin to the Establishment of their Chief Tribe at Sierra Leone*, etc. (2 vols., London, 1803), Vol. I, pp. 58–65, 76–77.
13. *Ibid.*, Vol. I, pp. 58–60.
14. *Ibid.*, Vol. I, pp. 58–65, 75–77.
15. Edwards, *History of West Indies*, Vol. 3, p. 306.
16. Dallas, *History of Maroons*, Vol. I, p. 123; Craton, *Testing the Chains*, pp. 81–96.
17. Public Record Office, London. *Colonial Office* 137/56: Trelawny to Newcastle, 30 June 1739; quoted in Barbara Kopytoff, 'The Development of Jamaican Maroon Ethnicity', *Caribbean Quarterly*, Vol. 22, Nos. 2 & 3 (June–Sept. 1976), p. 43.
18. Long, *History of Jamaica*, Vol. II, p. 347.
19. Kopytoff, 'Maroon Ethnicity', pp. 43–50.
20. Long, *History of Jamaica*, Vol. II, p. 346.
21. Craton, *Testing the Chains*, pp. 213–214.
22. Edward Brathwaite, *The Development of Creole Society in Jamaica 1770–1820* (Oxford, Clarendon Press, 1971), pp. 248–249, 250.
23. A. E. Furness, 'The Maroon War of 1795', *The Jamaican Historical Review*, Vol. V, No. 2 (November 1965), pp. 30–37; Robinson, *Fighting Maroons*, pp. 61–86, 104–105.
24. P.R.O. London, *C.O.* 137/96: Balcarres to Portland, 16 November 1795; quoted in Furness, 'Maroon War', pp. 38–39.
25. Long, *History of Jamaica*, Vol. II, p. 213.
26. Furness, 'Maroon War', pp. 38–39; Robinson, *Fighting Maroons*, pp. 87–93.
27. *Journals of the Assembly of Jamaica*, Vol. IX, 26 Sept. 1795, p. 384.
28. *Ibid.*, Vol. IX, 4 November 1796, p. 537; Furness, 'Maroon War', pp. 40–41; Robinson, *Fighting Maroons*, pp. 95–96, 126–132.
29. Furness, 'Maroon War', pp. 41–46; Robinson, *Fighting Maroons*, pp. 110, 120–125.
30. Furness, 'Maroon War', pp. 47–49; Robinson, *Fighting Maroons*, pp. 126–156; Craton, *Testing the Chains*, pp. 211–223.
31. *Accounts and Papers (Parliamentary Papers)*, 1832, Vol. 305, no. 127: 'The Select Committee of the House of Lords Appointed to Inquire into the Laws and Usages of the several West India Colonies in relation to the Slave Population. Minutes of Evidence'. Part II, p. 933. Evidence of T. F. Buxton.

172 OUT OF THE HOUSE OF BONDAGE

32. *Ibid.*, p. 933.
33. *Ibid.*, pp. 933–934.
34. *Ibid.*, pp. 933–934.
35. George Cumper, 'The Demographic Balance of the Maroon Communities in Jamaica, 1799–1830', unpublished paper presented at the Fourth Conference of Caribbean Historians, University of the West Indies, Mona, Kingston, Jamaica, 9–14 April 1972, pp. 1–12.
36. *Ibid.*, pp. 3–12.
37. Michael Ashcroft, 'Robert Charles Dallas: Identified as the author of an anonymous book about Jamaica', *The Jamaican Journal*, circa 1979, pp. 94–101.
38. Edwards, *History of West Indies*, Vol. 3, pp. 321–323.
39. Dallas, *History of Maroons*, Vol. I, pp. 104–107.
40. *Ibid.*, Vol. I, p. 84.
41. *Ibid.*, Vol. I, pp. 107–108.
42. *Ibid.*, Vol. I, pp. 108–110.
43. *Ibid.*, Vol. I, pp. 79–83.
44. Edwards, *History of West Indies*, Vol. 3, p. 320; Dallas, *History of Maroons*, Vol. I, p. 87.
45. *Lady Nugent's Journal of her Residence in Jamaica from 1801 to 1805*, Philip Wright, ed., A New and revised edition (Kingston, Institute of Jamaica, 1966), p. 70.
46. Edwards, *History of West Indies*, Vol. 3, p. 327.
47. Dallas, *History of Maroons*, Vol. I, pp. 86–87, 118–119.
48. Michael Scott, *Tom Cringle's Log* (London, J. M. Dent and Sons Ltd., 'Everyman's Library', 1938; first published in 1838), p. 137.
49. Cumper, 'Demographic Balance of Maroon Communities', p. 3; Michael Craton, *Searching for the Invisible Man: Slaves and Plantation Life in Jamaica* (Cambridge, Harvard University Press, 1978), pp. 104, 112.
50. Robert Renny, *A History of Jamaica*, etc. (London, 1807), p. 52.
51. B. W. Higman, *Slave Population and Economy in Jamaica, 1807–1834* (Cambridge, Cambridge University Press, 1976), pp. 122–123; George W. Roberts, *The Population of Jamaica* (Cambridge, Cambridge University Press, 1957), pp. 39–40.
52. Stanley L. Engerman, 'Some Economic and Demographic Comparisons of Slavery In the United States and the British West Indies', *The Economic History Review*, 2nd ser., Vol. XXIX, No. 2 (May 1976), pp. 258–275, especially pp. 270–272.
53. Richard B. Sheridan, *Doctors and Slaves: A medical and demographic history of slavery in the British West Indies, 1680–1834* (Cambridge, Cambridge University Press, 1985), pp. 222–248.
54. Lucille Mathurin Mair, 'A Historical Study of Women in Jamaica from 1655 to 1844', unpublished Ph.D. dissertation, University of the West Indies, Mona, Jamaica, October 1974, pp. 287–311, 343, 349.
55. Dallas, *History of the Maroons*, Vol. I, pp. 87–88.
56. *Ibid.*, Vol. II, pp. 339–340, 360–361.
57. Sheridan, *Doctors and Slaves*, pp. 148–184, 200–206, 222–248.

A Comparison between the History of Maroon Communities in Surinam and Jamaica*

Silvia W. de Groot

Resistance, passive and active, rebellion and marronage were inherent to the condition under which the plantation slaves in the American colonies lived. Marronage, that is the choice of a hard but free existence in the hinterlands of the plantation colonies, was the ultimate consequence of resistance. On the one hand, the slave-owners' attempts at getting back what they considered as their property and, on the other, the Maroons' attacks on the plantations to steal victuals, weapons, powder and additions to their numbers (especially women), led to escalating guerilla warfare. In most cases the Maroons got the worst of it and their communities ceased to exist. There were however a number of Maroon communities which managed to hold their own. Two of these will form the comparative subjects of this paper: the Maroons of Jamaica and those of Surinam. The similarities and differences in the development of both groups will be examined using a number of important historical events such as the origin of the groups, the guerilla wars, the relationship with the colonial communities, the concluded peace treaties, and the extent of their geographical, social and economic isolation. What is, in the first place, most striking is the extent of the similarities in the histories of both groups, and yet the results of these histories also show clear differences. I shall attempt to clarify how eventually the process of differentiation was accomplished.

Jamaica was developed into a plantation colony by the Spaniards, the first negro slaves being imported in 1517. The English established themselves in Surinam in 1650 and they too developed the country into a plantation colony using negro slaves. Jamaica was taken from the Spaniards by the English in 1655 and Surinam from the English by the Dutch in 1667. At the time there were about 1,500 slaves in the island and a number of Maroons. The English owned about the same number of slaves in Surinam, and most of these were removed by the departing colonists. Here, too, there were a few hundred Maroons in the interior. A century later the number of slaves had risen to 57,000 in Surinam (1738) and 130,000 in Jamaica (1753).

---

* This article was previously published in *OSO: A Journal for Surinamese Linguistics, Literature and History* (Journal of the Nijmegen Institute for the Advancement of Surinamese Studies), Vol. 3, No. 1, May 1984 (in Dutch).

174   OUT OF THE HOUSE OF BONDAGE

Between 1655 and 1807 about 350,000 slaves were imported into Surinam and 747,500 into Jamaica (Curtin, 1969: 160). In both territories the ratio of slaves to whites was about 20 to one. The administrative structure of the plantation system, the slave laws and the treatment of slaves were very much the same. The intentions of the whites were also similar, as the planters' main purpose was to return to their homeland with as much profit as possible. This was more successful in Jamaica than in Surinam. Absenteeism occurred less frequently in Surinam, and at a later date. In both territories the endeavours of the mother countries to exploit the colony as much as possible led to a self-seeking administration, which frequently gave rise to conflicts between planters, between planters and the local administration (often planters themselves), and between the local administration and the home governments.

Another source of conflict, which is of interest here, is the attitude to the Maroons. Both colonies were confronted with the fact that since colonisation, with the growing number of slaves, insurrections on the plantations and the formation of hostile groups of Maroons in the interior were a growing threat to the plantation system. In the 1730s an estimate put the number of Maroons in both territories at between a thousand and several thousand. The number of insurrections and guerilla attacks escalated in both Jamaica and Surinam from the end of the seventeenth century. The measures taken by the whites also escalated but they were usually insufficient, partly because of the planters' egoism and their reluctance to make either the financial or physical sacrifices required to organize and execute military expeditions. Another reason for the ineffectiveness of the measures was that the Maroons were militantly organized and competently led, they had a superior knowledge of, and were hardened to the geographical and climatic conditions. They were often supported, either passively or actively, by the slave population and were highly motivated as their freedom was at stake. Eventually the whites in both territories were forced to offer peace terms. Obviously, this was done grudgingly, but the fortifications, the military expeditions, the loss of lives coupled with little success and especially the high costs caused the planters to yield.

Peace had been made with small groups as early as the seventeenth century, in Surinam in 1686 and in Jamaica in 1670. In the 1730s new attempts were made. A half-hearted and unsuccessful attempt was made in 1734 to come to terms with the 'Leeward' group of Maroons in the mid-west of Jamaica. A renewed attempt in 1739 was successful. In the following year the same agreement was reached with the 'Windward' Maroons in the east. Agreements were reached with the Surinam Maroons in the south-east in 1760 and with those in the mid-south in 1762 and 1767, after abortive attempts in 1731 and 1749. I shall come back to these peace treaties later. The colonists had vain hopes that they could now peacefully apply them-

SURINAM, SHOWING LOCATIONS OF THE MAROONS

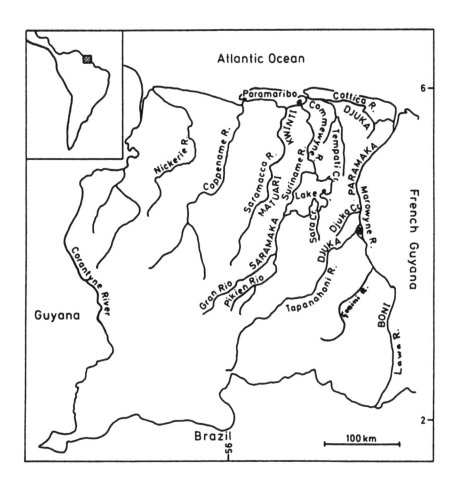

176 OUT OF THE HOUSE OF BONDAGE

selves to their own enrichment. Serious difficulties arose with the existing groups in Jamaica, and resistance and insurrections by slaves in both territories continued. In 1795 the dramatic rebellion by the 'Trelawny' Maroons took place, which was ended by deporting 500 Maroons to Halifax, Nova Scotia and some years later, in 1800, to Sierra Leone.

In Surinam a new group of Maroons had formed; they were the renowned Bonis, who, especially from 1765 until 1776 and to a lesser extent from 1785 to 1793, attacked plantations, thus inflicting heavy military and financial losses on the colonists. The Bonis were eventually driven out of Surinam to French Guiana and a century later – in 1890 – chose to be declared French.

To return to the peace treaties, the first treaty with the Maroons in Jamaica was concluded with Juan Lubola in 1660. He and his group had originally fought with the Spanish to defend the colony against the English, but later went over to them. In 1670 a treaty was concluded with another group, the Karmahaly, who broke the peace two years later. A further attempt in 1734, as already stated, was a failure. After a large-scale abortive campaign the colonists, urged by Governor Trelawny, offered peace terms to a group of Maroons led by Chief Cudjoe. The attempt was successful and the peace held. The articles of the proposed treaty were accepted after negotiation without major alterations. A similar treaty was concluded with the leaders of the Maroons who were entrenched in the Blue Mountains, in the eastern part of the island.

As has been stated, treaties were also made quite early – in 1686 – with a number of Maroons in Surinam (as well as with a group of Indians). The ever increasing new groups, however, caused Governor de Cheusses to make an attempt, which was unsuccessful, in 1731. Later, in 1749, Governor Mauricius – after a large-scale campaign – offered peace terms to one of the groups. Governor Mauricius took the treaties which had been concluded ten years earlier in Jamaica and literally copied the whole with only minor changes to accommodate the situation in Surinam. This attempt was successful at first but broke down a year later and once again the Maroons reverted to guerilla attacks. Ten years later, in 1760, a successful attempt was made with a second group and an 'eternal' peace was concluded with the same conditions. Two years later the first group followed and in 1767 peace was concluded with a third group.

It is important for my argument to look into the differences between the treaty provisions in Jamaica and Surinam.

First, the demarcation of the area conceded to the Maroons. The extent of the territory made it possible to agree to the unhindered movement of the Surinam Maroons in the area in which they lived but they had to stay at a distance of 'two days or 10 hours journey' from the nearest plantation. In Jamaica the distance was three miles and their territory was set at 1,500 acres.

MAROON COMMUNITIES IN SURINAM AND JAMAICA 177

In Surinam the number of Maroons who could visit the plantation area to trade was strictly limited. This was not so in Jamaica. The tradeable products also differed. In Surinam 'wood, live-stock and commodities' are named and in Jamaica coffee, cocoa, ginger, cotton and tobacco (with an embargo on sugar), cattle, goats and pigs.

Moreover, the Surinam Maroons were bound to give hostages, who had to be either sons or close relatives of the chief. In Jamaica, the chiefs were only obliged to wait upon the governor once a year. In addition, an agreement not mentioned in the treaty was that the Surinam colonial government would send presents to the Maroons regularly. The Jamaica Maroons were also obliged to keep their communities accessible by constructing roads. This was altered to making and keeping the rivers and creeks in Surinam navigable, for obvious geographical reasons. Finally, in Jamaica there was a cordon of defence posts around the Maroon villages; in Surinam such cordons were laid round the plantations.

It is clear that the Surinam administration was more concerned with the isolation of the Maroons than their Jamaican counterparts, because they were more afraid of attacks, even in times of peace, from existing or newly-formed groups. It was much easier to lead such an extremely isolated existence in Surinam than in Jamaica, as the Jamaican Maroons were closed in on all sides by whites. The Surinam Maroons themselves were also very much for keeping their distance as they thus felt much safer and freer.

The geographical situation was decisive for the difference in development in more ways than those already mentioned. The isolation of the Surinam Maroon communities and the lack of contact between the various groups made it possible for them to form autonomous communities upon which the colonial government had little influence. The exchange of products was also so limited (from the Maroons' side this was hardly more than wood) that their isolation or rather semi-isolation became durable. Moreover, many of the planters left the most remote areas, because of soil-exhaustion of their plantations and the constant threat of new attacks. In this respect Jamaica differed completely: contrary to the Dutch colony the English island developed itself in the third part of the eighteenth century. The colonists' hunger for land was insatiable, new plantations were continually laid out and the Maroons' territory became increasingly smaller.

The difference in freedom of movement and the size of the territory can explain another striking difference. In general, the Jamaican Maroons kept to the treaty article which made compulsory the handing over of runaways to the colonists; the destruction of newly-formed groups and the repression of slave insurrections. This was done to a much lesser extent in Surinam. The planters' complaints of the scanty co-operation of the Maroons in this province are manifold, and conflicts and threats were frequent. The Surinam Maroons handed over as few runaways as possible and took in

178   OUT OF THE HOUSE OF BONDAGE

newcomers gladly. They could do this, unlike their Jamaican brothers, as there was land, game and fish enough to allow them to take in small numbers of runaways. There were, however, limits. Large, newly-formed groups like the Bonis in the eighteenth and the Paramakkaners in the nineteenth centuries were excluded from the territory of the already established communities. The number that could be taken in was restricted by their method of overcropping, unlimited hunting and fishing, which required having large areas at their disposal. It was also of great importance that the rivers should be kept open in order to remain in contact with the coastal areas. The establishing of new groups would prevent such access. Thus a newly-formed group like the Bonis received the finishing stroke from one of the Maroon groups who felt threatened by their presence.

The same sort of situation also occurred in Jamaica in 1735. A group of about 300 'Windward' Maroons tried to join the 'Leeward' Maroons after a dramatic march across the island. The leader of the Leeward Maroons refused politely but adamantly to take them in and sent them back after a few months. His reasons were that the area could not support any more people, and he was afraid that the conduct of the newcomers would provoke attacks from the whites and that his own position of authority would be undermined. It would, however, be untrue to say that the Jamaican Maroons always handed fugitives and insurgents over willingly. Bryan Edwards (1801: 542–543) gives examples of Maroons who shirked this obligation. Nevertheless, the Jamaican Maroons are noted, and seemingly rightly so, for fulfilling this agreement. The above-mentioned reasons for not accepting runaways or Maroons were certainly valid after the peace treaties. There is also another point to consider: fugitives who had been accepted sometimes turned out to be informers. The Maroons' mistrust of the slaves was grounded in their supposed loyalty to their masters and for this reason they were usually pursued and handed over.

Another difference in the approach of the respective colonial governments is manifest in the treaty articles, especially with regard to the supervision of the Maroons' compliance with the treaty. In both territories white civil servants were placed in the Maroon communities (four in Jamaica, two in Surinam). These were called superintendents in Jamaica and postholders in Surinam. In Jamaica the stress was laid upon 'friendly correspondence with the inhabitants' and the form the supervision took was more or less left to the superintendents' discretion. In Surinam the latter point was also part of the treaty, but spying for the Government and setting up one group against the other, was stressed in the instructions for the postholders. Again it appears that the Surinam colonists were more apprehensive of a renewed guerilla war than their Jamaican counterparts and that they were less capable of timely intervention.

In fact, in both territories, the white civil servants did not have enough

MAROON COMMUNITIES IN SURINAM AND JAMAICA 179

authority to carry out their tasks. Their position with the Maroons was usually no sinecure and their authority depended on their own personal capacity. The Maroons of both territories saw ways of making their wishes known to the government through the offices of the civil servants, which was not entirely the original intention. It must be said that in Jamaica more thought was given to suitability when choosing superintendents than in Surinam. The difference in situation is a consideration here. In Surinam, where the geographical and psychological isolation was so much greater, the choice of person was more restricted than in Jamaica, where contact with the plantation area was easier.

In Jamaica the above-mentioned points resulted more or less naturally in ever-growing intervention: above the superintendent came a superintendent general; special, white officers were appointed to organize military expeditions to recapture runaways; and stewards, who supervised equipment, requisites and accounts, were attached to them. All of these forms of intervention did not occur in Surinam. Here the Maroons' aversion to, and the colonial governments' shrinking from, more contact than was strictly essential led to less intervention by the Surinamese authorities.

Both peace treaties were (whether intentionally or not) very vague as to the rights of the Maroons. Apart from the regulations of land rights, this found its expression in the nature of their self-government. In the Jamaican treaty with the Trelawny Town Maroons, Captain Cudjoe was acknowledged as commander-in-chief and all the Maroons who belonged with him were subject to him; he had 'full power to inflict any punishment ... death excepted', further they would 'enjoy and possess for themselves and posterity forever all the lands situated and lying between Trelawny Town and the Cockpits'. Nevertheless, there was frequent mention of their 'subjection' and 'submission' to the governor. Moreover, with the deaths of Cudjoe and those of his heirs who were mentioned in the treaties, the appointment of the chiefs devolved upon the governor. The real intention of the government, that of direct intervention, became clear in conflict situations. No new form of autonomous government replaced the Maroons' original form.

The government in Surinam was not able to limit the Maroons' autonomy in this manner. This was recognized from the very beginning. Although they would have preferred to keep to the Jamaican articles, the instructions given to the white negotiators of the treaties stated that the Maroons must have the right to elect their own chiefs, who only had to be 'approbated' by the governor.

The reason for the difference in attitude lay in the recognition that the Surinam Maroons were in a better bargaining position than their Jamaican brothers, who were closed in on all sides by whites and had been manoeuvred into accepting peace. The Surinam Maroons clearly negotiated

180   OUT OF THE HOUSE OF BONDAGE

from their own free will, and the chance that the terms offered would be rejected was considered great by the whites, with the ensuing disastrous effects.

Nevertheless, the later developments whereby the Surinam Maroon functionaries became, especially financially, more dependent on the colonial administration, caused an ambivalent position of authority in which the whites could exert indirect political pressure. This situation still exists today.

Differences and similarities can also be found in the attitude of the Maroons and whites towards each other. The Maroons in Jamaica saw themselves as conquered, and forced into accepting a peace treaty, since they were encircled and besieged. Cudjoe's alleged famous prostration when the treaty was concluded can therefore be explained. The typically African way of affirming his subjection was in no way 'abject' (Dallas, 1803, 1: 55–56). Having lost a fight is not the same as losing one's dignity or identity. They saw their new status as one of being under protection – under patronage – with the obligations and also the rights which were attached to that protection (Kopytoff, 1973: 254–5).

The attitude in Surinam was completely different. The Maroons felt in no way conquered. They had been offered peace because both parties had had enough of war. They negotiated with their opponents as equals and as free individuals in their own territory, without being encircled or besieged. The white negotiators were seriously taken to task about the objectionable behaviour of white plantation owners, which was one of the main reasons for the running away of slaves. Apart from taking oaths the Maroons demanded an additional token of trust: the negotiators all had to 'accept the company of one of the most distinguished negresses during their stay there' (Hartsinck, II, 1770: 798).

In both territories the solemn ratification of the peace was performed in almost the same way; the oath was taken according to white as well as to black customs. The practices of Jamaican and Surinam Maroons show a striking similarity in this respect: blood from a cut in the arm (hand) mixed with water and a little clay and rum was caught in a calabash and drunk by both parties (Hartsinck, 1770: 800; Williams, 1944: 389).

The result of the Jamaican Maroons' attitude of 'patronage' was that the whites saw them as subjects with a special status, in whose social structure they could intervene. In this way the Maroons' internal authority was weakened, and their dependence upon outside forces increased. The whites in Surinam recognized – grudgingly – that the Maroon communities formed a state within a state, with their own internal autonomy, social control and hierarchical structure. There was clearly more mutual mistrust in Surinam than in Jamaica. The Surinam Maroons were always viewed as potential enemies, who could best be kept at a distance. The Maroons never lost their

MAROON COMMUNITIES IN SURINAM AND JAMAICA 181

distrust of the colonial government, believing that the intention was to re-enslave them. All intervention in their internal affairs was averted. In Jamaica it was because of that very contact that conflicts could be resolved and even legal aid was available to the Maroons. The nature of the conflicts was also very different. In Jamaica they usually arose over land rights and in Surinam over smuggling with slaves or surrendering runaways. These controversies were the foundations of renewed treaties and measures, which were always imposed as white initiatives.

I would like to go into some of these renewed treaties briefly. Slavery was abolished in Jamaica in 1834. From that point onwards the whites had no more use for the Maroons. The obligations which the whites had taken upon themselves were considered a burden. They wanted to be relieved from the tasks of maintaining civil servants in the Maroon territory, of paying salaries to functionaries and the defence of the Maroons' property. In 1842, there-fore, the so-called 'Land Allotment Act' was promulgated. The main purpose of this act was to split the Maroons' territory into individual plots. The land had always been corporative and the colonials hoped in this way to weaken claims and break up the tenure. The resistance to these measures was so vigorous that the act was only put into practice in a few cases. Many conflicts resulted from this, some of which still endure to the present day.

As already stated, the problems in Surinam were of a different nature. The old treaties of 1760–62 were changed in 1835 and 1837. On the one hand, the restrictions on the number of Maroons allowed into the coastal area were relaxed but, on the other hand, stricter rules were laid down for the handing over of runaways. The latter point was the real reason for changing the treaty. There was, however, no appreciable change in the Maroons' attitude.

In the years previous to the inevitable abolition of slavery (which came about in 1863), the whites attempted to induce the Surinam Maroons to hire themselves out as labourers for the plantations, as lumberjacks or for rubber tapping. The Maroons rejected plantation work out of hand. They were prepared to hire themselves out for the other tasks for short periods, after which they returned to their communities. This had always been their way of working and in many cases still is. In 1856 the colonial administration made another attempt to induce the Maroons to more intensive contact with the coast. All former restrictions were lifted and the paramount chiefs were given a salary. This new ruling had, however, again very little effect on the Maroons' way of life.

They continued to live in their semi-isolation, travelling from time to time to the coast to take employment. When they had earned enough to buy the supplies needed by their communities they returned home. This was repeated whenever provisions were needed.

In conclusion, two main points emerge. Contact between the Maroons and the colonial administration was more intense in Jamaica than in Surinam. Furthermore, the nature of the conflicts which arose stemmed from a shortage of land in Jamaica but from a shortage of labour in Surinam. In Jamaica, this close contact between Maroons and officialdom created a form of integration, first in the form of an interchange of forms of labour. Second, from an early date, there existed a marketing mechanism for handling products including cash crops. Finally, there developed a distinct relationship at administrative and judicial levels. One aspect not dealt with here is religion, although there are syncretic elements present. The influence of Christianity on the religion of the Surinam Maroons has been very slight.

The Surinam Maroons' semi-isolation retarded integration. Colonial administration rarely intervened, and the Maroons' failure to produce tradeable products made a regular marketing mechanism impossible. Furthermore, the Maroon labour supply was always limited and temporary. Integration was set in train, although more gradually than in Jamaica, after World War II. More recently, the prospects for the Surinam Maroons look less promising than for their Jamaican counterparts, who have for centuries formed a relatively stable and integrated relationship with the surrounding society.

MAROON COMMUNITIES IN SURINAM AND JAMAICA

APPENDIX
COMPARATIVE STATISTICS
(Compiled from Curtin, Dallas, de Groot, Edwards, Long, Price, *loc. cit.*)

Jamaica	*Surinam*
11,000 km²	143,000 km²
1,900,000 inhabitants	400,000 inhabitants
150 inh./km²	2,3 inh./km²
1752: 2/3 uncultivated	1752: about 9/10 uncultivated
1774: 680 sugar estates	1774: about 150 sugar estates
(1,500 other estates)	(about 300 other estates)
145,000 slaves	55,000 slaves
1834: 646 sugar estates	1833: 105 sugar estates
1854: 330 sugar estates	1853: 87 sugar estates

Slave numbers		*Slave numbers*	
1662	552	1671	1,200
1708	45,000	1701	7,500
1740	99,000	1740	50,000
1787	250,000	1787	45,000
1795	219,000	1791	53,000
1830	357,000	1830	50,000

Total import 748,000	Total import 325,000

Maroon numbers (estimates)		*Maroon numbers* (estimates)	
1655	1,000 - 1,200	1680	a few hundred
1736	about 1,000	1740	a few thousand
1774	about 1,500	1863	6,000 - 9,000
1824	about 2,000	1924	18,000
1970	2,000 - 3,000	1964	27,500
		1970	39,000

184   OUT OF THE HOUSE OF BONDAGE

REFERENCES

Comitas, Lambros and David Lowenthal (eds.), 1973. *Slaves, Free Men, Citizens*. New York.

Dallas, R.C., 1803. *The History of the Maroons*, 2 vols. London.

Davis, David Brion, 1975. *The Problem of Slavery in the Age of Revolution*. Ithaca.

Debbasch, Yvan, 1962. 'Le Marronnage. Essai sur la désertion de l'esclave antillais'. *L'Année Sociologique*, (1961): 1–112; (1962): 117–95.

Debien, Gabriel, 1966. 'Le Marronnage aux Antilles Françaises au XVIIIe siècle'. *Caribbean Studies*, 6: 3–42.

Edwards, Bryan, 1801. *The History of the British Colonies in the West-Indies*. 3 vols. London.

Engerman, S., 1973. 'Some considerations relating to Property Rights and Man'. *Journal of Economic History*, 33: 43–65.

Engerman, S. and E. Genovese, 1975. *Race and Slavery in the Western Hemisphere*, Princeton.

Fouchard, Jean, 1972. *Les Marrons de la Liberté*, Paris.

Genovese, E., 1979. *From Rebellion to Revolution*, Baton Rouge.

Groot, Sylvia W. de, 1963. *From Isolation towards Integration: The Surinam Maroons and their Descendants, 1845–1863*, The Hague.

——, 1975. 'The Boni Maroon War, 1765–1793: Surinam and French Guyana', *Boletín de Estudios Latinoamericanos y del Caribe* 18: 30–48.

——, 1981. 'An Example of Oral History: The Tale of Boni's Death and of Boni's Head', *Lateinamerika Studien* 11: 181–216.

——, 1982. 'Surinaamse Marrons in kaart gebracht, 1730–1734' in Benno Francisco Galjart et al, *Een andere in een ander: Liber Amicorum voor R.A.J. van Lier*. Assen, Van Gorcum: 19–46.

——, 1984. 'Slaven en Marrons: Reacties op het Plantagesysteem in de Nieuwe Wereld. Een Schema', *Oso* 2: 173–82.

——, 1985. 'The Maroons of Surinam: Agents of their own Emancipation' in David Richardson (ed.), *Abolition and its Aftermath: The Historical Context, 1790–1916* (London, Frank Cass, 1985): 55–79.

Herskovits, Melville J. and Frances S. Herskovits, 1934. *Rebel destiny. Among the Bush Negroes of Dutch Guyana*. New York, S. Emmering.

Kilson, Marion, 1964. 'Towards Freedom. An Analysis of Slave Revolts in the United States'. *Phylon*, 25: 175–87.

Kopytoff, Barbara Klamon, 1973. 'The Maroons of Jamaica: An Ethnohistorical Study of Incomplete Polities, 1655–1905'. PhD diss., University of Pennsylvania.

Long, Edward, 1774. *The History of Jamaica*, 3 vols. London.

Meillassoux, C. (ed.), 1975. *L'Esclavage en Afrique précoloniale*. Paris.

Mintz, Sidney W., 1974. *Caribbean Transformations*. Chicago.

Patterson, Orlando, 1979. 'On Slavery and Slave Formations', *New Left Review*, 117: 31–67.

——, 1967. *The Sociology of Slavery*. London.

——, 1970. 'Slavery and Slave Revolts: A Socio-historical Analysis of the First Maroon War, 1655–1740'. *Social and Economic Studies*, 19: 289–325.

Price, Richard, 1973. *Maroon Societies*. New York.

——, 1975. *Saramaka Social Structure*. Puerto Rico.

Rout Jr., Leslie B., 1976. *The African Experience in Spanish America*. Cambridge.

Rubin, Vera and Arthur Tuden (eds.), 1976. *Comparative Perspectives on Slavery in New World Plantation Societies*, Part VI, New York.

Stedman, Captn. J.G., 1796. *Narrative of a five-years' expedition, against the revolted Negroes of Surinam, in Guiana, on the Wild Coast of South America from the year 1772, to 1777*. London, J. Johnson & J. Edwards.

Thoden van Velzen, H.U.E., 1966. *Politieke beheersing in de Djuka maatschappij: een studie van een onvolledig machtsoverwicht*. Leiden, Afrika Studiecentrum. Mimeo.

Williams, Eric, 1944. *Capitalism and Slavery*. Chapel Hill, N.C.

Bibliography

The references below include the principal printed sources used by the authors in this volume. The list makes no claim to completeness; such an undertaking would require at least a volume in itself. A fuller compilation is available in the annual bibliographical articles by Joseph Miller et al. in *Slavery and Abolition* (1980–1985). See also Joseph Miller, *Slavery: A Comparative Worldwide Bibliography* (forthcoming).

Accounts and Papers (Parliamentary Papers), 1832, Vol. 305, no. 127: 'The Select Committee of the House of Lord Appointed to Inquire into the Laws and Usages of the several West India Colonies in relation to the Slave Population. Minutes of Evidence', Part II, p. 933. Evidence of T. F. Buxton.

Ajayi, J. and Philip D. Curtin (eds.), *Africa Remembered: Narratives by West Africans from the Era of the Slave Trade* (Madison, University of Wisconsin Press, 1967).

Almeida, João de, *Sul d'Angola, Relatorio de um Governo de Distrito, 1908–1910* (Lisbon, 1912).

Amaral, Francisco J. Ferreira do, *As Colonias Agricolas em Africa e a Lei* (Lisbon, 1880).

Arrazola, Roberto, *Palenque, primer pueblo libre de América* (Cartagena, Ediciones Hernandez, 1970).

Ashcroft, Michael, 'Robert Charles Dallas: Identified as the author of an anonymous book about Jamaica', *The Jamaican Journal* 44 (1980): 94–101.

Beckles, Hilary, 'Rebels and Reactionaries: The Political Responses of White Labourers to Planter Class Hegemony in Barbados during the Seventeenth Century', *Journal of Caribbean History* 15 (1981): 1–21.

——, 'Emancipation by War or Law? Wilberforce and the 1815 Barbados Slave Rebellion' in David Richardson (ed.), *Abolition and its Aftermath: The Historical Context, 1790–1916* (London, Frank Cass, 1985): 80–104.

——, *Black Rebellion in Barbados: The Struggle Against Slavery, 1627–1837* (Barbados, Antilles Publications, 1984).

Bierck, Harold A., 'The Struggle for Abolition in Gran Colombia', *Hispanic American Historical Review* 33 (1953): 365–86.

186 OUT OF THE HOUSE OF BONDAGE

Bishop, P. A., 'Runaway Slaves in Jamaica, 1740–1807' (unpublished M.A. thesis, University of the West Indies, 1970).

Blassingame, John, *The Slave Community: Plantation Life in the Antebellum South* (rev. ed., New York, Oxford University Press, 1979).

Borrego Pla, María del Carmen, *Palenques de negros en Cartagena de Indias a fines del siglo XVII* (Seville, Escuela de Estudios Hispanoamericanos, 1973).

Brathwaite, Edward, *The Development of Creole Society in Jamaica 1770– 1820* (Oxford, Clarendon Press, 1971).

Brickell, John, *The Natural History of North Carolina* ... (Dublin, James Carson, 1737; reprinted Raleigh, N.C., Trustees of Public Libraries, 1911).

Brown, Richard Maxwell, *The South Carolina Regulators: The Story of the First Vigilante Movement* (Cambridge, Mass., Harvard University Press, 1963).

Buckley, Roger Norman, *Slaves in Red Coats: The British West India Regiments, 1795–1815* (New Haven, Yale University Press, 1979).

Campbell, Mavis C., 'Marronage in Jamaica: Its Origin in the Seventeenth Century' in Vera Rubin and Arthur Tuden (eds.), *Comparative Perspectives on Slavery in New World Plantation Societies* (New York, The New York Academy of Sciences, 1977): 389–419.

Capello, Hermenegildo and Roberto Ivens, *De Angola a Contra-Costa* (Lisbon, 2 vols., 1886).

Chandler, David L., 'Health Conditions in the Slave Trade of New Granada' in Robert Brent Toplin (ed.), *Slavery and Race Relations in Latin America* (Westport, Conn., Greenwood Press, 1974): 51–88.

——, 'Slave over Master in Colonial Colombia and Ecuador', *The Americas* 38 (1981–82): 315–26.

Clarence-Smith, W. Gervase, 'Slavery in coastal Southern Angola, 1875– 1913', *Journal of Southern African Studies* 2 (1976): 214–23.

——, 'Capitalist penetration among the Nyaneka of Southern Angola, 1760s to 1920s', *African Studies* 37 (1978): 163–76.

——, *Slaves, Peasants and Capitalists in Southern Angola, 1840–1926* (Cambridge, Cambridge University Press, 1979).

Clark, Walter (ed.), *The State Records of North Carolina* (Winston and Goldsboro, State of North Carolina, 16 vols., numbered 11–26, 1895– 1906).

Coleridge, Samuel T., 'Hints for a new Species of History' in Robert

BIBLIOGRAPHY 187

Southey and S.T. Coleridge, *Omniana; or Horae Otiosiores*, ed. Robert Gittings (Fontwell, Sussex, Centaur Press, 1969 [1st pub. 1812]).

Colmenares, German, *Historia económica y social de Colombia, tomo II: Popayán: una sociedad esclavista, 1680–1800* (Bogotá, La Carreta, 1979).

Comitas, Lambros and David Lowenthal (eds.), *Slaves, Free Men, Citizens* (Garden City, N.Y., Anchor Books, 1973).

Correio de Mossamedes (Mossamedes, fortnightly, 1903–1906).

Craton, Michael, *Searching for the Invisible Man: Slaves and Plantation Life in Jamaica* (Cambridge, Mass., Harvard University Press, 1978).

——, *Testing the Chains: Resistance to Slavery in the British West Indies* (Ithaca, N.Y., Cornell University Press, 1982).

Crow, Jeffrey J., *The Black Experience in Revolutionary North Carolina* (Raleigh, N.C., Division of Archives and History, 1977).

——, 'Slave Rebelliousness and Social Conflict in North Carolina, 1775 to 1802', *William and Mary Quarterly*, 3rd Ser., 37 (1980): 79–102.

Cumper, George, 'The Demographic Balance of the Maroon Communities in Jamaica, 1799–1830', paper presented at the Fourth Annual Conference of Caribbean Historians, Jamaica, 1972.

Curtin, Philip D., *The Image of Africa: British Ideas and Actions, 1780–1850* (London: Macmillan, 1965).

——, *The Atlantic Slave Trade: A Census* (Madison, University of Wisconsin Press, 1969).

——, *Economic Change in Pre-Colonial Africa: Senegambia in the Era of the Slave Trade* (Madison, University of Wisconsin Press, 1975).

Daaku, Kwame Yeboa, *Trade and Politics on the Gold Coast, 1600–1720: A Study of the African Reaction to European Trade* (Oxford, Oxford University Press, 1970).

Dallas, Robert C., *History of the Maroons, From their Origin to the Establishment of their Chief Tribe at Sierra Leone* (London, 2 vols., 1803).

Davies, Kenneth Gordon, *The Royal African Company* (London, Longmans, 1957).

Davis, David Brion, *The Problem of Slavery in the Age of Revolution* (Ithaca, Cornell University Press, 1975).

Davis, Ralph, *The Rise of the Atlantic Economies* (London, Weidenfeld and Nicolson, 1973).

188   OUT OF THE HOUSE OF BONDAGE

Debbasch, Yvan, 'Le marronage: essai sur la désertion de l'esclave antillais', *L'Année Sociologique* (1961): 1–112; (1962): 117–95.

Debien, Gabriel, 'Les marrons autour du Cap', *Bulletin de l'Institut Français d'Afrique Noire* 27, Serie B, (1965): 755–99.

——, 'Le Marronage aux Antilles Françaises au XVIIIe siècle, *Caribbean Studies* 6 (1966): 3–42.

——, 'Les esclaves marrons à Saint-Domingue en 1764', *Jamaican Historical Review* 6 (1969): 3–13.

——, *Les Esclaves aux Antilles Françaises* (Basse Terre, Société d'Histoire de la Guadeloupe, 1974).

Debien, Gabriel and Jean Fouchard, 'Aspects de l'esclavage aux Antilles françaises: le petit marronage à Saint-Domingue autour du Cap (1790–91)', *Cahiers des Amériques Latines* (1979): 27–64.

Dia, Gastão Sousa (ed.), *Artur de Paiva* (Lisbon, 2 vols., 1938).

Duffy, James, *A Question of Slavery* (Cambridge, Mass., Harvard University Press, 1967).

Edwards, Bryan, *The History, Civil and Commercial, of the British Colonies in the West Indies* (London, 3 vols., 1801).

Engerman, Stanley L., 'Some Considerations Relating to Property Rights and Man', *Journal of Economic History* 33 (1973): 43–65.

——, 'Some Economic and Demographic Comparisons of Slavery in the United States and the British West Indies', *The Economic History Review* 29 (1976): 258–75.

Engerman, Stanley L. and Eugene D. Genovese, *Race and Slavery in the Western Hemisphere* (Princeton, Princeton University Press, 1975).

Escalante, Aquiles, *El negro en Colombia* (Bogotá, Universidad Nacional, 1964).

Fouchard, Jean, *The Haitian Maroons: Liberty or Death*, trans. A. F. Watts (New York, E. W. Blyden Press, 1981 [1st pub. 1972]).

Furness, A. E., 'The Maroon War of 1795', *The Jamaican Historical Review* 5 (1965): 30–49.

Gaspar, David Barry, 'Runaways in Seventeenth-Century Antigua, West Indies', *Boletín de Estudios Latinoamericanos y del Caribe* 26 (1979): 3–13.

Geggus, David, *Bondmen & Rebels: A Study of Master–Slave Relations in Antigua* (Baltimore, The Johns Hopkins University Press, 1985).

——, *Slave Resistance Studies and the Saint Domingue Slave Revolt: Some*

BIBLIOGRAPHY 189

Preliminary Considerations (Miami, Florida International University, 1983).

Genovese, Eugene D., *From Rebellion to Revolution: Afro-American Slave Revolts in the Making of the Modern World* (Baton Rouge, Louisiana State University Press, 1979).

Goody, Jack, *Tradition, Technology and the State in Africa* (Oxford, Oxford University Press, 1971).

Gray, Richard (ed.), *The Cambridge History of Africa from c. 1600 to c. 1790* (London, Cambridge University Press, 1975), Vol. 4.

Greene, Lorenzo, 'The New England Negro as Seen in Advertisements for Runaway Slaves', *Journal of Negro History* 29 (1944): 125–46.

Groot, Silvia W. de, *From Isolation towards Integration: The Surinam Maroons and their Descendants, 1845–1863* (The Hague, Martinus Nijhoff, 1963).

——, 'The Boni Maroon War, 1765–1793: Surinam and French Guyana', *Boletín de Estudios Latinoamericanos y del Caribe* 18 (1975): 30–48.

——, 'An Example of Oral History: The Tale of Boni's Death and of Boni's Head, *Lateinamerika Studien* 11 (1981): 181–216.

——, 'Surinaamse Marrons in kaart gebracht, 1730–1734' in Benno Francisco Galjart et al., *Een andere in een ander: Liber Amicorum voor R.A.J. van Lier* (Assen, Van Gorcum, 1982): 19–46.

——, 'Slaven en Marrons: Reacties op het Plantagesysteem in de Nieuwe Wereld. Een Schema', *Oso* 2 (1984): 173–82.

——, 'The Maroons of Surinam: Agents of their own Emancipation' in David Richardson (ed.), *Abolition and its Aftermath: The Historical Context, 1790–1916* (London, Frank Cass, 1985): 55–79.

Gutman, Herbert G., 'The World Two Cliometricians Made', *Journal of Negro History* 60 (1975): 53–227.

——, *The Black Family in Slavery and Freedom: 1750–1925* (New York, Pantheon Books, 1976).

Hall, Neville, 'Maritime Maroons: Grand Maroonage from the Danish West Indies', paper presented at the Sixteenth Annual Conference of Caribbean Historians, Barbados, 1984.

Handler, Jerome, 'Slave Insurrectionary Attempts in Seventeenth Century Barbados', paper presented at the Thirteenth Annual Conference of Caribbean Historians, Guadeloupe, 1981.

Harms, Robert, *River of Wealth, River of Sorrow: The Central Zaïre Basin in*

190 OUT OF THE HOUSE OF BONDAGE

the Era of the Slave and Ivory Trade, 1500–1891 (New Haven, Yale University Press, 1981).

Hay, Douglas, et al., *Albion's Fatal Tree: Crime and Society in Eighteenth-Century England* (New York, Pantheon, 1975).

Herrick, C., *White Servitude in Pennsylvania* (Philadelphia, 1926, W. W. Norton reprint, 1974).

Herskovits, Melville J. and Frances S. Herskovits, *Rebel Destiny: Among the Bush Negroes of Dutch Guyana* (New York, McGraw-Hill, 1934).

Heuman, Gad, 'Runaway Slaves in Nineteenth-Century Barbados', paper presented at the Sixteenth Annual Conference of Caribbean Historians, Barbados, 1984.

Higman, B. W., *Slave Population and Economy in Jamaica 1807–1834* (Cambridge, Cambridge University Press, 1976).

——, *Slave Populations of the British Caribbean* (Baltimore, The Johns Hopkins University Press, 1984).

Hooker, Richard J., *The Carolina Backcountry on the Eve of the Revolution: The Journal and Other Writings of Charles Woodmason, Anglican Itinerant* (Chapel Hill, University of North Carolina Press, 1953).

Inikori, J. E. (ed.), *Forced Migration: The Impact of the Export Slave Trade on African Societies* (London, Hutchinson, 1982).

Jaramillo Uribe, Jaime, 'Esclavos y señores en la sociedad colombiana del siglo XVIII' in his *Ensayos sobre Historia Social Colombiana* (Bogotá, Universidad Nacional, 1968): 5–87.

Johnson, Michael P., 'Runaway Slaves and the Slave Communities in South Carolina, 1799 to 1830', *William and Mary Quarterly*, 3rd Ser., 38 (1981): 418–41.

Jones, Gwyilym Iwan, *The Trading States of the Oil Rivers: A Study of Political Development in Eastern Nigeria* (Oxford, Oxford University Press, 1963).

Jornal de Mossamedes (Mossamedes, fortnightly, 1881–1895).

Kaplow, Jeffry, *The Names of Kings: The Parisian Laboring Poor in the Eighteenth Century* (New York, Basic Books, 1972).

Kay, Marvin L. Michael, 'The North Carolina Regulation, 1766–1776: A Class Conflict' in Alfred F. Young (ed.), *The American Revolution: Explorations in the History of American Radicalism* (De Kalb, Northern Illinois University Press, 1976): 71–123.

Kay, Marvin L. Michael and Lorin Lee Cary, ' "The Planters Suffer Little or Nothing": North Carolina Compensations for Executed Slaves,

BIBLIOGRAPHY   191

1748–1772', *Science and Society* 11 (1976): 288–306.

——, 'A Demographic Analysis of Colonial North Carolina with Special Emphasis upon the Slave and Black Populations' in Jeffrey J. Crow and Flora J. Hatley (eds.), *Black Americans in North Carolina and the South* (Chapel Hill, Univ. of North Carolina Press, 1984): 71–121.

——, 'Slave Runaways in Colonial North Carolina, 1748–1775', *North Carolina Historical Review* 63 (1986), forthcoming.

Kea, Raymond A., *Settlements, Trade and Politics in the 17th Century Gold Coast* (Baltimore, The Johns Hopkins University Press, 1982).

Kilson, Marion, 'Towards Freedom: An Analysis of Slave Revolts in the United States', *Phylon* 25 (1964): 175–87.

Klein, Herbert S., *The Middle Passage: Comparative Studies in the Atlantic Slave Trade* (Princeton, Princeton University Press, 1978).

Klein, Rachel N., 'Ordering the Backcountry: The South Carolina Regulation', *William and Mary Quarterly*, 3rd Ser., 38 (1981): 661–80.

Kopytoff, Barbara K., 'The Maroons of Jamaica: An Ethnohistorical Study of Incomplete Polities, 1655–1905' (Ph.D. diss., Univ. of Pennsylvania, 1973).

——, 'The Development of Jamaican Maroon Ethnicity', *Caribbean Quarterly* 22 (1976): 33–50.

——, 'Jamaican Maroon Political Organization: The Effects of the Treaties', *Social and Economic Studies* 25 (1976): 87–105.

——, 'The Early Political Development of Jamaican Maroon Societies', *William and Mary Quarterly* 35 (1978): 287–307.

Kulikoff, Allan, 'The Beginnings of the Afro-American Family in Maryland' in Aubrey Land et al. (eds.), *Law, Society and Politics in Early Maryland* (Baltimore, The Johns Hopkins University Press, 1977): 171–96.

——, 'A "Prolifick" People: Black Population Growth in the Chesapeake Colonies, 1700–1790', *Southern Studies* 16 (1977): 391–428.

——, 'The Origins of Afro-American Society in Tidewater Maryland and Virginia, 1700–1790', *William and Mary Quarterly*, 3rd Ser., 35 (1978): 226–59.

Laslett, Peter, *Family Life and Illicit Love in Earlier Generations: Essays in Historical Sociology* (Cambridge, Cambridge University Press, 1977).

Latham, A. J. H., *Old Calabar 1600–1891: The Impact of the International Economy upon a Traditional Society* (Oxford, Oxford University Press, 1973).

192   OUT OF THE HOUSE OF BONDAGE

Law, Robin, *The Oyo Empire, c. 1600–c. 1836: A West African Imperialism in the Era of the Atlantic Slave Trade* (Oxford, Oxford University Press, 1977).

Lennon, Donald R. and Ida Brooks Kellam (eds.), *The Wilmington Town Book, 1743–1778* (Raleigh, N.C., Division of Archives and History, 1973).

Littlefield, Daniel C., *Rice and Slaves: Ethnicity and the Slave Trade to Colonial South Carolina* (Baton Rouge, Louisiana State University Press, 1981).

Long, Edward, *The History of Jamaica* (London, 3 vols., 1774).

Lovejoy, Paul, *Transformations in Slavery: A History of Slavery in Africa* (Cambridge, Cambridge University Press, 1983).

Mair, Lucille Mathurin, 'A Historical Study of Women in Jamaica from 1655 to 1844' (unpublished Ph.D. thesis, University of the West Indies, 1974).

Manigat, Leslie, 'The Relationship between Maroonage and Slave Revolts and Revolution in St. Domingue–Haiti' in Vera Rubin and Arthur Tuden (eds.), *Comparative Perspectives on Slavery in New World Plantation Societies* (New York, The New York Academy of Sciences, 1977): 420–38.

Manning, Patrick, *Slavery, Colonialism and Economic Growth in Dahomey, 1640–1960* (Cambridge, Cambridge University Press, 1982).

Martin, E.C., *The British West African Settlements, 1750–1821* (London, Longmans, 1927).

Meaders, Daniel E., 'South Carolina Fugitives as Viewed through Local Colonial Newspapers with Emphasis on Runaway Notices 1732–1801', *Journal of Negro History* 60 (1975): 288–319.

Meiklejohn, Norman, 'The Implementation of Slave Legislation in Eighteenth-Century New Granada' in Robert Brent Toplin (ed.), *Slavery and Race Relations in Latin America* (Westport, Conn., Greenwood Press, 1974): 176–203.

Meillassoux, Claude (ed.), *L'Esclavage en Afrique précoloniale* (Paris, François Maspero, 1975).

Meisel R., Adolfo, 'Esclavitud, mestizaje y haciendas en la provincia de Cartagena, 1533–1851', *Desarrollo y Sociedad* 4 (1980): 227–77.

Mellafe, Rolando, *Negro Slavery in Latin America* (Berkeley and Los Angeles, University of California Press, 1975).

Miers, Suzanne and Igor Kopytoff, (eds.), *Slavery in Africa: Historical and*

BIBLIOGRAPHY 193

Anthropological Perspectives (Madison, University of Wisconsin Press, 1977).

Mintz, Sidney W., *Caribbean Transformations* (Chicago, Aldine Publishing Co., 1974).

Mintz, Sidney and Richard Price, 'An Anthropological Approach to the Afro-American Past: A Caribbean Perspective', ISHI Occasional Papers in Social Change (Philadelphia, ISHI, 1976).

Möller, Peter, *Journey through Angola, Ovampoland and Damarland, 1895–1896* trans. from original Swedish edition of 1899 (Cape Town, C. Struik, 1974).

Moreau de Saint-Mery, Louis-Mederic-Elie, *Description ... de l'Isle Saint Domingue* (Paris, Société d'Histoire Colonies Françaises, 1958), Vol. 2.

Morgan, Philip D., 'A Profile of a Mid-Eighteenth-Century South Carolina Parish: The Tax Return of Saint James' Goose Creek', *South Carolina Historical Magazine* 81 (1980): 51–65.

——, 'Black Society in the Lowcountry, 1760–1810' in Ira Berlin and Ronald Hoffman (eds.), *Slavery and Freedom in the Age of the American Revolution* (Charlottesville, University Press of Virginia, 1983): 83–141.

——, 'Black Life in Eighteenth-Century Charleston', *Perspectives in American History*, New Ser., 1 (1984): 187–232.

Mullin, Gerald W., *Flight and Rebellion: Slave Resistance in Eighteenth-Century Virginia* (New York, Oxford University Press, 1972).

Nascimento, José Pereira do, *O Districto de Mossamedes* (Lisbon, 1892).

Newbury, Colin W., *The Western Slave Coast and its Rulers: European Trade and Administration among the Yoruba and Adja-Speaking Peoples of South-Western Nigeria, Southern Dahomey and Togo* (Oxford, Oxford University Press, 1961).

Northrup, David, *Trade without Rulers: Pre-Colonial Economic Development in South-Eastern Nigeria* (Oxford, Oxford University Press, 1978).

Norusis, Marija J., *SPSS, An Introductory Guide* (New York, McGraw-Hill, 1982).

Nugent, Maris, *Lady Nugent's Journal of her Residence in Jamaica from 1801 to 1805*, Philip Wright (ed.) (Kingston, Institute of Jamaica, 1966).

Palacios Preciado, Jorge, *La trata de negros por Cartagena de Indias, 1650–1750* (Tunja, Universidad de Colombia, 1973).

194 OUT OF THE HOUSE OF BONDAGE

Palmer, Colin, *Human Cargoes: The British Slave Trade to Spanish America, 1700–1739* (Chicago, University of Illinois Press, 1981).

Patterson, K. D., *The Northern Gabon Coast to 1865* (Oxford, Oxford University Press, 1975).

Patterson, Orlando, *The Sociology of Slavery: An Analysis of the Origins, Development and Structure of Negro Slave Society in Jamaica* (London, MacGibbon and Kee, 1967).

——, 'Slavery and Slave Revolts: A Socio-Historical Analysis of the First Maroon War, 1655–1740', *Social and Economic Studies* 19 (1970): 289–325.

——, 'On Slavery and Slave Formations', *New Left Review* 117 (1979): 31–67.

Pélissier, René, *Les Guerres Grises, Résistance et Révoltes en Angola, 1845–1941* (Orgeval, Editions Pélissier, 1977).

Perdue, Theda, 'Red and Black in the Southern Appalachians', *Southern Exposure* 12 (1984): 17–24.

Polanyi, Karl, *Dahomey and the Slave Trade: An Analysis of an Archaic Economy* (Washington, University of Washington Press, 1966).

Postma, Dirk, *De Trekboeren te St. Januario Humpata* (Amsterdam and Pretoria, 1897).

Price, Richard, 'The Guiana Maroons: Changing Perspectives in Bush Negro Studies', *Caribbean Studies* 11 (1971–72): 81–105.

——, (ed.), *Maroon Societies: Rebel Slave Communities in the Americas* (Garden City, N.Y., Anchor Books, 1973).

——, *Saramaka Social Structure: An Analysis of a Maroon Society in Surinam* (Río Piedras, Institute of Caribbean Studies, University of Puerto Rico, 1975).

Raboteau, Albert J., *Slave Religion: The Invisible Institution in the Antebellum South* (Oxford, Oxford University Press, 1978).

Renny, Robert, *A History of Jamaica* (London, 1807).

Reynolds, Edward, *Stand the Storm: A History of the Atlantic Slave Trade* (London, Allison and Busby, 1985).

Roberts, George W., *The Population of Jamaica* (Cambridge, Cambridge University Press, 1957).

Robinson, Carey, *The Fighting Maroons of Jamaica* (Jamaica, William Collins and Sangster (Jamaica) Ltd., 1969).

Rodney, Walter, *A History of the Upper Guinea Coast, 1545–1800* (Oxford, Oxford University Press, 1970).

BIBLIOGRAPHY 195

Rogers, George C., Philip M. Hamer, et al., (eds.), *The Papers of Henry Laurens* (Columbia, University of South Carolina Press, 1968–), 10 vols. to date.

Rout, Leslie B., *The African Experience in Spanish America* (Cambridge, Cambridge University Press, 1976).

Rubin, Vera and Arthur Tuden, (eds.), *Comparative Perspectives on Slavery in New World Plantation Societies* (New York, The New York Academy of Sciences, 1977).

Saunders, William L. (ed.), *The Colonial Records of North Carolina* (Raleigh, North Carolina, 10 vols., 1886–90).

Schaw, Janet, *Journal of a Lady of Quality ... 1774–1776*, edited by Evangeline W. Andrews and Charles M. Andrews (New Haven, Yale University Press, 1923).

Schuler, Monica, 'Day to Day Resistance to Slavery in The Caribbean during the Eighteenth Century', *African Studies Association of the West Indies Bulletin* 6 (1973): 57–75.

Schwartz, Stuart B., 'Resistance and Accommodation in Eighteenth-Century Brazil: The Slaves' View of Slavery', *Hispanic American Historical Review* 57 (1970): 313–33.

——, *Sugar Plantations and the Formation of Brazilian Society (Bahia, 1550–1830)* (Cambridge, Cambridge University Press, 1985).

Scott, Michael, *Tom Cringle's Log* (London, J.M. Dent and Sons Ltd., 1938).

Sharp, William F., *Slavery on the Spanish Frontier: The Colombian Chocó, 1680–1810* (Norman, University of Oklahoma Press, 1976).

Sheridan, Richard, 'From Jamaican Slavery to Haitian Freedom: The Case of the Black Crew on the Pilot Boat, Deep Nine', *Journal of Negro History* 67 (1982): 328–39.

——, *Doctors and Slaves: A Medical and Demographic History of Slavery in the British West Indies, 1680–1834* (Cambridge, Cambridge University Press, 1985).

Smith, Abbott, *Colonists in Bondage: White Servitude and Convict Labor in America, 1607–1776* (Chapel Hill, North Carolina University Press, 1947).

Smyth, J.F.D., *Tour in the United States of America* (London, 2 vols., 1784).

Sousa, Rodolpho de Santa Brígada de, 'Mossamedes', *Boletim da Sociedade de Geografia de Lisboa* 7 (1887): 396–414.

196 OUT OF THE HOUSE OF BONDAGE

Stedman, Captn. J.G., *Narrative of a Five-years' Expedition, Against the Revolted Negroes of Surinam, in Guiana, on the Wild Coast of South America from the year 1772, to 1777* (London, 1796).

Sydnor, Charles S., *American Revolutionaries in the Making: Political Practices in Washington's Virginia*

Thicknesse, Philip, *Memoirs and Anecdotes of Philip Thicknesse, late Lieutenant-Governor of Land Guard Fort, and unfortunately Father of George Touchet, Baron Audley* (Dublin, 1790).

Thoden van Velzen, H.U.E., *Politieke beheersing in de Djuka maatschappij: een studie van een onvolledig machtsoverwicht* (Leiden, Africa Studiecentrum, Mimeo, 1966).

Thompson, Alvin O., 'Some Problems of Slave Desertion in Guyana, c. 1750–1814', Occasional Paper No. 4, *ISER* (1976).

Thompson, E.P., 'The Moral Economy of the English Crowd in the Eighteenth Century', *Past and Present* 50 (1971): 76–136.

——, 'Patrician Society, Plebeian Culture', *Journal of Social History* 7 (1974): 382–405.

U.S. Bureau of the Census, *Historical Statistics of the United States: Colonial Times to 1957* (Washington, D.C., 1960).

Watson, Elkanah, *Men and Times of the Revolution ...* (New York, 1856).

Wax, Darold D., 'Preferences for Slaves in Colonial America', *Journal of Negro History* 58 (1973): 371–401.

Wieder, Padre, 'O Jau', *Boletim da Sociedade de Geografia de Lisboa* 11 (1892): 711–29.

Williams, Eric, *Capitalism and Slavery* (Chapel Hill, University of North Carolina Press, 1944).

Windley, Lathan A., 'A Profile of Runaway Slaves in Virginia and South Carolina from 1730 through 1787' (unpublished Ph.D. thesis, University of Iowa, 1974).

——, (comp.), *Runaway Slave Advertisements: A Documentary History from the 1730s to 1790* (Westport, Conn., Greenwood Press, 1983).

Wood, Betty, *Slavery in Colonial Georgia, 1730–1775* (Athens, University of Georgia Press, 1984).

Wood, Peter H., *Black Majority: Negroes in Colonial South Carolina from 1670 through the Stono Rebellion* (New York, Knopf, 1974).

INDEX

Advertising: for runaways, 2, 58, 76n, 95, 97, 104–5, 112, 114
Affiches Américains, 112, 114, 127
Africa: resistance, 2, 11ff; runaways in, 19
Africans: characteristics, 59–62; marronage in Saint Domingue, 120–3; as runaways, 5, 45–6, 48, 60, 69–73 passim, 98, 99, 103, 115
Angola, 3, 62; *see also* Southern Angola
Appea (escaped slave), 106
Arson, 82
Artisans: criminality, 51; proportion of slaves, 44; as runaways, 42, 43, 99–100, 125
Atkins, Governor, 92n

Bahia, 117
Balcarres, Earl of, 159, 160
Bambara slaves, 122
Bance Island, 13
Banditry; Southern Angola, 27–8
Barbadian, The, 97
Barbados, 4, 5, 6, 7, 96; maritime marronage, 79–94; rebellions, 80, 105; runaways, 95–111
Barbados Masters and Servants Law, 84
Barbados Mercury and Bridgetown Gazette, 97
Barracoons, 13–14, 18–19
Bata Bata (bandit stronghold), 30
Beckles, Hilary, 1, 5, 79–94
Beckles, Johnny (escaped slave), 104
Bentley, Martin, 82
Bight of Biafra, 62
Bishop, Pat, 99
Blake, Russell L., 77n
Boers, 23, 29
Bonis (Maroons), 176, 178
Bosman, William, 16, 17, 18
Bowman, Will, 82
Bridgetown, 100
Buc, M. de, 90
Buffy (slave), 104
Bussa's Rebellion, 105
Buxton, Thomas Fowell, 161, 167

Cali, 148, 151n; slave conspiracy, 144–5
Caribs, 89–90
Cartagena de Indias, 131, 134, 138, 148
Cartago, 148, 151n: *palenque*, 141–3
Carter, Thomas, 85

Cary, L. L., 4, 7, 37–56
Castrations, 49, 50, 51
Christianity: slaves, 135, 140, 144
Cimarrones, 132
Clarence-Smith, W. G., 3, 23–33
Clothing: runaways, 47–8; slaves, 59–60
Cockpit Country, 154, 156, 161, 179
Codrington, Colonel, 88
Coleridge, Samuel, 57
Collier, Commodore, 13
Colombia, 3–4, 7, 103; runaways and resistance, 131–51
Colt, Sir Henry, 80
Contract labour; Angola, 25–6; *see also* Indentured labour
Craton, Michael, 1, 106, 127n, 159
Creoles, 59, 98, 103, 119: marronage in Saint Domingue, 118–19; runaways, 60, 69, 115
Criminality, slave, 38–9, 49–53, 82
Cudjoe, Captain (Maroon leader), 154–5, 156, 176, 179, 180
Cumper, George, 162, 163
Cuttery, James (slave), 101

Dallas, Robert Charles, 157, 163, 164–5, 166, 169, 180
Debien, Gabriel, 112, 116, 121
Domestics, 44: criminality, 51; as runaways, 42, 43
Dominica, 86, 117

Edwards, Bryan, 163, 164, 166, 178
El Castigo (*palenque*), 135
Engerman, Stanley L., 168
Escapes: planning, 46–7, Southern Angola, 26–7; *seel also* Marronage, Runaways
Executions, 49, 85

Family feeling among slaves, 42, 73–4, 106–7
Fernando Martínez, Felix (escaped slave), 137–8
Field hands, 44: criminality, 51; runaways, 42, 43, 45
Fisheries, Southern Angola, 23, 26
Fouchard, Jean, 112, 114, 116, 117, 121, 125
French Revolution, 159
Frenquières, M. de Chevalier de, 90
Frument, Robert, 85

198   OUT OF THE HOUSE OF BONDAGE

Gautier, Arlette, 117
Geggus, David, 1, 112–28
Genovese, Eugene D., 1
Gold Coast, 62
Goman (Maroon leader), 126
Great Dismal Swamp (slave refuge), 40–1
Grenada, 89
Groot, Silvia W. de, 3, 95, 173–84
Guadeloupe, 117
Guerville, Poulain de, 90
Gutman, Herbert, 63

Haiti, *see* Saint Domingue
Hall, N.A.T., 92n
Hartsinck, —, 180
Hawkins, Sir John, 12, 21n
Healthcott, William, 81
Herero, 27, 28, 29
Herrick, C., 80
Heuman, Gad, 1–8, 95–111, 123, 127n
Higginbottom, Lt. Col. John, 81
Higman, Barry, 5, 63, 167
History of the British West Indies (Edwards), 163
History of the Maroons (Dallas), 163
Hyacinthe (voodoo priest), 126

Indentured servants, 79–80, 91: Irish, 83, 87–8, 91; maritime escapes, 86–7
Indians, (North American) and runaways, 40, 70
Inquisition, 137
Inventories, 62, 76n

Jackson, John (factor), 21–2n
Jackson, Josiah, 89
Jamaica, 3, 63, 87, 99, 117: Maroons, 152–84
Jamaica Servant Code, 85
Jaramillo Uribe, Jaime, 132, 149
Jesuits, 146, 147
Jewellery, 60

Kaholo (bandit stronghold), 29–30
Karmahaly (Maroons), 176
Kay, M.L.M., 4, 7, 37–56
Kin networks, 73–4, 106–7
Kopytoff, Barbara, 154, 155, 157, 180

Labat, Père, 89, 90
Land Allotment Act, Jamaica (1842), 181
Leare, Peter, 85–6
Leeward Islands, 154
Legislation, paternalistic, 25, 136–7, 146–8
Littlefield, D.C., 41
Long, Edward, 156, 157, 160
Los Remedios, 139, 148

Lubola Juan (Maroon leader), 176

McFarlane, Anthony, 3, 7, 131–51
Mair, Dr Lucille Mathurin, 169
Manumission, Southern Angola, 25
Maroon Wars: First, 155; Second, 158–61
Maroons: Colombia *see* Marronage; demography and health, 117–18, 123–4, 152–72 passim; description, 163–6, 169; Jamaica, 152–84; population, 157–8, 161–3, 167–8, 170; Saint Domingue *see* Marronage; St Vincent, 89–90; settlements, 40, 41, 154; Surinam, 173–84; treaties, 3, 134–5, 152, 156–7, 174, 176–7, 179–80, 181
Marriage *see* Family, Kin networks
Marronnage: Colombia, 131–51 passim; definitions, 92n; maritime, 5, 79–94; Saint Domingue, 112–28 passim; *see also* Maroons
Martínez, Felix Fernando (escaped slave), 137–8
Martinique, 89, 90
Maryland, 84
Massey (female slave), 105–6
Matthews, John, 19
Mauricius, Governor, 176
Mbundu (bandit leader), 28, 30
Mintz, Sidney, 7
Montego Bay, 159
Moore, Francis, 19
Moore, Thomas (planter), 81
Morgan, Philip D., 2, 57–78
Mozambique, 28
Mulattoes: runaways, 70
Mullin, G.W., 41, 42, 45, 108
Mullin, Michael, 97
Murders, 51–2
Mustees: runaways, 70

New Granada, 134, 135; *see also* Colombia
Newspapers: North Carolina, 41; *see also* Advertising
Newton, John (slave trader), 16, 17
North Carolina, 4, 37–53
Nugent, Lady Maria, 166
Nyaneka people, 28, 29, 30, 31

Occupations: slaves and runaways, 4, 42–4, 63–6, 77n, 99–100, 125
Ogé, Vincent, 123
Ormond, Henry (slave owner), 39
Owen, — (slave dealer), 17

Pablo (slave conspirator), 144–5
Palenques, 3, 132, 134, 139–43, 148, 149; of San Basilio, 134; treaty, 134–5

INDEX

199

Paramakkaners (Maroons), 178
Pass system, 83–4
Pennsylvania, 82
Phillips, Thomas, 14–15, 17, 21n
Plantations: Angola, 27, 29; runaways on, 100; statistics, 50–1, 74, 183
Poisoning case, 37
Portugal *see* Southern Angola
Price, Richard, 7, 95
Primus (escaped slave), 106–7
Prudencio (escaped slave), 142
Punishments, 49–53

Rathbone, Richard, 2, 11–12
Renny, Robert, 167
Roberts, George, 167
Runaways, 19, 67, 101, 102–3, 107, 109, 116, 126, 145; African, 59, 72; Barbados, 95–111; characteristics, 4, 41, 46, 47–8, 57–8, 60, 62, 69–71, 97, 98, 100, 109, 124; destinations and motives, 2, 4, 7, 48, 66–9, 100, 101, 136–8, 146–9; duration of absence, 103–4, 107; English and other linguistic skills, 46, 67, 126; group, 72, 78n, 126; harbouring, 5, 27, 71–2, 107–8; indentured servants, 81–5 passim; and Maroons, 158, 177–8; North Carolina, 39–53; occupations, 42–4, 63–6, 99–100, 125; recaptures, 116, 121–2; Saint Domingue, 112ff; sex ratios, 41–2, 98; South Carolina, 57–78; women, 42, 67, 115; *see also* Advertising, Maroons, Marronage, Slaves

Saint Domingue, 159: slave runaways, 4,6, 112–128
St Lucia, 86, 89
St Vincent, 86, 89, 91, 101
Sam (slave), 104
Sambo (slave), 37, 38
São Tomé, 23, 25
Schaw, Janet, 49
Scheuses, Governor de, 176
Schwartz, Stuart, 117
Scott, Michael, 167
Searle, Governor, 82, 83, 84, 85

Senegambia, 62
Sheridan, Richard B., 3, 152–72
Sierra Leone, 12, 18, 176
slave rebellions, 1–2; *see also* Maroons, Marronnage
Slave Registers, 97
Slave settlements: Africa, 19
Slaves: 183; absenteeism, 103–4, 107, 174; crimes, 7; languages, 21n; occupations, 4, 44, 77n; on board ship, 15–16; organisation, 143–4; paternalistic legislation, 136–7, 146–8; traditions, 18–19, 183; women, 4, 51, 52, 168–9; *see also* Runaways
Smith, A. E., 80
Smyth, J. F. D., 40
Snelgrove, W., 15–16
South Carolina, 40, 42, 45, 57–78
Southern Angola, 23–33
Stede, Governor, 84, 87, 88
Stono Rebellion, 40
Surinam, 3, 173–84
Sylvester, Giles (planter), 87

Thicknesse, Lieutenant Philip, 155
Tobago, 86, 89
Todd, Mr, 101
Tom Cringle's Log (Scott), 167
Tomba, Captain (slave), 14
Treaties *see* Maroons
Trelawny, Governor Edward, 156, 157, 176
Trelawny Town, 156, 165–6, 179

Upper Guinea, 19

Villavieja, 146–7
Virginia, 40, 42, 57, 73, 75n, 84
Visiting, 67, 68, 69, 70, 71, 72–3, 77n

Wadstrom, C. B., 20
Watermen, 43–5, 63
Watson, Elkanah, 41
West India Regiment, 107, 108
Windley, L. A., 41, 44
Windward Islands, 88, 91
Wood, Betty, 75n
Wood, Peter, 75n

Milton Keynes UK
Ingram Content Group UK Ltd.
UKHW031109180324
439528UK00015B/81